Islam, Standards, and Technoscience

Halal (literally, "permissible" or "lawful") production, trade, and standards have become essential to state-regulated Islam and to companies in contemporary Malaysia and Singapore, giving these two countries a special position in the rapidly expanding global market for halal products: in these nations, state bodies certify halal products as well as spaces (shops, factories, and restaurants) and work processes, and so consumers can find state halal-certified products from Malaysia and Singapore in shops around the world. Building on ethnographic material from Malaysia, Singapore, and Europe, this book provides an exploration of the role of halal production, trade, and standards. Fischer explains how the global markets for halal comprise divergent zones in which Islam, markets, regulatory institutions, and technoscience interact and diverge. Focusing on the "bigger institutional picture" that frames everyday halal consumption, Fischer provides a multisited ethnography of the overlapping technologies and techniques of production, trade, and standards that together warrant a product as "halal" and thereby help to format the market. Exploring global halal in networks, training, laboratories, activism, companies, shops and restaurants, this book will be an essential resource to scholars and students of social science interested in the global interface zones between religion, standards, and technoscience.

Johan Fischer is Associate Professor in the Department of Society and Globalization, Roskilde University, Denmark.

Routledge Studies in Anthropology

1 **Student Mobility and Narrative in Europe**
The New Strangers
Elizabeth Murphy-Lejeune

2 **The Question of the Gift**
Essays across Disciplines
Edited by Mark Osteen

3 **Decolonising Indigenous Rights**
Edited by Adolfo de Oliveira

4 **Traveling Spirits**
Migrants, Markets and Mobilities
Edited by Gertrud Hüwelmeier and Kristine Krause

5 **Anthropologists, Indigenous Scholars and the Research Endeavour**
Seeking Bridges Towards Mutual Respect
Edited by Joy Hendry and Laara Fitznor

6 **Confronting Capital**
Critique and Engagement in Anthropology
Edited by Pauline Gardiner Barber, Belinda Leach and Winnie Lem

7 **Adolescent Identity**
Evolutionary, Cultural and Developmental Perspectives
Edited by Bonnie L. Hewlett

8 **The Social Life of Climate Change Models**
Anticipating Nature
Edited by Kirsten Hastrup and Martin Skrydstrup

9 **Islam, Development, and Urban Women's Reproductive Practices**
Cortney Hughes Rinker

10 **Senses and Citizenships**
Embodying Political Life
Edited by Susanna Trnka, Christine Dureau, and Julie Park

11 **Environmental Anthropology**
Future Directions
Edited by Helen Kopnina and Eleanor Shoreman-Ouimet

12 **Times of Security**
Ethnographies of Fear, Protest and the Future
Edited by Martin Holbraad and Morten Axel Pedersen

13 **Climate Change and Tradition in a Small Island State**
The Rising Tide
Peter Rudiak-Gould

14 **Anthropology and Nature**
Edited by Kirsten Hastrup

15 **Animism and the Question of Life**
Istvan Praet

16 **Anthropology in the Making**
Research in Health and Development
Laurent Vidal

17 **Negotiating Territoriality**
Spatial Dialogues Between State and Tradition
Edited by Allan Charles Dawson, Laura Zanotti and Ismael Vaccaro

18 **HIV/AIDS and the Social Consequences of Untamed Biomedicine**
Anthropological Complicitics
Graham Fordham

19 **Environmentalism, Ethical Trade, and Commodification**
Technologies of Value and the Forest Stewardship Council in Chile
Adam Henne

20 **An Anthropology of Robots and AI**
Annihilation Anxiety and Machines
Kathleen Richardson

21 **An Anthropological Economy of Debt**
Edited by Bernard Hours and Pepita Ould Ahmed

22 **Ethnographies in Pan Pacific Research**
Tensions and Positionings
Edited by Robert E. Rinehart, elke emerald, and Rangi Matamua

23 **Anthropologies of Cancer in Transnational Worlds**
Edited by Holly F. Mathews, Nancy J. Burke, and Eirini Kampriani

24 **Magical Consciousness**
An Anthropological and Neurobiological Approach
Susan E.J. Greenwood and Erik D. Goodwyn

25 **Diagnostic Controversy**
Cultural Perspectives on Competing Knowledge in Healthcare
Edited by Carolyn Smith-Morris

26 **Transpacific Americas**
Encounters and Engagements Between the Americas and the South Pacific
Edited by Eveline Dürr and Philipp Schorch

27 **The Anthropology of Postindustrialism**
Ethnographies of Disconnection
Edited by Ismael Vaccaro, Krista Harper and Seth Murray

28 **Islam, Standards, and Technoscience**
In Global Halal Zones
Johan Fischer

Islam, Standards, and Technoscience

In Global Halal Zones

Johan Fischer

Routledge
Taylor & Francis Group
New York London

First published 2016
by Routledge
711 Third Avenue, New York, NY 10017

and by Routledge
2 Park Square, Milton Park, Abingdon, Oxon OX14 4RN

First issued in paperback 2017

Routledge is an imprint of the Taylor & Francis Group, an informa business

Library of Congress Cataloging-in-Publication Data
Fischer, Johan.
Islam, standards, and technoscience in global Halal zones / by Johan Fischer. — 1st [edition].
pages cm. — (Routledge studies in anthropology ; 28)
Includes bibliographical references and index.
1. Halal food industry. 2. Halal food—Social aspects. 3. Technology—Religious aspects—Islam. 4. Consumption (Economics)—Religious aspects—Islam. I. Title.
HD9000.5.F536 2016
381'.41091767—dc23 2015027666

ISBN 13: 978-1-138-06027-2 (pbk)
ISBN 13: 978-1-138-95418-2 (hbk)

Typeset in Sabon
by Apex CoVantage, LLC

To Sille, Anton, and Oscar

Contents

Figures

Acknowledgments

Most of all, I would like to thank my informants for their willingness to participate in and patience with my exploration of halal in a variety of contexts. I would also like to extend my gratitude to Singaporean, Malaysian, and European organizations and institutions that were most helpful during my fieldwork. In Singapore I was attached to Asia Research Institute at National University of Singapore as a visiting senior research fellow. I am most grateful for the encouragement I received from staff during that time, and in particular, I would like to thank Michael Feener for making this affiliation possible and for invaluable support and advice on the project. I would like to thank the Danish Council for Independent Research in Social Science that funded this project—I am most grateful for the help and support of the council. I am indebted to Bill Maurer for his comments and encouragement that helped this book come into being. A special thanks goes to Max Novick, Jennifer Morrow, and Katherine Ong at Routledge. Finally, I would like to thank my wife, Sille, and sons, Anton and Oscar, for enduring my absences during extended periods of fieldwork.

Frequently Used Abbreviations and Acronyms

AMLA	Administration of Muslim Law Act
GLC	Government-Linked Company
HDC	Halal Industry Development Corporation
HFCE	Halal Food Council of Europe
HMC	Halal Monitoring Committee
ICC	The Islamic Cultural Centre
IHRAM	The Institute of Halal Research and Management
JAKIM	Jabatan Kemajuan Islam Malaysia or Islamic Development Department of Malaysia
MATRADE	Malaysia External Trade Development Corporation
MUI	The Majelis Ulama Indonesia or Indonesian Ulemas Council
MUIS	Majlis Ugama Islam Singapura or Islamic Religious Council of Singapore
PAP	People's Action Party
PAS	Parti Islam SeMalaysia
PPIM	Persatuan Pengguna Islam Malaysia or the Muslim Consumers Association of Malaysia
SIRIM	Standards and Industrial Research Institute of Malaysia
SMCC	Singapore Malay Chamber of Commerce
UMNO	United Malays National Organisation
USIM	Universiti Sains Islam Malaysia or the Islamic Science University of Malaysia
WHF	World Halal Forum

Introduction

Halal between Islam, Standards, and Technoscience

In March 2010 I was in the audience for the 4th International Halal Food Conference held at the Sheraton Hotel in Brussels, Belgium. From around the world Islamic organizations, halal certifiers, and companies had come to attend this conference, titled "Establishing a Halal Quality Assurance System." In Arabic, *halal* literally means "permissible" or "lawful," and traditionally it signifies "pure food" with regard to meat, in particular, by proper Islamic practice such as ritual slaughter and pork avoidance. Yet in the modern and globalized industry for not only food but also biotechnology as well as care products, a number of Muslim requirements have been met, such as by an injunction to avoid any substances that may be contaminated with porcine residues or alcohol. These requirements are setting new standards for production, preparation, handling, storage, and certification. In the modern world halal is part of a huge and expanding globalized market. Optimistically, market players have estimated the value of the halal food market to be around at least $632 billion (Agriculture and Agri-Food Canada 2011). Based on multisited ethnographic fieldwork in Malaysia, Singapore, and Europe, I explore how global halal production, trade, and regulation are taking place. More specifically, I examine the halal state certification and standards of Malaysia and Singapore, on one hand, and companies, on the other hand. I also focus on global networks, training, science, and research and how Muslim activists in Malaysia, in particular, try to expand halal requirements to cover more and more products and processes, as well as manufacturing companies and shops. In each of these areas, halal production and trade sit uneasily between Islam, standards, and technoscience, that is, material technology and specialized social expertise (Ong and Collier 2005, 11).

In the rapidly expanding global market for halal products Malaysia and Singapore hold a special position; that is, they are the only two countries in which state bodies certify halal products, spaces (shops, factories, and restaurants) as well as work processes. In shops around the world, consumers can find state halal-certified products from Malaysia and Singapore that carry distinctive halal logos. Globally, companies are affected by the proliferation of halal that, to a large extent, is evoked by Southeast Asian nations such as Malaysia, Singapore, Indonesia, Brunei, and Thailand.

The morning at the 4th International Halal Food Conference starts with a recitation of the Koran by a representative from Jamia Islamia (an organization dedicated to disseminating knowledge about Islamic beliefs, history, and culture) and then a prominent Imam explains about halal in the Koran. Next the chairman of Islamic Food Council of Europe (IFCE),[1] which arranged the conference, delivers his welcoming address, introduced by *Assalamualaikum warahmatullahi wabarakatuh* (Peace be unto you and so may the mercy of Allah and His blessings). The chairman is also vice president of the influential halal-certification body, International Food and Nutritional Council of America (IFANCA),[2] based in Chicago. He was born in Malaysia, where he worked with Malaysia's state body for halal, and has been involved in setting up Malaysia's state regulated form of halal certification since the early 1980s. He explains that having key halal nations such as Malaysia (where halal has been institutionalized and regulated by the state longer than anywhere else), Singapore (an upcoming non-Muslim nation known for its efficiency and global attitude), and Indonesia (the most populous Muslim nation), as well as key industry players such as Nestlé and Novozymes (I have conducted fieldwork with both companies), present at the conference is a sign that not only is halal being recognized globally but, likewise, is the work and authority of IFCE. The chairman hoped the conference will open up opportunities for market access and the establishing of "networking" for the various players in the halal food industry worldwide. At the same time, Brussels is the place where 65 percent of European Union (EU) regulations are formulated, he goes on, and the EU as a major regulatory institution is increasingly focusing on the expanding market for halal.

Malaysia's ambassador to Belgium argues that it is of great importance to Malaysia to establish a national halal assurance system that matches the country's "long-term plan" incorporating the standards Malaysian MS 1500 (production, preparation, handling, and storage of halal food) and MS 2200 (consumer goods for cosmetic and personal care) as an international "benchmark" for the state certification of halal products. Malaysia has also set up halal research institutes at several of its universities that are developing technologies and techniques to detect pork gelatin and DNA, as well as alcohol in industrial processes, and I explore these points in Chapter 4. These issues are given special national attention at global network events held annually in Malaysia such as World Halal Forum (WHF; the leading global halal event that brings together Islamic organizations, certifiers, and companies) and Malaysia International Halal Showcase (MIHAS; the largest halal trade fair), where I did fieldwork.

During a short break everybody is encouraged to exchange visiting cards and "network." Then a representative from Jabatan Kemajuan Islam Malaysia (JAKIM), or the Islamic Development Department of Malaysia, Malaysia's halal state certification body, makes the case that to enhance market competitiveness mechanisms to monitor and audit halal must be in place. Certification is essential in this respect because it ensures that halal complies with standards. Companies wishing to be halal certified by the Malaysian state can apply online and pay the required fee online as well. For local Malaysian companies, the fee is lower than that for multinational companies. Applicants must declare that all ingredients are recognized by JAKIM or a certifier approved by JAKIM. In this process, ingredient specifications, supporting documents, company registration, and a business permit from local authorities, as well as a flow chart (a type of diagram that represents a process indicating the steps as boxes of various kinds and their order by connecting these with arrows), for each product must be made available for officers to check. Officers do an "on-site audit" and take note of any irregularities in the fields of documentation, processing, preparation, handling, hygiene, sanitation, storage, displaying, food safety, labeling, and layout of premises. The legal background is the Malaysian MS 1500 and MS 2200, as well as the Trade Descriptions Act of 1972, which stipulates the legal definition of halal. The mandatory internal Halal Committee consisting of Muslims in the company is responsible for providing auditors with required information. After this type of audit inspectors present a report to a panel of JAKIM directors that may pose additional questions before deciding to approve or fail the company in question. Certificates lapse after two years, and renewal applications are addressed within thirty working days. Companies must deliver control reports at least twice a year. If companies are found guilty in breaching halal requirements, forging the JAKIM halal logo, for example, they can be fined (Figure I.1). The JAKIM representative ends with stating that breaching halal regulations is also a breach of Syariah (Islamic law)[3] requirements.

A Néstle Malaysia representative now explains that the company has come a long way having taken halal to its global position today. Prior to state institutionalization of halal in Malaysia a plethora of Islamic revivalist groups produced uncertified halal products. Néstle established its halal policy in 1992 in close cooperation with the Malaysian state represented by JAKIM, as we shall see in Chapter 6. Around the same time many multinational companies in Malaysia and Singapore became halal certified.

The title of the talk by Singapore's halal state certification body, Majlis Ugama Islam Singapura (MUIS), or the Islamic Religious Council of Singapore, representative is "Experience in Administering Halal Certification in Singapore." She starts out by showing slides on key facts about Singapore, that is, its multiracial composition (Chinese, Muslims, and Indians), small size and population, very limited number of manufacturing companies, free-market economy, highly developed institutional infrastructure, cleanness, political and social stability, and pro-business environment. Out of Singapore's population of about 5 million people the majority are ethnic Chinese, and only 15 percent are Muslim, but despite being a Muslim minority country the focus on promoting halal is intensive and the growth in halal certified premises rose from 500 to 2,600 between 2000 and 2009. Multinational giants such as McDonald's have all been fully halal certified

Figure I.1 JAKIM's halal logo on a McDonald's restaurant in Kuala Lumpur, Malaysia

in Singapore since the 1990s (as is the case in Malaysia). In Singapore, Islam and halal are regulated under the Administration of Muslim Law Act (AMLA), and perpetrators can be fined or jailed. Exporters must have a valid certificate and logo issued by a recognized certifier (Figure I.2).

Figure I.2 The MUIS halal logo on a McDonald's restaurant in Chinatown, Singapore

MUIS "do rounds in supermarkets" and follow up on any suspicions. All applications submitted to MUIS must be done online, and subsequently MUIS looks into raw materials, standards of operating procedures and efficient monitoring, and staffing, in that all halal-certified premises must employ at least two Muslim staff, and it is mandatory for staff to attend MUIS's halal training. MUIS has adopted "state-of-the-art security information technology" to legally protect its halal certificate: anti-photocopy technology and microprint, as well as "other security technologies."

In the question-and-answer session that follows a Malaysian woman wants to know why and how it could happen that "halal pork" turned up in the Supermarket FairPrice NTUC (in which I have carried out fieldwork) in Singapore when everybody knows that pork cannot possibly be halal. The MUIS representative agrees that pork can never be halal and that it would compromise Syariah if it were labeled as such. She explains that the incident referred to arose because of a rumor in an e-mail that halal pork was on sale in Singapore. MUIS inspectors did not find any halal pork when investigating, and the MUIS representative calls this a "sabotage" incident. The subsequent police investigation could not place the responsibility. As we shall see, there is fierce competition over halal between Malaysia and Singapore, and more generally, there are historical and contemporary linkages and tensions between the two countries. Simultaneously, halal in both countries is framed by intensified flows of information about what halal is or should be.

Novozymes's global halal coordinator then took the stage. Novozymes is the leading enzyme manufacturer company globally. Virtually all the company's food enzymes[4] are halal certified. Since about 2000, Novozymes experienced a growing number of requests regarding halal certification from Southeast Asia, in particular. This was, to a large extent, the effect of a major food scandal in Indonesia, which I discuss in greater detail in subsequent chapters. To comply with divergent halal requirements set by Islamic organizations globally, the company's products are certified by five different certifiers. Novozymes trains all staff involved in halal production, that is, basic rules, approved ingredients/raw materials, and certification procedures. The global halal coordinator ended his talk by presenting a wish list aimed at the company's certifiers: quick and clear responses, precise and realistic requirements, realistic time frame for new requirements, specification of requirements—*not* how to comply with them—and common standards, as well as mutual full recognition between different certification bodies.

IN GLOBAL HALAL ZONES

The theme ("Establishing a Halal Quality Assurance System"), discussions, and audience of the 4th International Halal Food Conference in many ways bring out the central and larger questions raised and answered in this book. The complex interplay between Islam, standards, and technoscience that emerges from the above "network event" raises a number of questions subjected to ethnographic exploration. The research question answered in the book is this, "*Why and how is the global proliferation of halal markets taking place between Islam, standards, and technoscience?*" Thus, the central focus of this book is on "the bigger institutional picture" that frames everyday halal consumption, the contact zones or interface zones between Islam and markets through techniques like production, trade, and standards. In other words, I provide a multisited ethnography of the overlapping technologies and techniques of production, trade, and standards that together warrant a product as "halal" and thereby help to format the market.

My previous book was called *The Halal Frontier: Muslim Consumers in a Globalized Market* (Palgrave Macmillan 2011). From the perspective of anthropology of religion, I examined modern forms of everyday halal understanding and practice among Malay Muslims in London, that is, the halal consumption of middle-class Malays in the diaspora. More specifically, important themes were the politics of the national, diasporic identity, and ethnicity; economics in relation to Islam and Malaysia's role in the global market for religious/ethnic commodities; how the privileged position of science in a contemporary and secular setting such as London affects the role of Islam; authority, particularly linked to the power involved in halal certification embedded in contemporary Malaysian and Islamic institutional discourses and practices; and the ultimate complexity and contestation that grow out of the empirical material on halal consumption in the everyday lives of Malay middle-class Muslims.

The research on halal consumption in the everyday lives of Muslims raised a number of larger questions that are the central focus in this book: how organizations such as certifiers, Muslim consumer groups, Islamic universities, and manufacturing companies and shops understand and practice halal production, trade, and standards. A particular difference between the two projects is that the latter explores how standardization and certification regimes are emerging in the field of Islamic production, trade, and regulation. Throughout this book I bear in mind and move beyond the questions raised in my previous study. More generally, existing anthropological studies of halal and Islamic consumption overwhelmingly explore micro-social aspects such as the everyday consumption among Muslim groups.

For example, from an interdisciplinary perspective, the edited volume *Muslim Societies in the Age of Mass Consumption* (Pink 2009) argues that in spite of the intensifying globalization of markets and consumption, these processes have received modest scholarly attention. More specifically, this volume explores issues such as the changing spaces of consumption, branding, and the marketing of religious music as well as the consumption patterns of Muslim minority groups. Another important study is on urban Muslims in China, the Hui. Halal food and eating stood out as the most important identity markers in contradistinction to the surrounding Han majority. Besides nutritional and economic functions, food and eating practices expressed values and traits that they regarded as fundamentally Hui (Gillette 2000, 114). Finally, in Turkey the politics of identity among Islamists and secularists has been deeply influenced by an expanding consumer market, a "market for identities," in the context of the globalization of the 1980s and 1990s (Navaro-Yashin 2002).

An exception is the coedited volume *Halal Matters: Islam, Politics, and Markets in Global Perspective* (Bergeaud-Blackler, Fischer, and Lever 2015). Even if in this book I examine halal at different levels of the social scale among consumers, organizations, and state institutions I do not do so based on systematic ethnographic explorations of halal between Islam, standards, and technoscience comparing the two countries that arguably has the greatest influence on shaping trends in the global market for halal—namely, Malaysia and Singapore.

Current studies on the entanglements of capitalism, Islam, and the state in Southeast Asia explore, for example, how moderate Islamic "spiritual reform" movements in Indonesia combine business management principles and techniques from popular life-coaching seminars with Muslim practice. This form of "market Islam" and "spiritual economies" merge Muslim religious practice and capitalist ethics and effective self-management by attempting to make people "better from the inside" (Rudnyckyj 2009, 2010). Similarly, in the global and expanding market for halal Islam, standards, and technoscience fuse.

In Southeast Asia, regional technoscientific activity is imprinted with diverse colonial legacies and marked by cosmopolitan commitments, entrepôt experimental sites, complex trading zones, and flexible patterns of circulation (Warwick 2009). I take seriously Warwick's calls for more knowledge about the particulars and contingencies of Southeast Asian dwellings and journeys of technoscience and about how these hybrid shapes and assemblages inhabit interstitial spaces (Warwick 2009, 169). Fischer (2008, 539) rightly makes the case that anthropologies of science and technology should attend to both the cultural switches of the heterogeneous communities within which the sciences are cultured, technologies are peopled, and the reflexive social institutions within which medical, environmental, informational, and other technosciences must increasingly operate.

To my knowledge, the edited volume *Mediating Piety: Technology and Religion in Contemporary Asia* (Lim 2009) is one of the few studies that empirically explores the religion–science nexus in Asia. "Charismatic technology" refers to technology that inspires intense and often unquestioned confidence and optimism in it as the preeminent means for the improvement of quality of life (Lim 2009, 6). Charismatic technology is often, as it is the case in Malaysia and Singapore, regulated by a "technological clergy," that is, scientists, technicians, policymakers, and state leaders who adhere to the belief that there are technical solutions to most of humanity's problems (Lim 2009, 7). The pursuit and goals of transcendence in technology and religion can either converge or diverge from one another (Lim 2009, 23), and in the case of halal, I show that this is a case of current convergence globally. Similarly, there is a large and growing body of literature on Islamic banking (Maurer 2005; Kuran 1995, 1997; Haron 1997) and even accounting in Islamic banking and finance (Maurer 2002), but very little on halal production, trade, and standards. What is more, existing scholarship on the

Islamization of knowledge (Iqbal 2012) and Islamic technoscience (Furlow 2009; Lotfalian 1999) does not, in any systematic manner, explore halal production, trade, and standards.

I use "zones" to explain how not only Malaysia and Singapore but also the global markets for halal are composed of divergent zones inside and between which regulatory institutions and markets interact. I situate my analysis of halal between Islam, standards, and technoscience in a framework of new governing practices by different Southeast Asian countries such as Malaysia and Singapore (Ong 2006)—and global effects of these governing practices across global halal zones.

Exceptions to neoliberalism are central to these countries and neoliberal techniques combine with other cultural and economic forces in ways that evoke contingency, ambiguity, and instability. The spatial concentration of strategic political, economic, legal, and social conditions attracts foreign investment, technology transfer, and international expertise to particular zones of high growth such as Malaysia and Singapore (Ong 2006). In the halal zones of Malaysia and Singapore, regulatory institutions and global markets interact. At the same time, sovereign rule invokes the exception to create new economic possibilities, spaces, and techniques—for example, increased legal focus on halal in Malaysia and Singapore—and these countries are examples of how zoning technologies have carved out spaces to achieve strategic goals of regulation of halal in relation to market forces (Ong 2006, 7). What is more, spaces of government are not simply defined by geographies of territorial and national space but are also conceptualized in terms of zones formed through the circulation of technical practices and devices (Barry 2001, 3). Technology, standards, science, intellectual property rights, economy, and government all converge in such "technological zones" (Barry 2001).

The state in Malaysia and Singapore promotes these nations as landscapes that signify a localized form of "moderate Islam," that is, a form of modern Islam compatible with global capitalism. Halal production, trade, and regulation emerge in the interfaces between new forms of zoning, landscapes, state-driven visions, and at the same time global capitalism, that is, multinational companies, has made peace with cultural diversity (Wilk 2006, 197).

In the following chapters, "zones" signify not only national contexts for halal production, trade, and regulation but also zones within and between nations: major halal network events, halal training, science and research, how Muslim activists in Malaysia in particular try to expand halal requirements to cover more and more products and processes, and how local and multinational manufacturing companies, shops, and restaurants try to live up to rising halal requirements.

The connection between Malaysia, Singapore, and Muslim Southeast Asia more generally and the global proliferation of halal is no accident. As we shall see, halal has a particular and unique historical, political, and cultural trajectory in Malaysia and Singapore. This trajectory places these two countries at the forefront of developments in global halal zones.

WHAT IS MODERN HALAL?

Halal literally means "lawful" or "permitted." Industrial players, merchants and some Muslim scholars involved in halal trade and standardization have based their halal food rulings on statements from selected verses from the Koran, such as "Allah makes good things lawful to them and bad things unlawful" (7, 157), and

> [y]ou who believe, eat the good things We have provided for you and be grateful to God, if it is Him that you worship. He has only forbidden you carrion, blood, pig's meat, and animals over which any name other than God's has been invoked. But if anyone is forced to eat such things by hunger, rather than desire or excess, he commits no sin: God is Most Merciful and Forgiving. (Abdel Haleem, 2008, 2: 172–73)

It is repeated that

> [y]ou are forbidden to eat carrion; blood; pig's meat; any animal over which any name other than God's has been invoked; any animal strangled, or victim of a violent blow or fall, or gored or savaged by a beast of prey, unless you still slaughter it [in the correct manner]; or anything sacrificed on idolatrous altars. (Abdel Haleem 2008, 5: 3)

According to these scholars, halal is that which is beneficial and not detrimental to Muslims. Thus, the Koran and the Sunna (the life, actions, and teachings of the Prophet Muhammad) exhort Muslims to eat the good and lawful food God has provided for them, but a number of conditions and prohibitions are observed. Muslims are expressly forbidden from consuming carrion, spurting blood, pork, and foods that have been consecrated to any being other than God himself. These substances are haram ("unlawful" or "forbidden").[5] The lawfulness of meat depends on how it is obtained. Ritual slaughtering, *dhabh*, entails that the animal is killed in God's name by making a fatal incision across the throat. In this process, the blood should be drained as fully as possible. Among Muslim groups and individuals, the question of the stunning of animals prior to slaughter is highly contested; that is, some Muslims consider only meat from unstunned animals halal, whereas others accept that stunning is part of modern and ethical food production.

Sea creatures and locusts are considered halal. Because the sea is seen as pure in essence, all marine animals, even if they have died spontaneously, are halal. Despite the fact that they are not mentioned in the Koran, land creatures such as predators, dogs, and, in the eyes of some jurists, donkeys are haram. What is more, crocodiles, weasels, pelicans, otters, foxes, elephants, ravens, and insects have been condemned by the *ulama* (literally, those who know the law or religious scholars). Often some of these animals are seen as *makruh* or detestable and thus not haram (Denny 2006, 278). Divergences between jurists of the different schools of Islamic jurisprudence (Hanafi, Maliki, Hanbali, and *Shafi'i*, which is the school of thought dominant in Malaysia and Singapore) on halal understanding and practice exist.

Another significant Islamic prohibition relates to wine and any other alcoholic drink or substance, all of which are haram, whatever the quantity or the substance (Denny 2006, 279). As we shall see, alcohol has become a highly controversial question in mass production in divergent halal zones. With the advent of Islam, ancient negative attitudes toward pigs and pork were reinforced, as we saw earlier. Inspired by Jewish law, the Prophet Mohammad banned the flesh of pigs as the only animal to be prohibited, and in the Koran, the ban is repeated several times (Simoons 1994, 32). In effect, Muslims were distinguished from their Christian adversaries (Simoons 1994, 33). Some Muslim groups came to abhor pigs and pork to such an extent that everything touched by them was regarded as contaminated and worthless (Simoons 1994, 33). Under Western colonialism, pig abhorrence declined in many parts of the world, only to increase again with the end of European colonial rule after World War II, and especially with Islamic revivalism (Simoons 1994, 36). Historically, Arab traders spread Islam in peninsular Malaysia and Singapore in the thirteenth century, leading to a considerable reduction in keeping pigs and eating pork in this region (Simoons 1994, 58).

The reasons for the ban on pork within Islam largely follow the five main types of explanation advanced to analyze the origin of the Hebrew food laws. One is that these are arbitrary, make no sense to humans, and can only be understood by God. Another is that injunctions were based on sanitary concerns (Simoons 1994). A symbolic explanation proposed by Mary Douglas (see the later discussion) argues that acceptable animals represented proper human behavior versus the sinful behavior of banned animals. Yet another explanation is that Hebrew food laws originated in their rejections of cultic practices of alien peoples and of the worship of deities other than Jehovah. Involved in both the third and fourth hypotheses is the notion that the Hebrews wanted to set themselves apart from other peoples. Some anthropologists, most famously Marvin Harris, have argued for a fifth and recent explanation, according to which the prohibitions are grounded in economic, environmental, and/or ecological reasons (Simoons 1994, 64–65). According to Marvin Harris (1977, 1998) with the rise of Islam, the Israelite taboo on pigs was reconceptualized as a new set of sanctioned dietary laws "ecological" in essence; that is, religious ideas are traced to the cost/benefit of ecological processes.

The proliferation of halal can be seen as distinct sets of invocations of haram or taboo. Taboo can protect distinctive categories of the universe, consensus, and certainty about the organization of the cosmos, thus reducing intellectual and social disorder (Douglas 2004, xi). However, certainty and order easily mirror feelings of uncertainty and disorder. These doubts mostly surface in everyday strategies about how to go about practicing ever-intensifying demands for the Islamically proper in consumption. Elsewhere, Douglas (1975, 275) argues that when people become aware of encroachment and danger, dietary rules that control what goes into the body function as an analogy of the corpus of their cultural categories at risk.

The debate over the origins of the ban on pork in Judaism and Islam is far from resolved, and one central reason for this is that there is not sufficient historical evidence in existence. The prohibition of pork is one of the rare food taboos that live on in Islam, but the true reason for its prohibition is unknown. My brief discussion of anthropologists Douglas's and Harris's arguments serves the purpose of providing the reader with key arguments in a debate that has spanned decades and that still seems to inform scholarly and popular controversy over not only the prohibition of pork but also the nature of taboo itself.

In a Southeast Asian context, taboos distinguish between groups and individuals within their own society. Moreover, taboos operate in terms of the production, preparation, and distribution of food (Manderson 1986, 10). In modern Singapore, many Malays are fastidious about halal, but they practice this fastidiousness pragmatically in the context of the ethnic Chinese majority (Nasir, Pereira, and Turner 2009). Dietary laws among urban Malay Muslims in Malaysia are highly conscious, and halal is ubiquitous among them as a signifier in public as well as in private spaces or domains. During fieldwork in 2009–2010 in Singapore and Kuala Lumpur, I found a large number of food, as well as nonfood, products certified by that state in convenience stores, grocery stores, supermarkets, and hypermarkets (a combined supermarket and department store that carries a large range of products). What is more, virtually all of the large fast food chains such as McDonald's and Burger King are fully halal certified by JAKIM in Malaysia and the MUIS in Singapore, and this is also the case with many smaller restaurants, even those owned and run by ethnic Chinese.

The understanding and practice of halal requirements vary among import countries and companies producing halal food. This is the point made in the book *Halal Food Production* (Riaz and Chaudry 2004, vii). This book by two US scholars is a popularized guide to producing and marketing halal (foods) for professionals in an expanding global food market. Chaudry is president of IFANCA, a leading halal certifier based in the US, discussed earlier, and Riaz is a senior auditor in the same organization. Riaz is also the director of Texas A&M University's Food and Protein R&D Center. The IFCE that arranged the conference in Brussels is a kind of subsidiary of IFANCA in Europe. To my knowledge, this is the only book of its kind, and it is widely used by companies (e.g., Novozymes) worldwide that try to understand and comply with the current transformation of halal, and it is a unique piece of empirical material. It is *the* guide to modern and global halal. What is more, the book in particular focuses on Malaysia and Singapore as important halal nations or zones.

Modern halal cannot be understood simply as part of a stable taxonomy. In addition to halal and haram, doubtful things should be avoided; that is, there is a gray area between the clearly lawful and the unlawful (Riaz and Chaudry 2004, 6–7). The doubtful or questionable is expressed in the word *mashbooh* (Riaz and Chaudry 2004, 7), which can be evoked by divergences in religious scholars' opinions or the suspicion of undetermined or prohibited ingredients in a commodity. Hence, far more abstract, individual, and fuzzy aspects of context and handling are involved in determining the halalness of a product. The problem in certifying food and other products with regard to these substances is that they are extremely difficult to discover. The interpretation of these *mashbooh* areas is left open to Islamic specialists and state institutions such as JAKIM and MUIS.

To determine whether a foodstuff is halal or haram "depends on its nature, how it is processed, and how it is obtained" (Riaz and Chaudry 2004, 14). In the end, however, the underlying principle behind the prohibitions remains "divine order" (Riaz and Chaudry 2004, 12). Knowledge of the preceding requirements is, of course, essential to innovative companies that try to establish themselves in an expanding global halal market. The increased demand for halal products by conscious and educated Muslim consumers has urged developed countries to export halal products. In this way, developed countries have entered a market that was previously dominated by Muslim countries. Moreover, the proliferation of Western franchised food has changed the international food market and has subjected it to new standards of halal certification (Riaz and Chaudry 2004, 29–30).

In countries such as Malaysia, Singapore, and Indonesia, even paper/plastic labels and printing on food are seen as problematic. Glue used for labels, as well as edible printing and dyes used directly on food, may contain not permissible ingredients. Some halal-certifying bodies in importing countries feel that such seepage or cross-contamination may violate the halal status of food (Riaz and Chaudry 2004, 134). What is more, packaging food in a halal environment is essential (Riaz and Chaudry 2004, 134–135). Muslim dietary rules assumed new significance in the twentieth century, as some Muslims began striving to demonstrate how such rules conform to modern reason and the findings of scientific research. Another common theme in the revival and renewal of these dietary rules seems to be the search for alternatives to what are seen to be Western values, ideologies, and lifestyles, and this is reflected in globalized halal. Finally, standardization and technoscience have become essential to halal production, trade, and regulation in and across global halal zones.

HALAL STANDARDS AND CLASSIFICATION

Over the past three decades, Malaysia and Singapore have become world leaders in the global expansion of halal markets. This has come about in large part because the state governments of Malaysia and Singapore have taken on the role of halal-certifying authority within those countries. In effect, they have certified, standardized, and bureaucratized halal production, trade, and consumption in a way that made it possible to extend these standards abroad. However, even if halal symbolizes an ongoing social construction of quality the quest for a global halal norm has so far not been completed (van Warden and van Dalen 2013, 218).

In a broader perspective, I see halal and the vision to globalize it as a form of "standardization" (Scott 1998)—an attempt by the state to standardize production, trade, and consumption. This process of standardization is apparent in state halal certification, but standardization is also market driven. I take halal standards and standardization to mean several things. First, they can refer to the design and qualities of products, as well as proper conduct of states, organizations, and individuals, for example, with regard to the production, preparation, handling, and storage of halal. Standards and standardization can be seen to be instruments of control and forms of regulation attempting to generate elements of global order (Brunsson and Jacobsson 2000, 1). Unlike non-state-certifying bodies around the world, the Malaysian and Singaporean states can impose legal sanctions on companies that do not live up to standards.

What is more, standards can also refer to persons with certain qualifications, knowledge, or skills (Brunsson and Jacobsson 2000, 5). An example of this, as we shall see, is the mandatory requirement that companies set up what is called a Halal Committee in Malaysia and a Halal Team in Singapore. The purpose of this committee is not only to ensure the halalness of products but also to reduce the risk of non-halal contamination; that is, the committee is a form of standardized Muslim risk management. Hence, standards can generate and reinvigorate social norms and directives (Brunsson and Jacobsson 2000, 14). At the same time, the meanings of standards may evoke ideas of similarity and uniformity—the standardized is that which supposedly is similar and follows rules (Brunsson and Jacobsson 2000, 14). Such rules also specify what is proper behavior so that ideas of appropriateness become associated with standardization. Thus, the standard way of doing things is often understood as the most usual, generally accepted, normal, or "best way" (Brunsson and Jacobsson 2000, 15). Standards set by International Organization for Standardization (ISO), for example, provide states and large companies with rules about how to organize what policies to pursue, what kind of services to offer, and how to design products.

Busch (2000) argues that standards are part of the moral economy of the modern world that set norms for behavior and create uniformity. Standards standardize things or products; workers with regard to uniformity and discipline; markets in relation to fixed/uniform prices as well as the packaging of products; the way in which capitalists behave and use capital; standards themselves, that is, standardized methods that produce consistent results; the makers of standards such as scientists and technicians; consumers as a product of capitalist development and socially regulated consumption; and the environment—for example, halal parks, as we shall see. Through standards the moral economy is produced and reproduced (Busch 2000, 274). In this book I show how these trends are becoming increasingly important in the global market for halal as standardization processes in the making.

Last, a key argument that runs through this book is that halal standardization is inseparable from broader processes of classification and categorization. Such processes produce new identities, subjectivities, and forms of social organization (Ponte, Gibbon, and Vestergaard 2011, 1–2). Standards are one of the most important devices that are at play in rearticulations of the governance of economy and society that also discipline people, organizations, and states in the promotion of self-regulation (Ponte, Gibbon, and Vestergaard 2011, 299).

However, to understand halal regulation through systems of classification scholars need to move beyond a political economy approach. I am inspired by Bowker and Star's (2000) argument that classification systems and standardization often invisibly shape social order, morality, science, information/technology infrastructure, organizations, and their work processes. This point is essential in my exploration of emergent regulation of halal markets that in many ways escapes conventional logics of "secular" certification, standardization, and legislation. Formal and bureaucratic classifications and standards "trail behind" the permits, forms, numerals, and the visible work of people who adjust them to make organizations run smoothly. In that sense, classifications may become more visible, especially when they become objects of contention (Bowker and Star 2000, 2–3). In the case of halal, I explore ways in which the invisible forces of categories/classifications and standards are in play in the modern world and how these properties inform moral/social order and work practices (Bowker and Star 2000, 5).

A classification can be defined as a spatial-temporal segmentation of the world and a classification system generates knowledge (Bowker and Star 2000, 10). Classificatory systems are often contested, ignored, misunderstood, and mixed (Bowker and Star 2000, 11). Classifications and standards are closely related, but not identical. Classification systems often become standardized and a standard is in part a way of classifying the world (Bowker and Star 2000, 13).

My study of halal production, trade, and standards is inspired by the term *boundary objects*. Such objects inhibit several communities of practice and satisfy the informational requirements of each of them, travel across borders and maintain some sort of constant identity, are plastic and customizable, and have common identities across settings, and they are both ambiguous/constant as well as abstract/concrete (Bowker and Star 2000, 16). Boundary objects are disputed because they are subjected to entangled and crisscrossing classifications schemes of bureaucracies and this is especially the case with forms of ethical and religious classifications (Bowker and Star 2000, 21). Halal is no longer an expression of an esoteric form of production, trade, or consumption but is part of a huge and expanding globalized market in which standards and technoscience increasingly play important roles. In short, I study how these processes transform halal from an Islamic form of classification towards modern and global technologies and techniques of regulation.

HALAL THINKING AND PRACTICE IN ORGANIZATIONS

Organizations such as halal certifiers, Islamic universities, consumer/interest groups, and companies possess shared characteristics such as explicit rules, division of labor, aims that involve acting on or changing everyday life, and have governing ethos (e.g., making money or a management principle; Gellner and Hirsch 2001). Important themes in my study of how organizations think about and practice halal production, trade, and standards are conflicts, diversity, and power relations, as well as "the bigger picture," that is, competition between organizations and their relationship to the state and society at large.

I argue that halal organizations such as certifiers are being rationalized (Maznah 2010; Peletz 2002). I understand rationalization to be transformations that involve differentiation, systematization, specialization, and bureaucratic forms of social organization. An example of this is secularized Syariah bureaucracies in Malaysia and Singapore. A central question is how organizations think about and practice halal production, trade, and standards. I am inspired by Mary Douglas's point that organizations provide the categories of thought, which serve to define what things (patterns) are similar or not. Douglas argues that individuals' most elementary cognitive processes depend on social institutions. Halal regulation is premised on the ways in which halal certifiers may generate authority among individuals, for example, company representatives and participants in halal training, in their everyday working life (Douglas 1986).

Certifiers can gain legitimacy by a certain kind of "grounding in nature and reason," and these institutions try to promote "a set of analogies with which to explore the world and with which to justify the naturalness and reasonableness of the instituted rules" (Douglas 1986, 113). With reference to Durkheim, Douglas (1986, 113) argues that an institution must secure the social edifice by sacralizing the principles of justice. Halal classification and standardization can be seen as an institutional attempt to sacralize commodities in a religious market. Classifying or categorizing some commodities as halal sacralizes these commodities against others and invokes the (religious) authority of certifying institutions. The exchange of certified halal commodities illustrates the argument that every transaction is necessarily a "social strategy" (Sahlins 1972, 303). Sahlins (1972, 313) writes that "the economic flexibility of the system depends on the social structure of the trade relation." In the market for halal, a particular trade relation exists. Consumers buy commodities that ideally comply with certain religious standards, and the trader not only profits but also claims a measure of authority. Marking or tacking commodities or premises with halal logos helps to personalize this form of exchange or transaction, that is, ideally the producer, the trader, and the consumer all share the symbolic content of the halal logo.

Business is always personal at one level and impersonal at another, Hart (2005, 5) writes. Humans always experience society as personal and impersonal at once, and the halal market evokes the point that business and market relations more generally have a personal and social component (Hart 2005, 28). For example, shopping in standardized Malaysian and Singaporean supermarkets discussed in Chapter 7 is largely impersonal, but marking products as halal with logos emphasizes the religious, personal, and social component in proper Islamic consumption.

This is a form of "logo logic" that works by attaching political and moral messages to lifestyle brands and communicating these branded messages (Bennett and Lagos 2007, 194). In general, systems of certification have grown considerably, but the diversity of these systems often confuses consumers (Bennett and Lagos 2007, 204)—more and more products carry an increasing number of logos. There is a distinct element of political economy present in the way in which halal certification in complex ways links the different levels of the social scale, such as individual consumption, the marketplace, Islamic organizations, and the state. In a way, halal certification, standards, and logos can be seen as a form of moral economy (Busch 2000) in which the aim is to apply regulatory logics to the certification of virtue requiring that "virtue's characteristics be specified in increasingly formal ways." (Brown 2010).

Classification and classification systems organize and are organized by work practices of and in organizations (Bowker and Star 2000, 28). Classification schemes render work visible and thus allow for surveillance mechanisms such as audits and inspections (Bowker and Star 2000, 30). At the same time, classifications are powerful but relatively invisible technologies embedded in working infrastructures that contain multiple classification systems that are both invisible and ubiquitous. In turn, these link the individual with larger processes and structures (Bowker and Star 2000, 323). In sum, classifications are a key part of the standardization processes that are themselves the cornerstones of working infrastructures in organizations.

ISLAMIC AUDIT CULTURE

An important theme that runs through this book is the emergence and expansion of an audit culture around halal practice. Not only the state in Malaysia and Singapore, but also independent certifiers, such as the IFCE, regulate halal by performing "on-site" audits and inspections in shops, restaurants, and factories. There is a large body of literature on the rise of an "audit society," but there is need for further scholarship on the ways in which audits and inspections are understood and practiced in locally specific contexts.[6] The pervasiveness of an audit culture within and around halal practices is not well understood, but, as I show, it links Islam, standards, and technoscience.

Audit and inspection systems are a feature of modern societies. They exist to generate comfort and reassurance in a wide range of policy contexts (Power 1999, xvii). To a large extent auditing is about cultural and economic authority granted to auditors (Power 1999, xvii), based of course on the assumption that those auditors are competent and their practices effective. There is no general agreement as to precisely what auditing is or what it could be (Power 1999, 4), but there are some basic conceptual ingredients of any audit practice. These include independence from the matter being audited, technical work in the form of evidence gathering and the examination of documentation, and the expression of a view based on this evidence (Power 1999, 5). A central aspect of audit culture that is also highly relevant to the market for halal is the pushing of control and self-control farther into organizations to satisfy the need to connect internal organizational arrangements to public ideals (Power 1999, 10). The states in Malaysia and Singapore have become increasingly and explicitly committed to an indirect supervisory role in halal, and audit is both a solution to a technical problem and a way of redesigning the practice of government. Staff policies such as setting up a Halal Committee/Team to handle halal properly as well as establishing sections in companies that specialize in halal compliance are examples of the increasingly prominent role of internal control systems that can be audited.

Food scares and scandals relating to bovine spongiform encephalopathy (BSE) and salmonella, for example, have increased the public role of (halal) audits and inspections to control internal organizational arrangements and systems. Organizations and their procedures have become more auditable, and in practical terms, this involves formalized procedures of application and negotiation with a certifier, for example.

Audit culture has been explored from an anthropological perspective focusing on consensus endorsing government through economic efficiency and good practice. In this form of modern accountability, the financial and the moral converge to form a culture of what are deemed acceptable forms (Strathern 2000, 1). Audits and audit practices are discussed as descriptors applicable to all kinds of reckonings, evaluations, and measurements and as distinct cultural artifacts in the market that works as a platform for both individual interest and national politics (Strathern 2000, 2). A key question I explore is to what extent audit culture is compatible with the point made above that the underlying principle behind halal remains "divine order" and that the "halalness" of products is not easily verifiable: smell, texture, or taste cannot fully determine whether a product is halal. As we shall see in the following ethnography, audits/inspections seem to take on lives of their own. This point is comparable to Cobett's (2011) analysis of Islamic finance in South Africa. This study concludes that the representation of Islam by banks and financial institutions is not necessarily shared by Muslims in their everyday lives. Similarly, my own research shows that while some Malay Muslims are fastidious about halal consumption, others find the stress on piety through this form of consumption to be excessive and unnecessary (Fischer 2008b, 2011).

Ethnographies of inspections/audits are relatively sparse, especially in a religious context. However, a study of the United Kingdom government's inspection of the services provided by municipalities and other local units of administration (Miller 2003) is built on fieldwork on the actual process of auditing/inspections. Similar to my analysis, Miller's study explores the details of inspections with a focus on the terminology, stated aims, and observed practice of audit/inspection. Based on ethnography in an Indian shipyard a study shows how audit creates opacity, disorders the work process, and is part of value chains supported by diverse forms of charisma and racial distinction. Bear calls for a stronger focus on the disordered capitalism supported by audit regimes (Bear 2013). As I show in the case of the regulation of the halal market, both these studies demonstrate that audits/inspections seem to take on lives of their own.

IN AND ACROSS HALAL ZONES

Fierce competition exists between Malaysia and Singapore, not least in the race for world leadership in global halal production, trade, and regulation. Geographical proximity, history, and material flows all link the two countries. Arguably, these links are "eminently political creations" (Shiraishi 2009, 2). Since the 1980s, state-regulated Islam in both countries has standardized, certified, and institutionalized halal. Consequently, of all the countries involved in the proliferation of halal on a global scale, Malaysia and Singapore have developed the most extensive institutionalized state certification system.

Despite many similarities, the two countries are radically different in a number of respects including the political. Consequently, halal is classified in quite different ways in the two countries, even if the overall objective in both cases is to dominate the global halal market. Malaysia is a democratic, Muslim-majority country where politics is heavily influenced by the United Malays National Organisation (UMNO). This has been the case since independence from Britain in 1957. Singapore, meanwhile, is Chinese-dominated, arguably authoritarian, and led by the People's Action Party (PAP), which was formed in 1959. These differences in political economy have yielded certain distinct differences in the institutionalization of halal as it has expanded globally. In this ethnography I focus mainly on two of these institutional differences.

The first has to do with how each state, through Islamic bureaucrats and halal inspectors, subjects local and foreign businesses to its own set of expanding "Islamic" requirements and forms of regulation. What is more, JAKIM and MUIS have created lists of approved certifiers for dealing with imported food products. JAKIM and MUIS do not have the resources to carry out inspections globally and consequently have outsourced responsibilities to local Muslim organizations. In all this halal certification in the form of logos and certificates are essential. The IFCE, the organization that hosted the conference in Brussels, is approved by JAKIM. JAKIM has approved Islamic organizations in Australia, Argentina, Brazil, Brunei, China, Denmark, France, Germany, India, Indonesia, Japan, the Netherlands, New Zealand, Pakistan, Philippines, Singapore, South Africa, Taiwan, Thailand, the US, Uruguay, and Vietnam. However, these recognized Islamic organizations have been reevaluated by JAKIM following a tightening of legislation in Malaysia in 2011, and they continue to be so. All these countries are divergent halal zones in which local Islamic organizations approved by JAKIM regulate the proliferation of the global halal market. I have conducted fieldwork among two approved Islamic organizations—IFCE that held the conference in Brussels and Islamic Cultural Centre in Denmark. However, the majority of countries worldwide are not represented on this list.

The second institutional difference I explore has to do with how companies respond to the particulars of halal certification in each country. The ethnographic material is used to bring out the tensions and conflicts about halal production, trade, and standards. I analyze how powerful corporate discourses evoke state-regulated Islam and state-certified halal in Malaysia and Singapore to brand their commodities on a global scale. In Malaysia, in particular, the state provides infrastructure for the manufacturing firms that operate in the countries. The capability of state-regulated Islam to certify halal is essential to companies. Hence, these companies can be torn between desiring state certification, on the one hand, and being subjected to fuzzy and "Islamic" forms of disciplining, technoscience, inspection, and control on the other. For example, state halal inspections of companies are studied as techniques of disciplining and control that are essential to the understanding and practice of halal certification. To attract foreign companies and investment to Malaysia and Singapore, state bodies and bureaucracies such as JAKIM and MUIS must develop and refine methods of inspection, control, and discipline in production and trade. I also study technologies and techniques to control and avoid contamination of halal in production and handling. The problem in certifying food and other types of products with regard to non-halal substances is that such substances are extremely difficult to discover. These points reflect broader discussions of halal inspections, legal requirements, and expanding audit cultures that run through subsequent chapters.

In Malaysia and Singapore, local companies have become accustomed to state certification by JAKIM and MUIS. I compare responses to halal certification of local companies, often linked to the state, and foreign companies that may have limited experience in coping with increasing religious requirements, classifications, and standardization. As halal requirements proliferate, the state insists that Muslims must be involved in production. This insistence compels foreign companies to reconsider staff policies: to employ local Muslims in order to comply with increased demands for the proper "Muslim handling" of halal. I explore strategies of negotiating increasing requirements of halal and its certification among the earlier-mentioned types of companies. More specifically, I focus on strategies employed by these companies to negotiate or preempt what can be seen as excessive requirements. Halal requirements often mean additional costs for companies. So I examine the economies involved in halal. Finally, I consider the extent to which halal regulations have had an impact on often highly industrialized processes of innovation and development. Traditional Islamic requirements regarding halal have become increasingly complicated, abstract, and hazy, making production and trade (not to mention regulation) considerably more complex. The interpretation of these intricate and hence confusing stipulations is left to Islamic organizations and state institutions.

HALAL AS A GLOBAL ASSEMBLAGE

Modern halal is explored as part of "global assemblages"; that is, they are products of multiple and emergent determinations that are not reducible to a single logic (Ong and Collier 2005, 12). As a composite concept, "the term *global assemblage* suggests inherent tensions: global implies broadly encompassing, seamless, and mobile; assemblage implies heterogeneous, contingent, unstable, partial, and situated" (Ong and Collier 2005, 12). In short, I analyze how Islam, standards, and technoscience make up halal as a global assemblage. As we shall see, the proliferation of the halal market signifies broader global shifts in domains, such as circuits of exchange, systems of administration of governance, and regimes of ethics or values. These phenomena are distinguished by a particular "global" quality. They are abstractable, mobile, dynamic and move across and reconstitute "society," "culture," and "economy." Simultaneously, these phenomena are domains in which the forms and values of individual and collective existence are subject to technological (the problem of choosing the most appropriate means for achieving technoscientific, organizational, or administrative ends), political (concerning the appropriate form and scope of juridico-legal institutions), and ethical reflection on questions of value and morality (Ong and Collier 2005, 4).

Thus, exploring Malaysia and Singapore as particular zones in which halal as a global assemblage is taking place evokes a range of debates, including that of legality. In Singapore, for example, the AMLA that came into effect in 1968 and defined the powers and jurisdiction of Muslim institutions was in 2009 revised so that it is now a serious offence to display false halal logos, that is, false MUIS logos. The same tendency is seen in Malaysia and globally. Halal has not been systematically explored from the perspective of legal anthropology, and with this book I intend to fill this gap. This focus also entails broader questions such as the spectacle of attempts at intentional control and planning, and publicly rationalized imperative decision making (Moore 1978, 8), as well as emphasis on legal transactions, disputes, and rules seen in the dimension of time (Moore 1978, 256). An example of this is the hype surrounding the passing of a new Halal Act in Malaysia in 2010 that severely tightened halal regulation and enforcement.

A NOTE ON METHODOLOGY

The methodology of this study is based on participant observation and interviews undertaken between 2009 and 2012 with state bureaucracies in Malaysia and Singapore, Islamic organizations, at halal network events such as the WHF (an annual conference that includes major halal players globally) in Kuala Lumpur, companies/shops/restaurants, and Islamic universities that are developing technologies to detect pork gelatin/DNA and alcohol in industrial processes, as well as Islamic activists who want to proliferate halal further than state authorities. Companies were selected to obtain a good representative spread, that is, to cover types of companies with different histories, sizes, cultures, structures, hierarchies, and values to observe and analyze.

What is more, I also build on extended periods of fieldwork in Malaysia and Europe undertaken since 1996. Singapore is small in size, and there are not many manufacturing industries in the country. Hence, when focusing on halal in Singapore I mainly explore the working of MUIS, shops, and restaurants. In the chapters to come, the exploration of Malaysian halal takes up more space than does its Singaporean counterpart. The reason for this is that Malaysia is a bigger country with a large Muslim population in which halal has been an important question for many years. Thus, I explore why and how the historical, political, and institutional differences between the two countries mean that Malaysia is able to make the most difference in global halal zones. This can also be said to be a reflexive comparison (Herzfeld 2001) building on fieldwork in the two countries.

I endeavored to follow "the people" (bureaucrats, representatives from halal certifying bodies, scientists, activists, and company representatives), "the thing" (the circulation of halal commodities as manifestly material objects of study; Marcus 1995, 106), and as "the metaphor" (halal embedded in particular realms of classification, discourse, and modes of thought; Marcus 1995, 108). Thus, I follow people, halal things, and metaphors between Islam, standards, and technoscience, on one hand, and inside and across divergent zones, on the other. Despite the emergence of halal trade on a global scale, there have been few attempts to systematically disassemble halal as a global assemblage.

I have also conducted extensive archive studies on halal in Malaysia and Singapore, mainly through reading major newspapers with a long history, that is, *Straits Times* in Singapore (established in 1845) that was reestablished as *New Straits Times* in Malaysia following the separation of the two countries. These censored newspapers express state ideologies in the two countries. These ideologies thrive in the economic realm as financial nationalisms that promise future prosperity. In other words, the power of the state derives from its ability to define the national body as something primarily economic and set in the future (Williamson 2002, 403).

Newspapers in Malaysia and Singapore are primary vehicles of UMNO and PAP political discourse and control as cultural texts in which the state and 'the public' are represented (Gupta 1995, 377). Major newspapers in these two countries are all owned or dominated by state interest groups. My reading of newspapers and other types of documents such as political and legal documents compose a historical ethnography of halal understandings and practices in particular settings that reciprocally shape subjects and contexts allowing certain things to be said and done (Comaroff and Comaroff 1992, 31). At the same time, newspaper discourses are essential in transmitting halal classification systems and standardization that invisibly shape social order, morality, science, information/technology infrastructure, organizations, and their work processes (Bowker and Star, 2000). More specifically, I am inspired by Bowker and Star's (2000, 5) call to delve into the dusty archives of classification design to understand better how wide-scale classification decisions have been made.

In Malaysia and Singapore, censorship of the written and electronic media exists in the form of political control of technologies, organizations, audiences, and content (George 2006). Government regulation of the media allows the state to impose restraints on publication as well as access to ownership and operation (George 2006, 42). Political leadership in the two countries can rely on editors to act in the interests of the nation, the state, the government, and the party (George 2006, 49). I also explore the proliferation of halal in the media such as magazines, e-mails, websites, advertisements, pamphlets, and flowcharts in factories.

As we shall see, probability and statistics play important roles in halal production, trade, consumption, and standards. These insights are of particular relevance in my reading of newspapers and the way in which halal is classified and quantified based on assumptions about statistics and probability. Halal is constantly evoked as a global and growing market, and this fact legitimizes state involvement and regulation. The halal visions of Malaysia and Singapore are, to a large extent, driven by market research, statistics, and probability that attempt to map markets and predict the future. Modern statistics provides quantitative technology for empirical science—it is a logic and methodology for the measurement of uncertainty in the planning and interpretation of experimentation and observation (Stigler 1986, 1). Statistics and probability have a marked impact of scientific expertise on social issues, as well as the development of standards, for example (Stigler 1999), and this is also the case with halal as a global assemblage in and across divergent zones.

Statistics in economic, political, and social science are profound and wide ranging in changing the structure of power/knowledge (Gigerenzer et al. 1989, xiv). In halal discourse in the media and newspapers, in particular, statistics are constantly featured in connection with marketing, market research, quality control, accounting, economic forecasting, polling, and surveys. Thus, statistics and probability thinking play extraordinary roles in government, law, business, and other bureaucratic institutions with a responsibility to a wider public (Gigerenzer et al. 1989, 236), and this is the case with halal. To sum up on my methodology, I study the social life of halal certified things and services, that is, "things with a particular type of social potential" (Appadurai 1999: 6) that are premised on certification by a recognizable certifier.

NOTES

1. The IFCE later changed its name to Halal Food Council of Europe (HFCE).
2. IFANCA was founded in Illinois in 1982 with the objective of increasing awareness and understanding of Muslim dietary requirements, standards and regulation, and scientific research related to food, as well as nutrition and health. IFANCA provides halal supervision and certification for many companies worldwide.
3. *Syariah* is the local spelling of *Shari'a* in Malaysia and Singapore.
4. An enzyme is a substance that acts as a catalyst in living organisms, regulating the rate at which chemical reactions proceed without itself being altered in the process. Enzymes also have valuable industrial and medical applications; for example, the fermenting of wine, leavening of bread, curdling of cheese, and brewing of beer are reactions understood to be the result of the catalytic activity of enzymes. Enzymes have assumed an increasing importance in industrial processes that involve organic chemical reactions (Encyclopedia Britannica Online, Academic Edition, http://academic.eb.com.molly.ruc.dk/bps/search?query=enzyme&blacklist=189245).
5. These four prohibitions parallel those of *kashrut* (Jewish dietary law), which includes a number of additional prohibitions (e.g., many marine species). Compared to halal, kosher requirements have a longer history of systematic institutionalization, certification, and standardization.
6. For a study of Islamic audits in a "Syariah-compliant" national Islamic bank and local cooperative credit union in Indonesia, see Maurer (2002).

BIBLIOGRAPHY

Abdel Haleem, M. A. S. (translator) 2008. *The Qur'an*. Oxford: University Press.

Agriculture and Agri-Food Canada. 2011. Global *Halal Food Market*. Ottawa: Agriculture and Agri-Food Canada.

Anderson, Warwick. 2009. "Re-orienting STS: Emergent Studies of Science, Technology, and Medicine in Southeast Asia." *East Asian Science, Technology and Society: An International Journal* 3:163–171.
Appadurai, Arjun. 1999. "Introduction: Commodities and the Politics of Value." In *The Social Life of Things. Commodities in Cultural Perspective*, edited by Arjun Appadurai, 3–63. Cambridge: Cambridge University Press.
Barry, Andrew. 2001. *Political Machines*. London and New York: Athlone Press.
Bear, Laura. 2013. "The Antinomies of Audit: Opacity, Instability and Charisma in the Economic Governance of a Hooghly shipyard." *Economy and Society* 42(3): 375–397.
Bennett, Lance W. and Lagos, Taso. 2007. "Logo Logic: The Ups and Downs of Branded Political Communication." *The ANNALS of the American Academy of Political and Social Science* 611: 193–206.
Bergeaud-Blackler, F., Fischer, J. and Lever, J. 2015. *Halal Matters: Islam, Politics and Markets in Global Perspective*. Abingdon and New York: Routledge.
Bowker, Geoffrey C. and Star, Susan L. 2000. *Sorting Things Out: Classification and Its Consequences*. Cambridge and London: MIT Press.
Brown, Michael F. 2010. "A Tale of Three Buildings: Certifying Virtue in the New Moral Economy." *American Ethnologist* 37(4): 741–752.
Brunsson, Nils and Jakobsson, Bengt. 2000. "The Contemporary Expansion of Standardization." In *A World of Standards*, edited by Nils Brunsson and Bengt Jakobsson, 1–20. Oxford and New York: Oxford University Press.
Busch, Lawrence. 2000. "The Moral Economy of Grades and Standards." *Journal of Rural Studies* 16: 273–283.
Cobett, Elizabeth. 2011. "The Shaping of Islamic Finance in South Africa: Public Islam and Muslim Publics." *Journal for Islamic Studies* 31: 29–59.
Comaroff, Jean and Comaroff, John. 1992. *Ethnography and the Historical Imagination*. Boulder: Westview Press.
Denny, Frederick M. 2006. *An Introduction to Islam*. Upper Saddle River: Pearson Prentice Hall.
Douglas, Mary. 1975. *Implicit Meanings*. New York and London: Routledge.
Douglas. Mary. 1986. *How Institutions Think*. Syracuse, NY: Syracuse University Press.
Douglas, Mary. 2004. *Purity and Danger*. London: Routledge.
Fischer, Johan. 2011. *The Halal Frontier: Muslim Consumers in a Globalized Market*. New York: Palgrave Macmillan.
Fischer, Michael J. 2008. "Four Genealogies or a Recombinant Anthropology of Science and Technology." *Cultural Anthropology* 22(4): 539–615.
Furlow, Christopher. 2013. "Secularism in Malaysia." In *Making Sense of the Secular: Critical Perspectives from Europe and Asia*, edited by Ranjan Ghosh, 171–181. New York: Routledge.
Gellner, David N. and Hirsch, Eric. 2001. "Introduction: Ethnography of Organizations and Organizations of Ethnography." In *Inside Organizations: Anthropologists at Work*, edited by David N. Gellner and Eric Hirsch, 1–18. Oxford and New York: Berg Publishers.
George, Cherian. 2006. *Contentious Journalism and the Internet. Towards Democratic Discourse in Malaysia and Singapore*. Singapore: Singapore University Press in Association with University of Washington Press.
Gigerenzer, Gerd et al. 1989. *The Empire of Chance. How Probability Changed Science and Everyday Life*. Cambridge: Cambridge University Press.
Gillette, Maris B. 2000. *Between Mecca and Beijing. Modernization and Consumption among Urban Chinese Muslims*. Palo Alto: Stanford University Press.
Gupta, Akhil. 1995. "Blurred Boundaries: The Discourse of Corruption, the Culture of Politics, and the Imagined State." *American Ethnologist* 22(2): 375–402.

Furlow, C. A. 2009. "Malaysian modernities: Cultural Politics and the Construction of Muslim Technoscientific Identities." *Anthropological Quarterly*, 82(1), 197–228.

Haron, Sudin. 1997. *Islamic Banking: Rules and Regulations*. Petaling Jaya: Pelanduk Publications.

Harris, Marvin. 1977. *Cannibals and Kings. The Origins of Cultures*. New York: Random House.

Harris, Marvin. 1998. *Good to Eat: Riddles of Food and Culture*. Chicago, IL: Waveland Press.

Hart, Keith. 2005. *The Hit Man's Dilemma: Or, Business, Personal and Impersonal*. Chicago, IL: Prickly Paradigm Press.

Herzfeld, Michael. 2001. "Performing Comparisons: Ethnography, Globetrotting, and the Spaces of Social Knowledge." *Journal of Anthropological Research* 57: 259–276.

Iqbal, Muzaffar. 2012. *Islam and Science: Historic and Contemporary Perspectives*. Farnham: Ashgate.

Kuran, Timur. 1995. "Islamic Economics and the Islamic Subeconomy." *The Journal of Economic Perspectives* 9(4): 155–173.

Kuran, Timur. 1997. "The Genesis of Islamic Economics: A Chapter in the Politics of Muslim Identity." *Social Research* 64(2): 301–338.

Lim, Francis. K. G. 2009. "Charismatic Technology." In *Mediating Piety: Technology and Religion in Contemporary Asia*, edited by Francis Khek Gee Lim, 1–26. Leiden and Boston: Brill.

Manderson, Lenore. 1986. "Introduction: The Anthropology of Food in Oceania and Southeast Asia." In *Shared Wealth and Symbols. Food, Culture and Society in Oceania and Southeast Asia*, edited by Lenore Manderson, 1–25. Cambridge and Melbourne: Cambridge University Press.

Marcus, George E. 1995. "Ethnography in/of the World System: The Emergence of Multi-Sited Ethnography." *Annual Review of Anthropology* 24: 95–117.

Maurer, Bill. 2005. *Mutual Life, Limited: Islamic Banking, Alternative Currencies, Lateral Reason*. Princeton: Princeton University Press.

Maurer, Bill. 2002. "Anthropological and Accounting Knowledge in Islamic Banking and Finance: Rethinking Critical Accounts." *Journal of the Royal Anthropological Institute* 8(4): 645–667.

Miller, Daniel. 2003. "The Virtual Moment." *Journal of the Royal Anthropological Institute* (N.S) 9: 57–75.

Mohamad, Maznah. 2010. "The Ascendance of Bureaucratic Islam and the Secularization of the Sharia in Malaysia." *Pacific Affairs* 83(3): 505–524.

Moore, Sally F. 1978. *Law as Process. An Anthropological Approach*. London, Henley, Boston: Routledge.

Nasir, Kamaludeen Mohamad, Pereira, Alexius A. and Turner, Bryan S. 2009. *Muslims in Singapore: Piety, Politics and Policies*. Oxon: Routledge.

Navaro-Yashin, Yael. 2002. *Faces of the State: Secularism and Public Life in Turkey*. Princeton: Princeton University Press.

Ong, Aihwa. 2006. *Neoliberalism as Exception: Mutations in Citizenship and Sovereignty*. Durham and London: Duke University Press.

Ong, Aihwa and Collier, Stephen J. 2005. "Global Assemblages, Anthropological Problems." In *Global Assemblages: Technology, Politics, and Ethics as Anthropological Problems*, edited by Aihwa Ong and Stephen J. Collier, 3–21. Oxford: Wiley-Blackwell.

Peletz, Michael G. 2002. *Islamic Modern: Religious Courts and Cultural Politics in Malaysia*. Princeton, NJ: Princeton University Press.

Pink, Johanna. 2009. *Muslim Societies in the Age of Mass Consumption: Politics, Religion and Identity between the Local and the Global*. Newcastle upon Tyne: Cambridge Scholars Publishing.

Ponte, Stefano, Gibbon, Peter, and Vestergaard, Jakob. 2011. "Governing Through Standards: An Introduction." In *Governing Through Standards: Origins, Drivers and Limitations*, edited by Stefano Ponte, Peter Gibbon and Jakob Vestergaard, 1–24. Basingstoke: Palgrave Macmillan.

Power, Michael. 1999. *The Audit Society: Rituals of Verification*. Oxford: Oxford University Press.

Riaz, Mian N. and Chaudry, Muhammad M. 2004. *Halal Food Production*. Boca Raton: CRC Press.

Rudnyckyj, Daromir. 2009. "Market Islam in Indonesia." *Journal of the Royal Anthropological Institute* (N. S): S183–S201.

Rudnyckyj, Daromir. 2010. *Spiritual Economies: Islam, Globalization and the Afterlife of Development*. Ithaca: Cornell University Press.

Sahlins, Marshall. 1972. *Stone Age Economics*. London: Routledge.

Scott, James. 1998. *Seeing Like a State. How Certain Schemes to Improve the Human Condition Have Failed*. New Haven, CT, and London: Yale University Press.

Shiraishi, Takashi. 2009. "Introduction." In *Across the Causeway: A Multidimensional Study of Malaysia-Singapore Relations*, edited by Takashi Shiraishi, 1–10. Singapore: ISEAS Publishing.

Simoons, Frederick J. 1994. *Eat Not This Flesh: Food Avoidances from Prehistory to the Present*. Madison and London: The University of Wisconsin Press.

Stigler, Stephen M. 1986. *The History of Statistics: The Measurement of Uncertainty Before 1900*. Cambridge and London: The Belknap Press of Harvard University Press.

Stigler, Stephen M. 1999. *Statistics on the Table: The History of Statistical Concepts and Methods*. Cambridge: Harvard University Press.

Strathern, Marilyn. 2000. "Introduction: New Accountabilities." In *Audit Cultures. Anthropological Studies in Accountability, Ethics, and the Academy*, edited by Marilyn Strathern, 1–18. London and New York: Routledge.

Van Warden, Frans and van Dalen, Robin. 2013. "Halal and The Moral Construction of Quality: How Religious Norms Turn a Mass Product Into a Singularity." In *Constructing Quality: The Classification of Goods in Markets*, edited by Jens Beckert and Christina Musselin, 197–222. Oxford: Oxford University Press.

Wilk, Richard. 2006. *Home Cooking in the Global Village. Caribbean Food from Buccaneers to Ecotourists*. Oxford and New York: Berg.

Williamson, Thomas. 2002. "Incorporating a Malaysian Nation." *Cultural Anthropology* 17(3): 401–430.

1 In the Halal Zones of Malaysia and Singapore

In 2001, a major food scandal in Indonesia triggered a new phase of halal proliferation and standardization on a global scale leading it to cover areas such as enzyme production. The Majelis Ulama Indonesia (MUI), or Indonesian Ulemas Council (in English), set up by the Indonesian state in 1975, accused a Japanese company, Ajinomoto, of using pork products in the production of the flavor enhancer monosodium glutamate and demanded that the Indonesian government take appropriate action. It was a serious accusation: if true, the company would have violated halal rules. As a consequence of the scandal, several of the company's employees were arrested, and a public apology was issued. It is most likely that the flavor enhancer did not contain any pork products; instead, the company conceded that for economic reasons, it had replaced a beef derivative with the pork derivative bactosoytone in the production process. Bactosoytone was used as a medium to cultivate bacteria that produce the enzymes necessary to make monosodium glutamate. As the products of the company had previously been certified as halal by MUI, the scandal seemed to undermine or question the legitimacy of these religious scholars in the eyes of millions of Muslim consumers. The scandal also made it clear that even multinational companies can come into conflict with the rising number of Muslim consumers and organizations if they overlook or disregard religiously inspired customs. Indeed, the Indonesian scandal generated inquiries at companies worldwide. Novozymes, a company that specializes in producing enzymes for a wide range of applications, including scientific research and food processing, was one such company. Customers of Novozymes became more aware of the validity of halal certifications and the company eventually chose to have its products certified by Islamic Food and Nutrition Council of America (IFANCA). Around that time, many other companies also decided to have their products certified as halal by various Muslim organizations, and I return to this example and other companies in greater detail in Chapter 6.

The media hype over the scandal was massive in neighboring Malaysia and Singapore. JAKIM confirmed that Ajinomoto products in Malaysia were halal after a team inspected the company's factory. JAKIM advised Muslims to refer to its recommendations should they have any doubt over food products carrying the halal sign. Ajinomoto Malaysia's general manager assured Muslim consumers that its products were halal and that it did not use bactosoytone.[1] However, the Persatuan Pengguna Islam Malaysia (PPIM), or, in English, the Muslim Consumers Association of Malaysia, an organization that protects the interests of Malay Muslim consumers and entrepreneurs, called on the authorities to conduct scientific tests on Ajinomoto's food seasoning products to confirm products were actually halal. Its executive secretary said claims made by the company and JAKIM that the products did not contain pig enzymes were not enough and called on the domestic trade and consumer affairs ministry to conduct tests and make the findings public to instill confidence among consumers.[2] A couple of days later Ajinomoto Malaysia reassured Muslim consumers that its products were halal responding to the call from PPIM.[3] After having carried out tests on Ajinomoto flavoring powder, JAKIM confirmed that it was halal.[4] The food scandal in Indonesia in 2001 triggered a new phase of halal proliferation and regulation on a global scale. The hype in Singapore was comparable to that of Malaysia, MUIS advised Muslims to be careful, and inspectors checked supermarkets for Ajinomoto products.[5]

Two representatives from MUI were also present at the halal conference in Brussels that was discussed in the introduction. The chairman and the executive director of MUI stressed that one of its main targets was to "harmonize" halal standards among certification bodies, and I could not help hypothesizing that these aims indirectly addressed issues and procedures in the wake of the Ajinomoto scandal. This incident highlights many of the central themes explored in this book, namely, how halal markets in the wake of the Ajinomoto incident proliferated in the global interface zones between Islam, standards, and technoscience. In a broader perspective, halal, to a large extent, is about state assurance of the halalness of products, often following rumors about products or services not being halal, and this tendency was reinforced after the Ajinomoto scandal. However, the historical and institutional background for the effects of this scandal in Malaysia and Singapore is not well understood, and I address these aspects later.

Thus, this chapter serves as an introduction to the halal zones of Malaysia and Singapore. I mainly focus on powerful halal discourses, visions, and policies in the two countries while ethnographic explorations of the extent to which these are translated into actual practice are found in subsequent chapters. The chapter also shows why it is that Malaysia compared to Singapore is the dominant halal zone, and the global implications of this. As we shall see, a major reason for Malaysia's dominance is that large Malay middle-class groups have helped format the halal market in Malaysia and beyond while this is not the case in Singapore. Thus, in addition to the fact that Singapore is small in size and lacks large-scale manufacturing, Malaysia is dominant in global halal zones for a number of historical, political, and institutional differences that will become clear. Discussions in this chapter are based on my previous studies in Malaysia, secondary sources, and the reading of *New Straits Times* in Malaysia and *Straits Times* in Singapore. These papers express state ideologies in the two countries, and they show how discourses are essential in transmitting and expressing halal classification systems and standardization.

THE MALAYSIAN HALAL ZONE

In this section I discuss the way in which Islam has been nationalized and halal regulated in Malaysia. These processes have taken place through Malaysia's bold vision to become the world leader in halal production, trade, and standardization. Interestingly, the Singaporean halal vision is comparable to that of Malaysia, but it takes place in a radically different country right across the causeway, namely, the one-kilometer long causeway that links the city of Johor Baru in the southern part of peninsular Malaysia and Singapore. These discussions provide the reader with a broader context for exploring Malaysia as a particular halal zone in which regulatory institutions such as JAKIM and markets interact and diverge.

Building on anthropological fieldwork in urban Malaysia, I argued that the more cultures of consumption assert themselves, the more controversies over what Islam is, or ought to be, are intensifying.[6] As new consumer practices emerge, they give rise to new discursive fields within which the meaning of Islam and Islamic practice are being debated. Exploring consumption practices in urban Malaysia, this study showed how diverse forms of Malay middle-class consumption of food, clothing, and cars (Fischer 2015), for example, are understood, practiced, and contested as a particular mode of modern Islamic practice. This study illustrated ways in which the issue of "proper Islamic consumption" for consumers, the marketplace, and the state in contemporary Malaysia evokes a whole range of contradictory Islamic visions, lifestyles, and debates articulating what Islam is or ought to be. One key effect of these transformations is the deepening and widening concern for halal commodities among Malay Muslims that I called "halalization," that is, a major preoccupation with the proliferation of the concept of halal in a multitude of commodified forms. I also draw on more recent research (Fischer 2011) that explores halal as a globalized religious market among middle-class Malays in the diaspora.[7]

Of the Malaysian population of around 28 million in 2010, about 67 percent are indigenous Malays (virtually all Muslims) and tribal groups that together are labeled *bumiputera* (literally, sons of the soil), 25 percent are Chinese, and 7 percent are Indians (http://www.statistics.gov.my). Since Malaysia gained independence from Britain in 1957, Malays have constitutionally only been Malays if they are Muslims, speak the Malay language, and adhere to Malay culture/customs. Malaysia is not an Islamic state, but Islam is Malaysia's official religion and is professed by more than 50 percent of the population. In principle, Islam's "official" role was for ceremonial purposes and public occasions while the nation would remain a secular state (Nagata 1994, 67). However, some scholars argue that it is probable that Malaysia will become an Islamic state (Mutalib 1994). In contrast to Malaysia's current form of government, an Islamic concept of state is enshrined in religious texts and based on the implementation of Islamic law.

At the time of independence, the United Malays National Organisation (UMNO) stressed the constitutional position of Islam as the religion of the country within the framework of a secular state (Funston 2006a, 54) at least in the eyes of more Islamically oriented groups. Economically, Malaysia has sustained rapid development within the past three decades during which the meaning of Islam has become ever more contested. The rise of divergent *dakwah* (literally, invitation to salvation) groups in the wider resurgence of Islam in Malaysia challenged the secular foundation of the Malaysian state. *Dakwah* is both an ethnic and a political phenomenon, which has transformed Malaysia for both Muslims and non-Muslims. From the 1970s onward, Parti Islam SeMalaysia (PAS), the Islamic opposition party that still enjoys widespread popularity, together with *dakwah* groups, criticized the policies of the government led by UMNO for having un-Islamic colonial traditions and secular practices that separated religion from political, social and economic issues (Jomo and Cheek 1992, 85). Conversely, the state views dogmatic forms of *dakwah* as the decline of Islam because of the arrogant rejection of secular knowledge by *ulama* (religious functionaries; Mauzy and Milne 1999, 84).

My fieldwork in suburban Malaysia took place in a middle-class suburb about 15 kilometers west of Malaysia's capital, Kuala Lumpur. From my 14th-floor condominium flat I had two quite distinct views beneath me: to one side, my fieldwork site and, to the other side, a view over the lush and "rural" greenery of Sungai Pencala. Sungai Pencala had the status of a Malay reserve, meaning that, formally, only Malays could buy land in this area. Sungai Pencala was also the home of the commune of Darul Arqam (the group has now dispersed and a highway runs through the area). Darul Arqam, or the House of Arqam, was an Islamic group whose believers sought to follow the behavior of the Prophet Muhammad in everyday life. Followers appeared to engage in an ascetic lifestyle and deny themselves Western luxuries such as furnishings, television, radio, and other amenities. Established in 1971, Arqam developed into a commune comprising about 40 houses on eight acres of land. The group set up its own *surau* (prayer house), medical clinic, school, and a number of workshops. Arqam cultivated and marketed an Islamic vision of Malay independence and prosperity through the production of a wide range of halal food products. Ideally, this vision was to ensure the group full independence from any kind of non-Muslim control. Arqam successfully promoted this vision of communal self-sufficiency, and their halal goods were traded throughout the Malaysian peninsula.

The Malaysian National Fatwa (opinion concerning Islamic law issued by an Islamic scholar) Council banned the organization in 1994 reasoning that the movement and its leader, Ustaz (religious teacher) Ashaari, believed in the imminent appearance of the *Mahdi* (or hidden imam, a Muslim man who leads the prayers in a mosque), a key idea in Shia belief. From the viewpoint of Malaysian Sunni orthodoxy, this notion implies unseen power and sectarian secrecy (Ackerman and Lee 1997, 49–51). The state had effectively curbed Arqam as the vanguard of halalization. As we shall see in Chapter 5 on halal activism in Malaysia, this phenomenon can be seen as a continuation of *dakwah* engagement, but with a particular focus on proper Islamic consumption and halal and not so much Islamic theology.

To preempt *dakwah* groups such as Darul Arqam and PAS, the state started to "nationalize" Islam (Fischer 2008a). In fact, today, Malaysian Islam may be the most monolithic and most state regulated in the Muslim world (Bakar 2008, 82). Thus, the state's attempt at molding a modern form of Malayness is intimately linked to challenging Islamic discourses or *dakwah*, each with particular ideas and standards of how to combine consumption and Islamic practice. The nationalization of Islam means the increased centrality of Islam as a national and ethnic signifier in Malaysia. The logic of this nationalization is to see Islam equated with Malayness being the naturalized core of the Malaysian nation. This nationalization of Islam has initiated a broader fascination with the proper and correct "Islamic way of life." For example, this Islamic way of life entails consuming specific halal goods, which are seen to have a beneficial impact on domains such as the family, community, and nation. Halal is both a result of the increase in revivalism and an instrument of that resurgence that leads to ever greater involvement with Islam helping to promote the movement that produced it.

Ironically, Islamic revivalist critiques of "secularism" and the "secular state/government" in Malaysia have helped shape and reinforce not only a unique type of powerful UMNO-driven state nationalism in Malaysia but also a highly commercialized version of Islam in which halal plays a significant role. Although this type of state-driven nationalism can be said to be secular in nature, it feeds into and is, in itself, fed by a whole range of divergent Islamic discourses. The growing centrality of Islam in Malaysian society is also reflected in the bureaucratization of Malay ethnicity (Ackerman and Lee 1997, 33), that is, an officially ethnically plural state in which Malays are a favored ethnicity. An example of an Islamic bureaucratic body set up by the state is Institut Kefahaman Islam Malaysia, or the Institute for Islamic Understanding, established in 1992. The priority of state organizations such as the Institute for Islamic Understanding is to guide Malays to correct and rightful Islamic practices in everyday life even as religious views are challenged by persistent secularists.

In Malaysia halal is promoted as bridging the religious and the secular, as an example of the compatibility of the ethnicized state, modern Islam, business, and proper Islamic consumption. In a way, the Malaysian state's promotion of halal among Malays in Malaysia and on the global stage can be seen as a form of buycott (Fischer 2007) that encourages Muslim consumers to buy locally manufactured, standardized, and state-certified halal products.

Halal Bureaucracies and Regulation

After coming to power in 1981, the charismatic and outspoken prime minister, Mahathir Mohamad, set off the wave of institutionalizing and regulating halal and the strict halal requirements of today are product of this process. Mahathir was in many ways the architect behind modern Malaysia and the social engineering policies aimed at manufacturing a Malay middle class. Mahathir actively nationalized the proliferation of halal and concentrated its certification in the realm of the state where it has remained. In 2003, Mahathir resigned after 22 years as prime minister. Reforms under Prime Minister Badawi, who succeeded Mahathir and was in office from 2003 to 2009, focused on nurturing smaller *bumiputera* (literally, 'sons of the soil') enterprises. This included encouragement of competitive advantage in the Malaysian economy by developing niche markets for halal and Islamic products through a vendor system in which companies were tied to government-linked companies (GLCs), companies controlled by the government and multinationals (Gomez 2012, 68). These policies were continued by PM Mohammad Najib, who succeeded Badawi in 2009, through liberalization of the economy coupled with promoting Malaysia as a hub for halal and Islamic services (Gomez 2012, 72). Arguably, Malaysia has also become a halal hub because of Islamic tourism from the Middle East in particular (Henderson 2003).

In 1982 the Malaysian state set up a committee to evaluate the certification of halal commodities under the Islamic Affairs Division (later JAKIM) in the prime minister's department (Riaz and Chaudry 2004, 54). This committee was exclusively responsible for instilling halal awareness among food producers, distributors, and importers. Another responsibility was mandatory halal certification of all imported meat. More specifically, the Islamic Affairs Division of the prime minister's department and the Department of Veterinary Services should approve all meat plants exporting to Malaysia (Riaz and Chaudry 2004, 52).

It is of great importance to Malaysia to establish a national halal assurance system that matches the country's halal vision incorporating the standards Malaysian MS 1500 (production, preparation, handling, and storage of halal food) and MS 2200 (consumer goods for cosmetic and personal care) as an international benchmark for the state certification of halal products. As part of Malaysia's vision to become the world leader of halal, Malaysia's prime minister from 2003 to 2009 Badawi (2006, 172) describes how Malaysia aspires to become a global halal hub, and to do so, the country has established the standard MS 1500: 2004 as an international benchmark for the certification of halal products.

Malaysia is a model country in terms of complying with halal standards and has strong halal activity in food processing and the export/import trade as reflected in its systematization and standardization of halal certification. In response to the expansion of food service establishments and the opening of international restaurants in Malaysia from the 1970s onward, a thorough enactment of laws, diverse procedures, and guidelines was worked out. For example, the Trade Description (use of expression "halal") Order of 1975 made it an offense to falsely label food as halal, and the Trade Description Act (halal sign marking) of 1975 made it an offense to falsely claim the food to be halal on signs and other markings (Riaz and Chaudry 2004, 54)

Current general "Requirements for Halal Certification" are far more elaborate than the two acts discussed earlier: every producer or manufacturer/food premise/slaughterhouse must produce only halal products; every company that applies for the Halal Confirmation Certificate must ensure that the source of ingredients is halal and they must choose suppliers or subcontractors that only supply halal goods or have Halal Confirmation Certificates; all companies must ensure that halal procedures are observed in all aspects as underlined in the Malaysian Halal Certification Procedure Manual; and a company listed under the Multinational and Small & Medium Industry category is required to establish an Internal Halal Audit Committee and appoint an Islamic Affairs Executive (Islamic Studies) to oversee and ensure compliance of halal certification procedures. Moreover, it is required to have a minimum of two permanent Muslim workers of Malaysian nationality in the kitchen/handling/food-processing section; products/equipment/appliances must be clean and may not contain non-halal ingredients during preparation, handling, processing, packaging, or transfer; transportation used must be specifically for halal product delivery only; and cleanliness must be ensured through Good Manufacturing Practices (http://www.halal.gov.my/v3/index.php/en/about-halal-certification/general-requirements).

Standards and standardization are also evident in the anthology *Food and Technological Progress: An Islamic Perspective*, edited by Sallah and Sobrian (2006b), produced by a Malaysian publisher. It illustrates the powerful halal discourses in Malaysia. One contribution in the book argues that in the modern Muslim world, food scares and food security are inseparable from halal concerns. This contribution argues that in Muslim majority Malaysia, the halal/haram dichotomy is being handled with great care by the relevant authority (Sallah and Sobrian 2006a, x). All this shows that halal regulation in the form of certification and standardization has become the central concern of the Malaysian state. Thus, from the 1980s onward, rationalized organizations specialized in halal regulation technologies and techniques.

Between JAKIM and HDC

The Halal Industry Development Corporation (HDC) was established on September 18, 2006. Its main purpose was to take over JAKIM's responsibilities and to coordinate the overall development of the industry with its main focus being the development of halal standards, audit, certification, capacity building for halal products and services, as well as to promote and facilitate growth and participation of Malaysian companies in the global halal market (www.hdcglobal.com). These moves reflect a further specialization of halal institutions, but also the consequent tensions that followed in the wake of such halal specialization. Because of power struggles between JAKIM and HDC, JAKIM, in 2009, regained its role as the principle state body involved in halal regulation. During my fieldwork with HDC and JAKIM, many of the differences between the two types of bodies came out. HDC is management oriented and it does not reflect the theological authority and ethos of JAKIM.

I discussed the vision and responsibility of HDC with one of its senior managers when we met at the HDC headquarters located only a short walk from the suburb outside Kuala Lumpur, where I did fieldwork in 2001–2002 among Malay Muslim middle-class families; the Islamic revivalist group Darul Arqam's commune, in which halal was first mass-produced; and Nestlé Malaysia's headquarters—a global leader in halal as is shown in Chapter 6. This local setting comprises a potent zone in which halal exists and expands between Islam, the state, and the market in contemporary Malaysia. This senior manager is an example of a middle-class bureaucrat that received his tertiary education in Britain, had worked for a bank, and is very well networked among both other state bodies and companies and activists. I was referred to this contact person by a member of one of the halal activist or interest groups. The senior manager was not directly involved in *dakwah*, his office did not, in any way, display any Islamic paraphernalia such as plaques with Islamic calligraphy, and he was wearing ordinary office dress.

While previous generations of *dakwah* revivalists, to a large extent, were driven by purism and piety much of the current stress on halal is more "managerial," that is, regulative rather than strictly theological. His main vision and responsibility in HDC was to develop halal "integrity," "branding," and "to take halal to the next level." Moreover, the focus of HDC is to support and assist business enterprises to be more competent and efficient in the halal industry with the ultimate aim of "ushering" as many participants as possible into the global halal economy. A central topic in our discussion is the shift from JAKIM to HDC regulation that took place in 2006 but was reversed in 2009. Unsurprisingly, this led to institutional uncertainty and confusion. Conversely, JAKIM representatives reflect a more "Islamic," or theological, ethos, even if much of their work overlaps with that of HDC.

One of the main challenges HDC and JAKIM face, the Senior Manager tells me, is the allocation of resources to hire and employ halal inspection/audit officers and ultimately "political goodwill." "The political decision," the manager stresses, to "expand" halal must be backed with appropriate resources to hire more inspectors in order to enforce halal properly, and this is a major topic in the popular debate on halal in Malaysia; that is, to regulate halal properly, much tighter legislation and punishment is needed.

These discussions have a long history within the Islamic bureaucracy and in the media in Malaysia. It is to this point I now turn.

In 2002 JAKIM became the sole state body responsible for regulating halal in Malaysia,[8] but the setting up of HDC in 2006 was arguably done to strengthen international halal certification, training, research, and development.[9] HDC was described as the only body in the country authorized to issue halal certificates, and the organization was established to streamline halal operations previously handled by JAKIM (certification) and Ministry of International Trade and Industry (MITI; promotions, marketing, and exhibitions). JAKIM officers involved in certification had been "absorbed" into HDC.[10] However, this major restructuring was disrupted when the management and issuance of halal certificates reverted from HDC to JAKIM in 2009. This was explained as a "cabinet directive" aimed at separating the role of the issuance of halal certificates and the development of the regional and global halal market between the two agencies. Now JAKIM would again play its original role of issuing halal certificates for products and services, and JAKIM officers on secondment to HDC would return to JAKIM.[11] These events caused friction within the state bodies, with companies, and other halal certifying bodies around the world. Interest groups in Malaysia soon called for a strong "master plan" and "leadership" applicable to all stakeholders in the industry to address the inability of government agencies to work together.[12]

A central theme related to these discussions of halal bureaucracies and regulation in Malaysia is authority embedded in contemporary Malaysian and Islamic institutional discourses and practices. Most of all, these formal procedures signify a celebration of the state's authority, capability, and techniques to market and regulate halal as a brand or logo of Malaysian nationalized Islam. However, discussing bureaucracies in the plural, for example, between JAKIM and HDC, stresses the internal friction the regulation of halal is undergoing. Within three decades, local halal production, trade, and consumption in Malaysia has become part of a huge and expanding globalized market, and one of the main challenges faced by the state is how to regulate such a market that essentially is divine in nature. Simultaneously, Malaysia's bid to become the world leader in rapidly expanding halal markets on a global scale is entangled in complex webs of national and political significance.

Halal Visions

From the 1990s onward, Malaysia's vision to become a world leader in globalized halal markets intensified. This happened in conjunction with an increased focus on a range of broader issues and questions such as upgrading food-processing technology, automation, and food quality, as well as increased safety and health standards to meet consumer preferences and tastes.[13] Continuously, Malaysian halal producers and traders were called on to explore and make the most of the halal food industry.[14] Another important issue in the popular halal discourse is joint ventures between Malaysian companies with knowledge of halal and foreign companies that want to benefit from halal certification in particular.[15] The emergence of localized forms of Islamic regulation, technoscience, or charismatic technology, as it were, runs through these discourses.

The growing awareness among Muslims in Malaysia to follow their religious tenets strictly and concerns about halal "issues" is constantly evoked as the driving force behind the emergence and success of the halal industry in Malaysia.[16] These points are supported by my own research (Fischer 2008b, 2011) showing that many, but by no means all, Malays are fastidious about halal. Most important, these articles show that for the local halal industry to prosper, the state and powerful political and Islamic discourses try to instill halal as a disciplined form of consumption in Muslim consumers.

In the late 1990s, the state came up with the idea of locating halal industries in particular areas or "parks," as it was later called,[17] and these plans coincided with an increased focus on strategies to make the country an "international halal food hub" with an "image" that can "convince" the 1.2 billion Muslim population that Malaysian-made food products are guaranteed halal.[18] In addition to traditional halal requirements such as pork avoidance, standards of hygiene, safety, "goodness," raw materials, and processed items became prominent issues.[19] Similarly, the state called on the halal industry to focus on "standards" and "quality" that were "universally accepted" as this would broaden the halal market "beyond" that of Muslim consumers in "the vastly untapped global market."[20] All these issues reflect the transformation of halal from divergent forms of classification into a more standardized global assemblage.

The Institute of Islamic Understanding Malaysia (IKIM), an Islamic bureaucratic body established in 1992 by the Prime Minister's Office with its main objective being to guide Malays on correct and rightful Islamic practice, argued that the halal concept was very much related to religious commandments but that it was still lacking in practice, for example, only a few hotels had JAKIM certification.[21] In fact, this was a call for developing more elaborate regulation techniques. The vision of making Malaysia a halal hub was further developed when six areas in five states were identified as suitable for halal production,[22] but a formal body was needed to regulate these efforts. Moreover, Malaysian Institute of Industrial Research and Standards (SIRIM) wanted more focus on standards applied to imported products[23] in order for the local halal industry to become a "global player."[24] At the same time, there were state concerns that lacking industry initiatives kept Malays(ians) out of the international halal food business[25] as well as industry concerns about lacking political backing among companies on the international halal scene.[26] The central dilemma was that as halal emerged as a global assemblage, it was lifted out of its conventional Muslim base, and this point warranted Muslim regulation techniques in the form of standardization and certification. Consequently, as regulation intensified halal products transformed into boundary objects subjected to entangled and crisscrossing classifications schemes of bureaucracies. In the eyes of the state, the vision to make Malaysia a global halal hub rested on the creation of "glocal" Malay entrepreneurs with a "first-class mentality" who could "think globally and act locally."[27] Halal hubs played a major role in this vision[28] and so did the development of accreditation standards,[29] biotechnology, and biodiversity.[30] Malaysian companies should forge strategic partnerships with international corporations in the halal industry as a way to fast-track their entry into the global halal market. Moreover, halal was targeted as a particular focus area in the tabling of the nation's budget.[31]

Entrepreneurs were called on to explore halal as a "niche area,"[32] and small and medium-sized enterprises were urged to take advantage of this.[33] These halal visions based on probability and statistics play a powerful role in Malaysian discourses on halal, often moralistic in nature, but at the same time, state bureaucrats, activists, and company representatives are well aware that one thing is visions and quite another thing is translating these into actual practices.

Of Law and Logos

A major issue in Malaysian halal from the 1990s onwards is the linking of law, logos, and certification. Many consumer groups and Islamic organizations such as PPIM called on the state to introduce laws governing the use of the halal "sign" at eateries because the "enforcement" of its use was still considered weak. This lack of enforcement was seen as a consequence of the Trade Descriptions Act of 1972 that was not capable of enforcing halal signs specifically, it was argued. If this sign was left "unchecked" it could lead to "confusion" among consumers and companies. At the time, Pusat Islam's (the Islamic center set up to reduce vice and upgrade Malay Muslim morality and not to regulate halal in any systematic manner) condition for the use of the halal sign was relatively loose. Another problem with halal regulation was overlapping national certification by Bahagian Hal Ehwal Islam (Islamic Affairs Division) in the prime minister's department versus committees in individual Malaysian states.[34] Similarly, it was argued that to ensure consumer confidence, on one hand, and Association of Southeast Asian Nations (ASEAN) recognition on the other certification could not possibly be left to manufacturers. Instead, there should be government support of setting up an ASEAN or global halal standard.[35] Hence, halal legality was still relatively unregulated and overlapping in the 1990s.

A central issue in late 1996 was the Malaysian state's role as a protector of halal food safety for *bumiputeras* to avoid "loopholes" in the use of halal logos on food products.[36] Malaysia's bold vision to become a leader in halal was intimately linked to the role of certification, not least for small and medium-sized industries.[37] However, there were constant calls for simplifying bureaucratic halal procedures. The government should explain rules, regulations, and protocols involved in halal certification to companies to ensure Malaysia's rightful position as a global halal hub.[38] Malaysian halal certification gained momentum in the 1990s, arguably because of greater awareness by international organizations that certification standards would open the door to patronage by Muslims and wider acceptance by hotels, fast-food outlets, restaurants, and airlines.[39]

In 1998, the government privatized halal certification and inspections and outsourced responsibilities to a company that was criticized for excessive fees. Several of the company representatives I discuss later recalled that these moves were confusing and costly. Hence, the state had to look into the level of fees companies had to pay.[40] Unlike restaurants that must display the JAKIM logo, shops were not subjected to this ruling. Proposed amendments to the Food Regulations on labeling should tackle both the nutritional aspect as well as religious sensitivities of consumers.[41]

JAKIM experienced that more and more companies were applying for halal certification to enable them to tap the global halal market. One major reason for this, JAKIM argued, was that in Singapore, as we shall see, the decision to go halal by fast-food operators such as Delifrance, Pizza Hut, Taco Bell, and local entrepreneurs brought about higher profits to these operators.[42] Moreover, Muslim businessmen and entrepreneurs should not depend only on the halal label of their products to compete in the domestic and international markets they should also take the opportunity to turn Malaysia into a "halal hub" for the international market.[43]

Concurrently, there were calls to standardize halal certificates because companies too freely could use the halal logo for their products on wrappers, tins, and boxes in different sizes and formats.[44] Closely related to this, the Ministry for Domestic Trade and Consumer Affairs argued that different forms of halal certification in Malaysian states should be regulated under one new company to achieve a national standard certification easing the job of enforcement officers.[45] The proliferation of halal certification led to the appointment of 79 religious enforcement officers who all received one month of training.[46]

In 2003 JAKIM introduced a new, standardized logo for national halal certification. The logo only bears the word *Malaysia*, in Roman and Arabic, around the large word *halal* written in Arabic. The earlier logo had the department's name or name of the respective state Islamic religious department around a large word *halal* in Arabic and the name Malaysia printed in green. There was a code printed within the circle to indicate the issuer of the certification, and the logo was in black and white to enable certificate holders to choose any color they wished to suit the color of their product packaging. The new logo shows not only that halal regulation was further nationalized and standardized but also that this was a move to make halal products more auditable. The current halal logo issued by JAKIM or other state Islamic religious departments could still be used.[47] However, the prime minister once more warned the industry not to rely solely on the halal label to stay competitive. For Malaysia to be a halal food hub, manufacturers must produce high-quality and nutritious products.[48]

In 2004 it was mandatory that all meat produce should carry the JAKIM logo registered and approved by the Intellectual Property Corporation under the Trade Marks Act 1976.[49] In light of forged halal logos, JAKIM announced that it would issue halal "stickers" that would come with microchip features and that this should provide extra safety to consumers when buying from non-Muslim traders and companies.[50] This point evokes the way in which an institution such as JAKIM thinks about halal enforcement as premised on Islamized forms of technoscience.

In 2010 the question of fake halal logos and a nationalized halal logo was still being debated. The difference, however, was that at the time everyone was waiting for a proposed Halal Act, that is, a piece of legislation that once passed in Parliament would ensure that halal certification was not abused and that sanctions against halal offenses were far more heavily enforced.[51] Hence, the Halal Act would empower JAKIM to not only manage and issue halal certification, but also stronger enforcement on misuse. JAKIM was drafting the law together with the prime minister's department and the attorney-general's chambers.[52] The Halal Act came into being on November 1, 2011, and it contained amendments to the Trade Description Act of 1972 and provided stiffer penalties for those using fake halal certificates or logos.[53] The Trade Descriptions (Certification and Marking of "Halal") Order 2011 came into operation on January 1, 2012. This law was signed by minister of domestic trade cooperatives and consumerism, and it states that food, goods, and services are halal if certified by the competent authority and marked with a specified logo. Food supplied by non-Muslims must be properly certified and food imported into Malaysia must be certified and marked by a foreign halal certification body recognized by JAKIM. (Attorney General's Chambers 2011, 1–4).

Owners of eateries could be fined up to RM 5 million or sentenced to a maximum of 10 years in jail, or both, if they fail to display halal logos and certificates on premises selling "Syariah-compliant" food.[54] While the Halal Act was being drafted, JAKIM planned to set up halal certification units nationwide to standardize procedures.[55] Under the amended Trade Descriptions Act, only JAKIM and state religious departments were agencies approving and issuing halal certificates and logos; that is, existing halal certificates would be void, and traders were advised to start applying for new ones. Companies and individuals that failed to comply would be fined up to RM 250,000 or jailed for three years, or both. Another important consequence of the Halal Act, as we shall see, was that imported goods must also carry certification and halal logos from JAKIM or obtain these from the 53 foreign halal certification bodies recognized by JAKIM.[56] This network of halal certifiers gave shape to halal as a global assemblage. It was in this tense climate of actors hoping for or fearing (foreign companies, for example, that saw this as yet another increase in bureaucracy and enforcement they had to adapt to) the Halal Act that my fieldwork took place.

Sanctions and Seizures

There is an abundance of examples of how food was seized for not complying with halal requirements. The Domestic Trade and Consumer Affairs Ministry claimed to have acted in 35 cases under the Trade Descriptions Act 1972 and RM 15,820 worth of food items were seized between 1990 and 1996 and collected RM 8,500 in fines.[57] "Non-Muslims" (Chinese) especially figure prominently in these accounts of seized food, and an example of this is mixing up halal and non-halal processed chicken at the same food stalls.[58] Other instances of food seized and premises raided concerned noodles when a company was "misusing" the JAKIM halal logo[59] and packed powdered milk imported from Australia with the same problem.[60] Retailers could also suffer heavy penalties for failing to display "prominent" halal signs in their stores informing Muslim consumers of products made from non-halal materials such as pigskin leather.[61]

A particular case concerns casings for sausages in IKEA's food outlet that was raided by the domestic trade and consumer affairs ministry and JAKIM officials. Reportedly, the 34-member team seized 60 boxes of halal sausages on suspicion that they were enclosed in animal casings. This happened in the wake of another raid on two factories manufacturing sausages using the same casings. One of the factories supplied the sausages seized from IKEA. Both factories had been ordered closed for violation of the Food Act 1983. Besides using animal-based products for casings, the companies' halal certificates had expired. The halal logo on the packets of sausages was also found to be a forgery, and there was a discrepancy between the logos on the boxes and the logos on the packets of sausages inside the boxes. Halal casings for sausages have to be made from cellulose, that is, fibers from plant tissue.[62] In the wake of these incidents, members of Parliament (MPs) called for harsher penalties such as jail and whipping for those misusing the halal logo, but the government chose only to blacklist errant companies.[63]

Another example is 572 cans of minced pork bearing the halal inscription in Jawi (an Arabic alphabet for writing the Malay language) imported from China seized in a supermarket. It was "understood" that the supermarket had relabeled the items from China. The enforcement division also confiscated 62 boxes of frozen chicken parts bearing forged halal logos and inscriptions in a raid on a shop here.[64] Malaysian authorities threatened to stop import of Australian beef because of "thoracic piercing," a stunning method that arguably did not conform with Islam.[65] In Port Klang, the customs department seized two containers of oxtail, cow's tongue, and offals that required an import license from the veterinary department and halal certification.[66] Another example was a company that did not follow regulations and sold non-halal chickens even though the workers were Muslims and were assumed to be knowledgeable about proper halal procedures.[67]

There are also cases of banned companies because of issuing halal certificates and halal logos never authorized or recognized by Islamic authorities. Food outlets obtain halal certification and logos to ensure that raw food materials must have valid halal certification and to employ the services of at least two Muslim cooks.[68] Similarly, enforcement officers suspended an abattoir's halal certificate due to the behavior of "rowdy" abattoir operators.[69] In another case JAKIM "revoked" the halal certification of QBB Pure Ghee (clarified butter) because it allegedly contained "suspicious elements" that could not be consumed by Muslims.[70] All these examples show how halal regulation is enforced in Malaysia, and as we shall see, companies work hard to comply with rising halal requirements and to avoid prosecution or ending up as having been "sanctioned" in the media. These discussions also demonstrate that halal regulation technologies/techniques and legislation were accompanied by far more stringent enforcement measures that became favorite topics in the media.

Global Politics of Halal

In Malaysia, the state certifies Nestlé's production, as I discuss in greater detail in Chapter 6. Imported products manufactured by Nestlé are certified by the IFANCA, for example, which is recognized by JAKIM. JAKIM has a list of recognized Islamic bodies globally, that is, Islamic organizations to which local regulation and inspection of halal are "outsourced." An example of this is the Islamic Cultural Centre in Denmark and Halal Food Council of Europe (HFCE), with which I did fieldwork. The global proliferation of halal necessitates that JAKIM outsources halal regulative responsibilities, as this institution cannot in practice perform halal regulation on a global scale. Hence, JAKIM not only recognizes a body such as Islamic Cultural Centre but also "inspects" such organizations in their local setting. A wide range of certifying bodies are competitors in the global market for halal, and a company such as Nestlé is meticulous about selecting certification that is acceptable in particular regional, national, and local markets. Similarly, JAKIM and MUIS carefully choose recognized certification bodies globally. When the Halal Act was passed, this list of approved certifiers was modified and this had global effects among companies.

JAKIM states that Muslims should not doubt state halal certification and that consumers should refer to JAKIM if they have doubts about the authenticity of halal certification instead of believing rumors.[71] An example of a rumor that was rejected by the state was that Red Bull drinks (halal certified since 1993) contained alcohol and/or cocaine.[72] However, the state indirectly contributes to such confusion among consumers when stating that neither *kopitiam* (traditional breakfast/coffee shops) operators go for halal certification and that logos at restaurants and companies may either be fake or be issued by private companies.[73] Imported products such as milk are often susceptible to confusion or rumors that call for state reassurance.[74]

The events of September 11, 2001, taking place only a few months after the Ajinomoto scandal, transformed Islam into both an agent and a product of globalization, making Islam a global phenomenon that demands an opinion about itself (Devji 2005). What is more, Islam has come to occupy the language of faith globally (Devji 2008, 191). As a sign of this, a newspaper article asserted that post 9/11, the halal market grew from "a tributary concern of the devout to the mainstream of the multitudes." Politics combined with demographics to manufacture a global demand while supply was struggling to catch up.[75] The events of September 11 had become a global concern reconfiguring domestic politics in Malaysia and consolidated the country's position as a moderate Islamic state (Shamsul 2001, 7). Hence, post 9/11, the powerful state and corporate halal discourse in Malaysia identified this "moderate" Muslim country as a key player in the proliferation of global halal. Ironically, the demonization of Islam and Muslims that followed in the wake of 9/11 was complemented by the recognition that Muslims were also consumers with certain demands that were open to commercialization. It is in this context this multisited ethnography should be seen; that is, the emergence of modern halal in the new millennium has become part of a standardized and globalized religious market.

One of the most pervasive themes in the Malaysian halal discourse is the country's position in a globalized market for halal and Islam more broadly. Imported products such as meat from India (Malaysia's top supplier in 2000) were subjected to calls for improving its halal "quality."[76] Conversely, joint ventures, with Australia, for example, promised to combine the quality of foreign products and Malaysia as a "modern and progressive Islamic country."[77] Since 2002 China became a prominent topic in the halal discourse in Malaysia. China was described as being very interested in halal production and certification in Malaysia in particular.[78]

In many cases broader foreign policy issues are entangled with halal. For example, the conflict in the Middle East is described as having had repercussions on its people and the way they do business so that these countries are skeptical about the United States and Europe, and they are now looking to other potential trading partners such as Malaysia in the halal market.[79] In the halal discourse there is constant alert about competing countries such as the Philippines, Thailand, China, Brazil, Britain, and Australia that have established halal research and development programs.[80]

In 2004, the Malaysian prime minister Badawi at a meeting in the Organisation of the Islamic Conference, an organization of 57 member states that represents Muslim interests, "rallied" member countries to work together for the good of all. More specifically, the prime minister outlined areas of potential economic cooperation in halal-based products and Islamic financial services stressing Malaysia's strong competitive position in these fields.[81]

Moreover, making Malaysia the number one Muslim tourist destination in the world with attractions such as a halal hub, food, culture, world-class mosques, infrastructure, and Muslim-friendly accommodation, was a priority of the government. In 2008 more than 200,000 tourists from the Middle East visited the country.[82]

The state in Malaysia often calls on these Muslim countries to "unleash" their potential in halal and Islamic finance, which is more developed in parts of Southeast Asia.[83] Cooperation in halal markets also includes countries such as Zambia and Bosnia-Herzegovina.[84] When the state compares Malaysia's success in the global market for halal to other countries, often the "high standard" of halal certification sets the country apart.[85] These comparisons in many cases also include a focus on modern and moderate Islam in Malaysia.[86] In 2009 relations between Malaysia and Brunei improved after a long-standing debate over territorial claims on the border town of Limbang in the western part of Malaysia. Halal was discussed as an obvious area where the two countries could now expand their cooperation.[87] Around the same time, the Malaysian state argued that the global economic crisis stressed the need for increased focus on Islamic finance and the halal market.[88]

The complex interplay between Islam, states, global politics, and markets makes modern halal part of global assemblages, that is, "the bigger institutional picture" that frames halal production and regulation. In Malaysia, all this takes place in the contact zones or interface zones where regulatory frameworks meet the market. These tendencies were reinforced by the food scandal in Indonesia and 9/11. The preceding discussions evoke halal as a truly global assemblage subject to technological, political, and ethical reflection on questions of value and morality.

The Ethnic Other

In contemporary Malaysia, even many Chinese shops and restaurants have started putting up halal signs and selling state-certified halal products, and they are thus recognized as "halalized." At the same time, pig farming, for example, in Malaysia is traditionally an ethnicized Chinese business and one that, because of Islamic revivalism and Malay cultural politics, has been subjected to enactments to oversee the pig industry (Neo 2008, 262). In other words, not only are Chinese shops now subjected to state-controlled halalization; this is also the case with many other types of businesses.

The powerful halal discourses in Malaysia are discussed in *Halal Haram: A Guide by Consumers Association of Penang* (2006) published by a local Malaysian consumers' association that has status as a nongovernmental organization (NGO). The book states that Malaysia is a multiracial country with various ethnic groups and thus the issue of halal/haram is of great importance, "as many non-Muslims do not understand the Islamic dietary rules" (Consumers Association of Penang 2006, 19).

In Malaysia, ethnic distinctions are often expressed through food. In the eyes of rural Malay fishermen, Thai and Chinese are quintessential pork eaters regardless of actual dietary practice. Thus, these ethnic groups are expressive of ritual contamination that can only be negated by conversion to Islam (Firth 1966). In the eyes of some Malays, the Chinese may be omnivorous, whereas Malays, in line with halalization, are particular and sensitive about food. Logically, the halalized food domain must be protected from the "pollution of indifference." It is a generally held idea among many Malays that the Chinese are skilled and cunning networkers. Once these business or social networks of Chinese entrepreneurs have been conceptualized, such networks become real and only bring benefits for those inside them (Yao 2002, 143). As part of the state discourse on halal, Malays have a moral obligation to support Muslim businesses, as the Chinese have always supported their own ethnic group through complex networks of loyalty, questionable moral business standards, and a concealed system of credit given only to Chinese. All this is formative of a ritual economy that has halal at its center (Fischer 2008a).

Two discourses dominate halal and Chinese ethnicity in the popular media in Malaysia. First, an abundance of articles happily reports that traditional Chinese foods have (unproblematically) become halal. An example of this is the promotion of halal Chinese food that is "just as flavourful and creative" as non-halal food.[89] Many articles report that halal mooncakes, a Chinese bakery product traditionally eaten during the Mid-Autumn Festival, are now available in a halal version.[90] Another example is a Chinese or "non-*bumiputera*" company that has done well in the halal food sector. The manager explained that the business "boomed" after the company switched from non-halal products to those that appealed to Muslims.[91] Yet another example of Chinese ethnicity is the availability of Chinese food at eating outlets at the country's public universities. The management at one of Malaysia's largest universities had closed down a Chinese food stall, but then after all agreed to allow Chinese chefs to prepare the food at the stall as long as they abide by the university rules to ensure the food is "halal and clean."[92] Another set of discourses targets the state's desire to increase *bumiputera* or "bumi" participation in the halal sector, for example, with regard to women.[93] The news that more non-*bumiputera* companies were applying for halal certification than *bumiputera* companies led to the remark "It's the kind of information that would make you scratch your head."[94]

In a wider perspective, these ideas fit an analysis of the everyday conceptualization of fixed and uncontested Chinese economic success. Thus, the hardworking, economically successful Chinese come alive in the twilight zone between reality, ideological construction, and social imagination (Yao 2002, 3–4). The requirement to form a Muslim committee in companies owned or run by foreigners or local Chinese can be seen as a way that Malay Islamic bureaucrats can regulate or "halalize" Chinese capitalists.

In the Halal Zone

Halal has spurred new forms of space making in the form of halal "centers," "areas," "zones," or "parks."[95] An example of this is the vision to construct Malaysia International Halal Park, which is being promoted as the first International Halal Park offering a world-class global gateway for halal industries, trade, and services, according to the company behind the endeavor (www.myhalalhub.org). Malaysia International Halal Park is driven by a vision to establish a halal supply chain between Malaysia's Port Klang Free Zone, which is a mix of an industrial park and a free-trade zone conveniently located close to Malaysia International Halal Park and the Port of Rotterdam, now a halal-certified zone that is trying to position itself as a halal gateway into the European Union. All this testifies to a more general tendency in both Malaysia and Singapore, as well as elsewhere in Southeast Asia, to see that proper halal production, trade, and regulation increasingly hinge on context and handling, for example, the requirement that Muslims must be involved in production processes and management in shops and factories.

The vision to set up halal centers and parks in many Malaysian states intensified from 2003.[96] To attract foreign companies and investment to these halal parks state bodies and authorities such as JAKIM and HDC are refining their methods of inspection, control, and discipline in scientific production. Politicians, Islamic bureaucrats, and corporate figures now promote moderate Islam in Malaysia not as a problem, but as a sanitized Islamic innovation. Hence, the ethos of moderate Islam has helped foreign companies develop a vibrant high-tech manufacturing sector (Ong 2006, 36). In these halal parks or zones, Islam, standardization, and technoscience fuse.

Middle-Class Innovation

In the 1970s, the Malaysian state launched the New Economic Policy (NEP) to improve the economic and social situation of the Malays vis-à-vis the Chinese, in particular. The NEP entailed a number of benefits for the Malays and other indigenous groups, such as increased ownership of production and preferential quotas in the educational system. The number and proportion of Malays engaged in the modern sector of the economy rose significantly as a result of these policies. Ideologically, the overall objective was to produce an educated, entrepreneurial, shareholding, high-consuming, and socially/physically mobile Malay middle class, which the state elite view as a necessary prerequisite for economic, national, and social cohesion. Mahathir became the proponent of this policy. This piece of grand social engineering is essential for understanding the middle-class terrain of Malaysia and the social and physical mobility of these Malays.

At the same time, the NEP of the Malaysian state has forged a new class of Malay entrepreneurs, Melayu Baru or New Malays. This group of highly educated and relatively affluent Malays is centrally located in the Islamic bureaucracy that manages and regulates halal and as employees in local and multinational companies in Malaysia. According to Mahathir Mohamad (1995, 1), the New Malay embodies an aggressive, entrepreneurial, and global "we can" mentality. In 1991, Mahathir unveiled Vision 2020, which pictured Malaysia as a fully developed nation by 2020, and this New Malay mentality is seen as essential for achieving this goal. The coining of this term by Mahathir signifies the concretion of a hardworking and entrepreneurial urban Malay middle-class mentality. In effect, the novel Islamic ethos in Malaysia is tied to allegiance to the state evoked as a form of cultural kinship through religion (Ong 1999, 226). My informants within the state, Malaysian companies, activist groups, and education/science can be seen to belong to this group of New Malays.

As a consequence of the growing middle class in Malaysia, consumption has been subjected to state and business interventions in the form of extensive market research and the political institutionalization of consumption, an example of this was the setting up of the Ministry of Domestic Trade and Consumer Affairs in 1990. Clearly, this is a sign of the state's bid to become an apparently "honest broker" of consumption (Zukin 2004) that protects the entitlements of Malaysian consumers against what the state and consumers increasingly see as confusing and excessive consumer culture. What is more, since the 1980s, shopping spaces have been "standardized"; that is, supermarkets and hypermarkets have become favorite outlets among middle-class groups.

For a developing economy such as Malaysia, the emergent middle class and the New Malays have become an almost mythical national signifier of mental and material development. This myth is very much alive and has been internalized as a significant point of self-understanding among the Malaysian middle class and political elites. The state elite views the creation of such a class as a necessary prerequisite for economic, national, and social cohesion (Embong 1998, 85). This Malay Muslim middle class is a driving force behind the prominent status of halal in Malaysia. On one hand, these groups, to a large extent, generate moral panic about halal and "excessive" consumption more generally. For example, in 2005 a hype focused on the abuse of the halal logo. Muslim consumers and state agencies called on JAKIM to introduce foolproof halal stickers. In the wake of suspicion that the casings of halal sausages in IKEA mentioned earlier was not halal, casings now have to be made from cellulose—fibers from plant tissue—to be halal calls for increased credibility, particularly with respect to the JAKIM halal logo.[97] It became publicly known that JAKIM had only six enforcement officers involved in checking the validity of halal logos and certificates.[98] As a consequence of this, the domestic trade and consumer affairs ministry produced a halal directory covering all halal establishments.[99]

Another recurring theme on halal related to the Malay Muslim middle class is product and service innovation/quality. Adabi halal food products were voted a superbrand for 2002 by the Malaysian Superbrands Council, and its products were the first to receive the halal certification from the Islamic Affairs Division of the prime minister's department and were among the first to be formally standardized.[100] Many articles discuss the emergence of halal nonfood products, such as halal spa products,[101] and halal food, nonfood products, and services were increasingly advertised online.[102] This trend continues with mobile phone applications that can locate halal restaurants and hotels and check the halal status of products developed by HDC and a local telecommunications operator.[103]

The Malay Muslim middle class is both shaped by and actively shaping state and market in Malaysia. From halal requirements concerning food, these ideas have deepened and widened to cover a whole range of commodities and technologies/techniques of regulation. Arguably, Malaysian Islam may be the most monolithic and most state regulated in the Muslim world and the same goes for halal in Malaysia. However, Islam and halal in Singapore are also highly state regulated but in a quite different socioeconomic context, and to this point I now turn.

THE SINGAPOREAN HALAL ZONE

In 2009–2010 I was a visiting senior research fellow at National University of Singapore (NUS). Previously, my work had been focusing on Islam, consumer culture, and halal in Malaysia and Europe, but NUS asked if I would be interested in developing a Singapore "angle" on halal, because halal was becoming a major priority for the government. When I first started at NUS in 2009 I spotted a notice by the MUIS, or the Islamic Religious Council of Singapore, in a canteen food stall at NUS campus: "Halal certification pending approval" it read. In early 2010 the stall had put up a MUIS halal certificate stating that the stall

> [s]erves food/drinks that are Halal to Muslims according to Islamic law. . . . This Halal certificate is issued under Section 88A of the Administration of Muslim Law Act (Cap. 3). It is non-transferable and not allowed to be used for food catering services.

This certificate was issued under MUIS's Eating Establishment Scheme (hawker) and signed by the mufti of Singapore on behalf of MUIS. This focus on halal in Singapore caught my interest, and I soon started doing fieldwork, as we shall see. The Singaporean halal vision is in many ways comparable to that of Malaysia, that is, to become a world leader in halal, but it takes place in a radically different country and context right across the one-kilometer-long causeway that links the two countries geographically, politically, and historically. This section provides the reader with a broader context for understanding halal in the Singaporean zone and the way in which this is comparable and different to what we have seen in Malaysia. Out of 3.77 million Singapore residents in 2010, Chinese composed about 74 percent; Malays, 13 percent; and Indians, 9 percent, while "Others" accounted for the remainder (http://www.singstat.gov.sg/pubn/popn/c2010acr/key_demographic_trends.pdf). These ethnic groups are also found in Malaysia but in quite different proportions: Singapore is a Chinese-majority country while Muslims, most of whom are ethnic Malays, constitute the largest minority, and this has a significant bearing on halal production, trade, consumption, and regulation.

Because of racial and religious tensions in Singapore, the state has responded to religious diversity by preventing religious "labels" playing an overt public role (Nasir, Turner, and Pereira 2010, 3). I show that while this rightly may be the case on a more general level in relation to a local version of "multiculturalism," Islamic "labels" in the form of halal logos and certificates are ubiquitous in Chinese-majority Singapore. As we shall see, local Malays, who are often seen as an indigenous "problem" in terms of social, educational, and economic performance, play an instrumental role—as patriotic consumers who support the local market for halal products and services, bureaucrats, and inspectors/auditors with MUIS as well as members of companies' mandatory Halal Team that must include at least one Muslim staff. All this is to market and standardize halal as what I called proper Islamic consumption. While promoting halal as a form of ethnicized or indigenous Islamic market, legislation carefully tries to balance ethnicity between Chinese, Malays, and Indians. An example of this is the Maintenance of Religious Harmony Act from the 1990s, which should prevent the use of religion for political ends and include punishment for being found guilty of causing racial conflicts and political activities under the guise of practicing religious activities. One of the most important questions answered here is why and how halal, inseparable from Islam and Malays in the local context, has been reclassified from being a sensitive issue about dietary requirements of an indigenous minority group to become subjected to forms of standardization technologies and techniques. Hence, I explore Singapore as a zone in which regulatory institutions in a nondemocratic Chinese-majority setting strategically employ Malays to dominate global halal markets.

Nation Management

Singapore's history of nation building and state formation is inseparable from its colonial past, on one hand, and Malaysia's development, on the other. Singapore is a former British colony that achieved self-governance in 1959. Its colonial history dates back to 1819 when the British East India Company chose it as a settlement because it was centrally located for trade. In 1959, the People's Action Party (PAP) formed the government led by Lee Kuan Yew, who was the first prime minister of the Republic of Singapore.

Lee governed for three decades until 1990, and he can be said to be the architect behind Singapore's impressive performance and continuous economic growth, not unlike that of Mahathir in Malaysia. The reasons for this growth are many, but his strategies to use technology with multinational corporations have helped the country achieve first-world status. To this day, the PAP governs Singapore, driven by the pursuit of economic growth, which it delivers, and this is the PAP's "performance" principle and single legitimacy to rule. The party will go to all lengths including curtailing conventional democratic rights and practices to "deliver the goods" to the people (Chua 2003b, 3). Singapore exports almost everything it produces and imports almost everything consumed, and this is an example of globalization of commodity distribution and consumption (Chua 2003b, 5). The country was born of the modern age of mercantile and global service capitalism, and at the same time the absence of precolonial traditional or tribal culture conditioned a form of cultural modernity of capitalism (Chua 2003b, 19).

A referendum decided that Singapore should form part of Malaysia, and the merger took place in 1963. However, as soon as in 1965 the new nation witnessed the painful separation of Singapore from Malaysia. Arguably, one of the main reasons behind the split was that Lee showed an incomplete understanding of the Malaysian theater of politics and Malay rights (Mauzy and Milne 2002, 22). While the Malaysian prime minister at the time seemed more focused on special rights of the Malays, PAP and Lee stressed the making of provisions for an effective common market, rationality, and equity (Mauzy and Milne 2002, 23). To this day, these differences shape local politics within the two countries, their often turbulent relationship, and halal production, trade, regulation and consumption in these two adjacent zones.

Some general trends characterize the new nation of Singapore. I briefly discuss Singapore's form of government because it is quite unique in the modern world, and it has a direct bearing on the way in which Islam and halal are regulated. Certain laws and controls on political participation and civil rights such as freedom of the press can be said to determine that Singapore is not a liberal democracy but, rather, some form of authoritarian state. More broadly, authoritarianism is intimately linked to the political history of Singapore and the PAP's quest for political dominance (Chua 1995, 204). What is more, the "moral performance" of the PAP state defines the political rule and shapes the quality of social and political life (Yao 2007, 180). Simultaneously, Singapore's judicial system has received high international acclaim, and this is also relevant to the way in which religion, and in connection with halal in particular, Islam is regulated and managed legally.

"Tripartism," a local form of government–union–business relationship in which the government plays the role of balancing the other two, is essential for Singapore and halal production, trade, and regulation. All unions are under an umbrella organization called the National Trades Union Congress

(NTUC) of the government that supervises its activities. The NTUC owns Singapore's largest supermarket chain, at which I did fieldwork (I return to this in Chapter 7). Moreover, through government-linked companies and private holding companies with close ties to the government (comparable to what we saw in Malaysia) the state has a near monopoly on the press and political activity in general (Hefner 2001, 41). Thus, my reading of Singapore's highest-selling newspaper, *Straits Times*, detailed later, reflects state ideology in censored form.

In Singapore public service and governance reforms relate to the context of Singapore's "developmental state," striving to reinvent itself in light of changes brought about by globalization challenges. Major administrative reform programs to strengthen institutional capacity for innovation and leadership and to alter attitudes towards change are part of a larger state-managed project to develop a corporate state that can maintain the state–economy complex under strong government leadership. Global competition in the market for halal has legitimized strategic moves by the PAP government to reinvent the structure of interventions and to create a new agenda and rationale for state-directed political, administrative, and economic governance (Cheung 2002, 258). The close networking among government, civil service, trade unions, and key institutions, such as the press, is important for Singapore's halal policy; that is, once a policy is determined as the only "sensible" course, it is filtered through these interlocking channels and then any further debate or opposition is almost impossible (Clammer 1993, 271). Singapore as a zone embodies a remarkable combination of capitalism (investment of multinationals and foreign banks facilities) and state control (desire to regulate such activities). There is a persistent intervention of government in all areas of economic activity and the Singaporean economy is one of the most regulated in the world. Such direct state intervention in the economy is marked through large statutory bodies (Clammer 1993, 276). MUIS is a state-linked statutory board, and it is powerful because it is tasked with managing Islam and halal in Singapore. "Appropriation" is a key principle as in the case of halal only the state can take any important initiatives, or it co-opts alternative initiatives (Clammer 1993, 269–270). An example of this, as we shall see, is a legally enforced ban on alternative forms of halal certification. More generally, the state, dominated by the PAP, penetrates many aspects of social life, and central PAP ideologies are pragmatism, meritocracy, multiracialism, Asian values, communitarianism, and elitism.

Since the early 1980s, not unlike what we have seen in the case of how Islam was nationalized and halal standardized in Malaysia, the Singapore nation-building project moved towards a more "ethnic-cum-racial" form with the conceptions of "Chinese" ethnicity and a peculiar Singaporean notion of "Chinese values" playing increasingly important roles (Barr and Skrbis 2008, 5). What is more, this ethnicization includes the upholding of Singapore's two main national myths, that is, multiracialism and meritocracy that facilitate and legitimize rule by a self-appointed Chinese elite (Barr and Skrbis 2008, 5). Interestingly, halal aspirations emerging since the 1980s took place parallel to the stress on Confucian ethics and, more broadly, on a form of Chinese ethnicization of society. Confucian ethics include obedience to benevolent and paternalistic hierarchical authority and emphasize societal duties and obligations. This powerful narrative about the hardworking and economically successful Chinese, especially vis-à-vis the lazy and problematic Malay comes alive in the "twilight zone" among reality, ideological construction, and social imagination (Yao 2002, 4) in both Malaysia and Singapore. Ironically, this transformation plays a key role in the proliferation of halal in Singapore and beyond.

The Malays in Singapore enjoy special recognition of a mostly symbolic nature as an indigenous population in the Singaporean Constitution. There seems to be a (legal) replay of this indigenous ethnicity in the way in which Malay Muslims are evoked as proper and instrumental handlers and protectors of halal in Singapore. What is more, the indigenousness has both a colonial trajectory in the way in which ethnicity was solidified, essentialized, or "frozen," and the PAP-led government has to a large extent enhanced ethnic consciousness, identities, and boundaries.

Paradoxically, to keep religion and politics apart, the state must actively intervene in the "religious market" to guarantee that religious services (e.g., preaching, teaching, healing, and praying) are compatible with security and national goals (Nasir, Pereira, and Turner 2009, 3). Similarly, the state promotion of halal in Singapore presents a paradox: halal as an ancient Muslim taboo on specific foods is promoted as a national and neutral brand that benefits the economy, while the moral implications are downplayed—especially in a Chinese-majority cultural context where Chinese social, religious, and economic rituals are unavoidably intertwined. Gambling, eating pork, and drinking alcohol are important ways of establishing identity and group membership, and rituals involving these things permeate all aspects of Singapore life (Stimpfl 2006, 74).

In this context Malay Muslims are called on to handle halal properly. In other words, no matter how forcefully halal is promoted as a highly lucrative global market in which countries such as Malaysia and Singapore want to find their rightful place, halal is essentially an Islamic injunction or binary based on halal–haram, always moral and not socially neutral in nature. Before halal became part of a global and growing market the state in Singapore considered it an expression of excessive religiosity and minority rights that separate Muslims and non-Muslims in a "multiracial context." Compared to Malaysia, *dakwah* groups and individuals do not place great emphasis on halal in Singapore. So not only are the number of Muslims in Singapore limited, but most of these are also relatively relaxed about everyday halal consumption. The state overtly tries to demonstrate that no one racial community is especially privileged or disadvantaged and that all groups have equal status in contrast to Malaysia's pro-*bumiputera* policies

(Nasir, Pereira, and Turner 2009, 7). The tight management of all religions in Singapore is a means to achieve social stability that the state sees as a prerequisite for the ultimate goal—capital accumulation or economic growth, and it is in this context the Singaporean halal vision should be seen. Thus, in contradistinction to Malaysia, where the halal consumption of local Muslims is essential, the driving force behind the halal market in Singapore is the "tapping" of the global halal market.

MUIS and Halal Regulation

Islam is heavily state-regulated in Singapore. In contradistinction to Malaysia, where JAKIM and HDC together with a host of *dakwah* and Malay interest groups at federal and state levels struggle over authority, there is only one halal bureaucracy in Singapore. MUIS is the state Islamic institution, its main decision-making body is the council headed by a president, and it comprises the mufti of Singapore and persons nominated by Muslim organizations. The state in Singapore promotes religiosity even though Singapore is officially a secular state; that is, the "religious economy" is heavily regulated and governed by a very pragmatic state (Pereira 2005, 172).

Three MUIS clusters regulate different aspects of Islam: first, Islamic development, education, mosques, and public outreach; second, "assets management" such as halal certification, *haj* (pilgrimage) services, *zakat* (almsgiving), and *wakaf* (endowments); and, last, corporate services such as finance, human resources, and information systems. MUIS raises most of its own funds but still receives budgetary assistance (Funston 2006b, 73). There are close workings (and tensions) with other Muslim groups including Singapore Islamic Scholars and Religious Teachers (PERGAS). Thus, while MUIS is a centralized and hegemonic religious bureaucracy that administers Islam in Singapore, an uneasy relationship exists between MUIS and PERGAS, for example, over the representation of Islamic authority. Consequently, Islamic administration by the state shrinks the space in which new ideas, interpretations, and contestations in the Muslim community can take place (Kadir 2004, 364).

When AMLA was enacted in 1965, it allowed for the establishment of MUIS in 1968 and the consequent culmination of the fusion of Malay and Muslim identities in Singapore (Kadir 2004, 360). The management of Islam in Singapore is undertaken through the institutionalization of AMLA and the formation of MUIS. MUIS's functions, duties, responsibilities, and powers are clearly defined in AMLA. MUIS's halal services formally started in 1978 and were driven by the increasing demand for halal certified products, eating establishments, and the need to regulate the halal industry. MUIS is solely responsible and performs a regulatory function in halal under the state. MUIS also facilities halal food trade through certifying local exporters to export their products to a global halal market; and local establishments as well as participating in forums on standardization of halal certification (Riaz and Chaudry 2004, 53). An amendment of AMLA was passed in 1999, giving MUIS new powers to regulate, promote, and enhance the halal business. In other words, this bill empowers MUIS to regulate the halal certification of any product, service, or activity in Singapore. Prior to the AMLA amendment, MUIS could only rely on the Sale of Food Act and only with respect to false labeling (Riaz and Chaudry 2004, 217). On December 1, 2009 (during my fieldwork) a further amendment of AMLA with specific reference to halal certificates took effect, so it was now a serious offense to display false halal logos, that is, false MUIS logos. Singapore's halal regulations and import requirements are governed by three major legislations administered by three state and quasi-state agencies. These regulations govern the import of food and agricultural products.

MUIS's is vested with the powers to act as the sole authority to administer and regulate Halal certification in Singapore, and this is clearly stipulated in section 88A(1) of the AMLA. Persons who, without the approval of the MUIS, issue or misuse a halal certificate in relation to any product, service, or activity are guilty of an offense and shall be liable on conviction to a fine not exceeding S$10,000[104] or to imprisonment for a term not exceeding 12 months or both. In 2009, MUIS certified more than 2,600 premises (http://www.muis.gov.sg/cms/services/hal.aspx?id=1714). MUIS regulation of halal includes a whole range of audit and inspection technologies and techniques. The following are general halal requirements: meat and poultry must be slaughtered by qualified Muslims and sourced from a halal-certified vendor; all imported meat and meat by-products must be halal certified by foreign Islamic authorities recognized by MUIS; during the course of slaughtering, preparation, processing, transporting, and storage all food products must be clearly and visibly segregated from and not come into contact with non-halal food products; at least two Muslim employees of sufficient seniority must be involved in procurement, verification, and production processes, and their role is vital to ensure all aspects of the preparation processes are in compliance with Islamic requirements (Riaz and Chaudry 2004, 223); mixing of utensils and equipment of halal and non-halal during preparation, collection, washing, or storing must be avoided; separate washing and drying equipment/premises must be provided for MUIS-appointed officials when they ritually cleanse utensils and equipment (Riaz and Chaudry 2004, 223); and to be halal certified, only halal food is to be served. Non-halal food must not be served or used in any of the ingredients for the food and beverages. Employees are not allowed to bring any non-halal food or beverages into "halal-designated" premises (Riaz and Chaudry 2004, 223–224); fast-food chains with multiple outlets or restaurants operating under a franchise scheme must submit applications for all outlets; and applicants are advised to operate "100% halal" and employees must be "comfortable" with the halal requirements set by MUIS (Riaz and Chaudry 2004, 224).

A number of requirements are related to audits and inspections specifically. On submission of applications and in course of being halal certified random audits and "surprise" inspections are performed at the applicant's premises to ensure compliance with the halal requirements. These audits check on concerns such as seriousness of intention to go halal, the authenticity of information and supporting evidence submitted, halal compliance and internal control systems, effectiveness and consistency of implementation, the role and efficacy of the Muslim staff in guiding and ensuring compliance in the production process, educate and reinforce understanding of halal requirements and compliance by employees, risk of noncompliance, and areas for improvement (Riaz and Chaudry 2004, 224).

In an MUIS publication the definition of the mandatory Muslim staff or Halal Team is outlined. The Halal Team appoints personnel responsible for implementing, monitoring, and maintaining halal systems. The Halal Team is led by an appointed management representative and includes at least one Muslim staff and members from a "multi-disciplinary background, who possess relevant knowledge and expertise" (MUIS 2007, 11). The company must ensure that the Muslim staff and at least one other member of the Halal Team are sent for halal training recognized by the MUIS. On the establishment of the Halal Team MUIS writes that the management must ensure that the terms of reference of the Halal Team are fully established and the roles and responsibilities of each member are clearly defined. Members must be fully committed and responsible in developing, implementing, and maintaining an effective halal system (MUIS 2007, 12).

As we saw it in the case of Malaysia, the state intensified its focus on halal from the early 1990s onward, and this is reflected in popular discourses. An example of this is that for hygienic reasons the environment ministry and primary production department wanted to "phase out" fowl slaughtering in wet markets by early 1992 and move this to abattoirs. Now, Muslim consumers could no longer see the slaughtering take place at the wet markets, and MUIS ensured Muslims that the abattoirs only employed slaughterers with MUIS certificates.[105] This point is important because it reflects a shift from face-to-face interaction and visibility between seller and buyer toward more abstract and impersonal exchange and standardized mass production in the market place that necessitates third-party involvement and regulation by MUIS. Mandatory Muslim involvement in halal was discussed in a MUIS handbook outlining requirements for slaughtering at abattoirs that replaced the "live slaughtering" of poultry at wet markets. Requirements for an abattoir to obtain the halal certification include a "sufficient number" of Muslim employees, qualified Muslim slaughterers who passed an MUIS "test-interview" on halal slaughtering methods, and a Muslim supervisor who is responsible for the whole process of halal slaughtering and halal labeling, as well as tagging of chickens with a green-colored label that says "Approved by MUIS." Finally, MUIS ensured proper segregation in the abattoirs between halal and non-halal chickens.[106]

Another MUIS handbook targeted fast-food restaurants and requirements: all outlets must serve halal food only, there must be two authorized Muslim employees at each outlet who are responsible for verifying that all food prepared meets the manner prescribed by MUIS, and a file must be opened to compile delivery orders, invoices, and recognized halal certificates to be verified by the Muslim staff in charge. This is to be made readily available to an MUIS officer for inspection. There must be neither pork nor alcohol on the menu; all meat served must be slaughtered by Muslims and bear recognized halal certificates; animal-based ingredients such as gelatin and animal shortening must derive from halal sources only; all crockery and utensils must be *sertu* (ritually cleansed) if they had been used previously for serving non-halal foods; halal foods must be stored separately from non-halal items; and staff must not take non-halal food into the premises.[107] In the 1990s a wave of fast-food restaurants, including McDonald's, became halal certified in Singapore, and the preceding guidelines are aimed at regulating this transformation.

Simultaneously, the MUIS advised Muslims, government departments/statutory boards/armed forces, and companies, hotels, and restaurant chains on proper Islamic consumption such as the prohibition of eating frogs' legs or turtle soup and the wearing of perfume containing alcohol. A simple guidebook was needed as Singapore became more open to "international influences," MUIS argued.[108] MUIS also guided Muslims on halal investment because "wealth" must be halal and from a halal source and "the items traded must also be halal."[109] Islam and halal are regulated by the Singaporean state and this tendency seems to be reinforced in the context of visions of Singapore's rightful place in globalizing market for halal products and services. The previous discussions show how MUIS played an essential role in managing overlapping techniques and technologies of production, trade, and regulation that together warrant a product as halal and thereby helped to format the market in the Singaporean zone.

Halal Visions

From the early 1990s onward, Singapore was presented as a "logical choice" as a processing and trading center for halal food based on strong trading and cultural links in the Muslim world. This involved modern, efficient, and cost-effective infrastructure; technologically advanced food products industry; the availability of halal certification by competent authorities; and an export-oriented food industry.[110] In 1997 it was estimated that over the preceding six years, the number of halal certificates issued by MUIS jumped from 19 to 271 and that this expansion included new products such as mooncakes.[111] As the global market for halal expanded in the 1990s, MUIS envisioned a new service certifying nonfood products endorsing makeup, for example, "to ease the doubts of Muslims."[112]

Interestingly, a recent article in *Straits Times* summarizes many of the points discussed in this book. It reports that in the context of the "booming" global halal market, Singapore's halal industry is "on a roll," with the number of halal-certified premises rising fivefold within the last 10 years to 2,650 in 2011. Expectedly, the number will go up to 5,000 by 2015, and the trend has prompted MUIS to move beyond certification. Together with organizations such as International Enterprise Singapore, MUIS will build the country's halal brand through product development, trade, and consultancy. At stake is a global halal market worth US$661 million. MUIS's president explained that "going halal" can increase takings by 20 to 25 percent for businesses. The minister in charge of Muslim affairs, who is also minister for information, communications, and the arts, added that the quintupling of halal certified premises over the last 10 years is also a boost for tourism, especially with regard to Muslim tourists from Malaysia, Indonesia, and the Middle East staying in halal hotels. The minister launched an MUIS Singapore Halal Eating Guide iPhone app (a digital version of the hard copy available at bookstores and some mosques), which can be downloaded for free. At the same time, multinational fast-food chains, such as Delifrance (halal certified since 2001), had a 20 percent boost in revenue since then, and a local Chinese owner of a pizzeria had the same experience—once the challenge of buying only halal-certified raw materials was overcome, business prospered.[113]

Considering Singapore's size and history, halal visions and halal altogether take up much space in the Singaporean media. Compared to Malaysia, the vision in Singapore is basically the same. However, in Singapore, actions speak louder than words, especially in a political context, where halal is relatively uncontested and comfortably situated in a form of bureaucratized authoritarianism. Halal is constantly evoked as a global and growing market, and this fact legitimizes state involvement and regulation. The halal visions of Singapore are, to a large extent, driven by market research, statistics, and probability that attempt to map markets and predict the future.

Of Law and Logos

The enforcement of state halal certification and logos is a favorite topic in the Singaporean media. As early as 1978, the year when the first MUIS halal certificate was issued, MUIS stated that it would not hesitate to prosecute any firm for willfully deceiving Muslims by putting misleading and deceptive products for sale. Firms and manufacturers intending to classify their products as halal should apply to the MUIS for the certificate before putting their products on sale in the market.[114] After MUIS established its form of national Singaporean halal certification in 1978 the halal discourse focuses on the multiplicity involved in regulating and enforcing this type of standard. For example, MUIS asked a fast-food restaurant that claimed to have halal certificates to explain itself. MUIS's public relations officer argued that having halal certificates of slaughter does not make the restaurant halal.[115] MUIS now conducts its own "investigations" into restaurants and food stalls exhibiting halal signs "indiscriminately."[116] These points show that as an organization, MUIS was rationalized to develop and refine halal regulation techniques.

The PAP launched a new series of dialogue sessions to gather feedback on issues affecting the Malay Muslim community, and a key issue was the use of false halal certificates by some restaurants and hawkers.[117] This point relates to the way in which the halal discourse intensified in the early 1990s and a central theme is the proliferation and regulation of halal into more and more areas, for example, the beginning of MUIS certification of abattoir poultry.[118] When these abattoirs apply for halal certification they must comply with MUIS requirements and ensure that they have enough Muslim workers to comply with these guidelines. Only Muslim staff can attach the halal labels.[119] This is an important point because it testifies to the trend that Muslims must be involved in proper handling and not only the actual ritual slaughter in light of rising halal requirements. Another important issue here is techniques and technologies of certification and logos. When the move from wet market to abattoir slaughter was completed logos in the form of "paper tags" tore when wet and had to be replaced by stallholders. Poultry hawkers in some wet markets resorted to "do-it-yourself" tagging. Hawkers called for waterproof plastic or aluminum tags to be used instead of the paper ones delivered. In these markets, stallholders must sell only poultry labeled by the abattoirs. The penalty for not doing so is a fine of up to S$1,000 for the first offense and S$2,000 for the second and subsequent offenses.[120]

An important theme is MUIS dissatisfaction with the licensing of halal food that is not "backed by legislation." The rationale was that as long as the vendor is a Muslim, regardless of race, the "onus" of ensuring that the food served is halal rests on him, because MUIS has no legislative powers to stop any halal restaurants from operating or to subject it to a test or inspection.[121] A particular case is related to Muslim handling of halal in a seafood restaurant listed as a non-Muslim owned restaurant that was not issued with a halal certificate. MUIS had to clarify that this was incorrect and that the restaurant was Muslim-owned and thus did not need to apply for a halal certificate at that time.[122] Another seafood restaurant was accused by customers for not displaying a MUIS halal certificate while promoting itself in an ad as halal; that is, "no pork or lard will be used."[123]

From the mid-1990s the halal discourse focused on calls to tap the growing global market for halal production, trade, and consumption through MUIS certification; that is, from around that time the state and companies in Singapore realized that halal had grown into a truly global assemblage with immense business potential. In 1994, Singapore's exports of halal food amounted to S$1.2 billion, making up 24 percent of the country's total food and beverage exports of S$5 billion.[124] In 1995, MUIS introduced its first logo that was to standardize existing logos labeled on halal food products. Previously, food manufacturers with halal certificates merely used the Arabic halal symbol to indicate that their food was halal and not a "standard" logo. Food manufacturers now had three months to change their halal logo to the new one issued by MUIS.[125] Thus, centralized regulation transformed diverse classifications of logos into one national standard. With the amendments to the AMLA, MUIS's role as the highest Islamic authority in Singapore was "expanded" and "strengthened," and MUIS could form part of companies as well as joint ventures. Moreover, MUIS was given the authority to issue halal certificates and punish those who violated the rules.[126]

In the late 1990s the halal discourse focused on the successes of halal certified companies. MUIS reported a steady increase in issued halal certificates. The certificate was said to "draw business" because Muslims were assured that their food was halal, especially in Malay areas. This success reinforced MUIS requirements that companies have to pass stringent checks before they are given the certificates. Food must be prepared properly for Muslim consumers and companies must use equipment free from contact with non-halal food. A coordinator from a certified catering firm explained that this process was not easy—the firm spent about S$4,000 to restructure the kitchen and had to look for new halal suppliers but profited in the end.[127]

With the massive proliferation of halal certification and markets came new calls for reviewing halal certification laws. When firms misuse halal certificates, they get away with fines, but individuals who do the same thing face jail because the law prosecutes the company and not its staff, and this should be changed, a high court judge argued. This call appeared in the wake of a court case where a Singaporean company had used MUIS's halal logo on chicken nuggets imported from Thailand. The product was in fact halal, but the company had used MUIS's logo without its approval. The AMLA provided for a maximum fine of S$10,000 or a jail term of 12 months for such an offense.[128]

MUIS wanted a more rigorous scheme for certifying products as halal that would help local companies to market products overseas. In 2007 the global halal market was estimated at more than US$2.1 trillion. The new certification scheme developed by MUIS was called the Halal Quality Management System, or HalMQ (pronounced "hallmark"), and it took effect March 1, 2008. Suppliers going for certification for the first time will have to comply with all HalMQ terms from that date and existing holders of halal certificates had until January 1, 2010, to comply. While the current halal certification requirements were product focused, the new certification scheme went further and set standards for business operations in addition to ensuring that the ingredients and the preparation of food or health goods are halal. HalMQ required companies to appoint people to monitor and document the preparation of halal products and recommend corrective actions if the products are tainted by alcohol or other prohibited ingredients.[129] The proposed changes to AMLA should give halal certification laws "more bite" and provide MUIS with "more clout" in supervising and enforcing halal certification at a time when the global halal food industry and exports to Middle Eastern markets were growing. The new law was to "resolve" an "anomaly in the current law" so that individuals who misuse halal certificates are liable to a jail term, but companies that do the same thing only liable to fines.[130]

In August 2009, a dispute among the MUIS, the supermarket NTUC FairPrice, and a local halal consultancy organization surfaced. MUIS had "taken issue with a claim by supermarket chain FairPrice that its new halal auditing program will give greater consumer assurance." MUIS's president stressed that the council is the sole authority that can certify establishments and products as halal. FairPrice announced the plan in connection with the launch of their newest outlet in Joo Chiat Complex, which was also their first to undergo a halal audit. However, MUIS had not yet certified the Joo Chiat outlet.[131] During my fieldwork in Singapore, the FairPrice director of food safety and quality explained to me that "[a] specific halal counter is not enough. There has to be a mindset in terms of a system," and the implementation of this "system" is the focus of attention in Chapter 7.

Since the issuing of MUIS's first halal certificate in 1978 some major transformations in the realm of certification, logos, and legislation transpired. Halal has become a global market in which legality plays an increasingly important role. What is more, since the early 1980s, Singapore nationalized and standardized the proliferation of halal and concentrated its certification in the realm of the state and MUIS, where it has remained.

Sanctions and Seizures

There is an abundance of examples of how food was seized for not complying with halal requirements. However, as late as 1984, MUIS admitted that it did not have enough people to check on eating places to make sure that all food marked halal meets Muslim requirements.[132] This shows that in the early days of halal regulation there was not sufficient institutional capacity to regulate halal, and this did not change until the 1990s. In this decade the halal discourse starts to target more actual offenses backed by law, for example, two people who were fined a total of S$5,700 relating to the forgery of halal certificates for cooking oil.[133] Moreover, warnings about legal sanctions are frequent.[134] The first jail sentence appeared in 1993 when a perpetrator was jailed for a week and fined S$2,000.[135] A particular case concerns a catering company that lost its halal certificate for a food-preparation area for six months because it failed to comply with halal requirements. MUIS looked into the case after having received complaints about the company from the public.[136] By 2004 MUIS had "hauled" 33 companies and restaurants to court within the last five years, and all were fined. MUIS also issued warnings to 28 companies for breaking halal regulations in 2003. At the same time, the number of halal certificate holders amounted to 6,769 in 2004 compared to 2,329 in 1999. The global halal market was estimated at about US$350 billion (S$600 billion), and the industry was expected to be worth about US$460 billion by 2005.[137]

In a recent case, MUIS filed a police report over a gift shop selling food that was labeled with a non-MUIS halal logo. MUIS was alerted by a "member of the public".[138] This incident raises the important point that not only smaller companies, but also multinationals such as McDonald's have become extremely sensitive to such alerts by the public. For example, in 2010 McDonald's pulled a pig toy from its latest toy promotions in Singapore. The pig soft toy was expected to have been part of a 12-character Doraemon set depicting the animals of the Chinese zodiac calendar. But following complaints McDonald's decided not to include the pig toy to avoid offending Muslim customers. This move caused controversy in Singapore.[139] I have shown that the increased backing by legislation, on one hand, and the global proliferation of halal, on the other, have given impetus to much stricter enforcement of halal in Singapore. To the more global aspects I now turn.

Global Politics of Halal

Another example of the way in which the market for halal has been globalized is Singapore's participation in halal events such as the 4th International Halal Food Conference[140] in which Malaysia and Indonesia also participated. Malaysia is frequently discussed in the popular discourse on halal in Singapore. When the Malaysian state banned the sale of non-halal meat at all hotels, restaurants, and rest houses owned by the government,[141] these increased requirements were seen as a type of new standard for halal regulation that MUIS and Singapore must take into consideration because of competition between the two countries. Since the early 1980s both countries have been alert to halal developments across the causeway. Another example is the mufti of Singapore's statement that food declared haram in Malaysia was also haram for Muslims in Singapore. A certain brand of jelly was found to contain gelatin derived from pigs and was therefore haram.[142] Many articles focus on the success of halal in Malaysia.[143]

As early as 1981 MUIS wrote to the Federation of Australian Muslim Councils to seek clarification on the contents of Australian beef exported to Singapore following inquiries from Muslims after reading reports about Australian beef being contaminated or mixed with kangaroo meat.[144] From the 1990s onward, the global aspects of halal were often formulated in terms of business opportunities; for example, China figured prominently in this type of discourse.[145] Transnational guidelines for halal among ASEAN countries were another important issue.[146]

As the halal market globalized and included new products, MUIS also became involved in regulating labels and television advertisements, such as with the company Halal Foods Diet Formula, for example. "Scantily-clad" models could not appear any more in advertisements that were found "too sexy."[147] MUIS also advised Muslims not to drink a soft drink that allegedly contained alcohol.[148] From the 2000s, MUIS became more and more involved in countries such as Australia, France, Switzerland, and Germany, and reportedly these countries were "asking" MUIS for advice on halal certification and Muslim marriage laws.[149] Similar trends were detectable in the Middle East.[150]

A powerful narrative or discourse in Singapore stresses the nation's vulnerability as a small state, especially with regard to its large Muslim dominated neighbors Malaysia and Indonesia (seen as a potentially failed state), and the need for Singapore society to be rugged and equipped with morally strong fiber when squeezed between these large Muslim majority countries. The advantage of smallness, however, as we have seen, is that halal in Singapore was relatively easily centralized with MUIS. What is more, PAP and its form of political culture and nationalism have been highly successful in promoting and combining economic growth and acceptance of authoritarian and paternalistic government in return for providing societal stability—again especially vis-à-vis Malaysia and Indonesia. These two countries are major competitors in the run for leadership in halal, and at the same time, they are major markets for Singaporean-halal-certified products. Even today, relations with Malaysia are not easy or comfortable, and Singaporean reliance on water from Malaysia is a constant source of tension between the two countries. Citizens in the two countries have prejudices about each other—Malaysia tends to regard Singapore as inferior because of its small size and absence of resources while Malaysia seems to be envious of Singapore's economic growth (Mauzy and Milne 2002, 177).

Like Malaysia, Singapore is outspoken on the international stage in support of "moderate" Islam in the context of the Shafi'i school of Sunni jurisprudence in a secular state framework. Unquestionably, the *dakwah* movement increased Islamic religiosity and created greater interest in dress and diet (Funston 2006b, 74) but not to the extent it happened in Muslim majority Malaysia. However, *dakwah* across the Muslim world is a major reason behind the proliferation of halal as a global assemblage. All this takes place in the contact zones or interface zones where regulatory frameworks meet the market.

Instrumental Muslims

Singapore exists in a "double minority" setting: Chinese are a majority in Singapore, but minority in the region whereas the Malays are a minority in Singapore, but a strong majority in the immediate region (Mauzy and Milne 2002, 99–100), and this complex relationship is essential to understanding halal in Malaysia and Singapore. As we have seen, Malay Muslims are the largest ethnic minority in Singapore and pose important challenges to the state as this group lags behind in terms of education and low-skill jobs (Mauzy and Milne 2002, 109). The "Malay problem," which pervades the mind of the nation as a kind of state-generated other, requires a more nuanced/complex view between blaming the state and blaming the Malays

(Nasir 2007). The low rate of Malays involved in entrepreneurship in the Singapore economy has reaffirmed the false supposition that Malays are indolent, rural, and poor (Lee 1989, 138–139).

Traditionally, cooked food is an important sector of Malay and Chinese petty enterprise. Malays have a guaranteed market, because Muslims generally do not buy Chinese food for fear of contamination by pork. Many Singapore Chinese also buy Malay food and thus widen the market and support Malay business (Lee 1989, 139). The state has very strict health rules as well as a strongly enforced licensing scheme for small businesses such as food and drink hawkers (Stimpfl 2006, 68). While many Malays are fastidious about halal in modern Singapore, they practice this fastidiousness pragmatically in the context of the ethnic Chinese majority (Nasir, Pereira, and Turner 2009). Pious middle-class Malays display a strong "halal consciousness," and they often prefer to abstain from eating if they have doubts about the halal status or certification of a particular food. Preferences for Muslim cooks and kitchen staff, desire to avoid sitting too close to people who are not eating halal food, and halal(-certified) environments are commonplace. Yet most Malays feel comfortable eating in environments that are not fully halal as long as certified halal food is available. Thus, the halal certification contributes to the integration process (Nasir and Pereira 2008).

Research shows that some non-Muslim Singaporeans may misunderstand the practice of defensive Malay dining strategies as antisocial or even offensive (Marranci 2012, 94). When Malay Muslims' halal practices are read within everyday contexts and interactions with the Chinese majority, in particular, dining strategies can be seen as less effective and even divisive. MUIS's centralized certification of halal food has provided a protected meta-space in which Singaporean Malay Muslims can feel reassured and free to interact with non-Muslims without concerns about non-halal food contamination that would perhaps prevent sharing dining spaces and activities. Younger generations in particular are becoming used to the green MUIS halal logo (Marranci 2012, 93), and often the only reliable means of discerning what is halal is the halal logo on products or the halal certificate at food stalls and restaurants.

The effects of 9/11 in Singapore subjected Muslims to further scrutiny and suspicion and reinvigorated questions about their loyalty to the nation (Mutalib 2005, 62), but at the same time, the Ajinomoto scandal coupled with the promotion of moderate Islam generated interest in halal and intensified the flows of people, things, and metaphors associated with halal. Generally, minorities such as Malay Muslims do not display individual or community differences publicly (Chua and Kian-Woon 2001, 116); for example, there is virtually no public criticism of the way in which the vision to become a world leader in halal is transforming Singaporean society in terms of ethnic relations, audit culture, or legislation. The state evokes halal as integral to national and patriotic sentiments as well as ways in which Malay ethnicity is tied to the state. Thus, while the state saw halal requirements as a sensitive minority issue of some indigenous Malays, halal is now considered part of a lucrative globalized market; it is a patriotic duty to "tap," a word that is often used in popular discourse. Moreover, Malays in Singapore who traditionally have been involved in the food industry became instrumental to the state halal vision.

Race in Singapore can be said to be a structural and sociopolitically constructed phenomenon within an environment of coercive political control and strong economic growth. The constant reinforcement of race classification is a potent means of political mobilization and structuring of life (Tan 2004, 66). In the case of halal this means that indigenous Malay Muslims are seen as quintessentially proper handlers of halal in a Chinese-dominated bureaucratic context. The Singaporean state turned constitutional multiculturalism into an ideological basis for the rationalization of policies and administrative practices on issues of race (Chua 2003a, 58).

In popular media discourse, the question of halal in the context of the Malay Muslim minority and a Chinese-dominated nation stands out. In the early 1980s when halal was still mainly a question of (excessive) minority rights, a special panel was set up to upgrade the religious consciousness of some 5,000 Muslims who worked in the food and beverage industry. One of its aims was to dispel the belief that they were "immoral" and to teach them the correct Islamic ethics.[151] At the time, Malays had not yet been articulated as "proper indigenous handlers of halal" but was mainly a "problem," as it were. In the mid-1980s the prime minister had to apologize for "over-simplicity" when he remarked that the tendency was that for some Muslims to live up to the teachings of Islam they merely dressed, ate, and behaved as Muslims in the Middle East. Moreover, the prime minister linked the behavior of some Muslims, for example, their preference not to dine with non-Muslims who do not eat halal food, to "pressures from the Arab countries."[152]

Not until later in the 1980s did the media start to happily report that Chinese-style seafood was becoming popular among Malays, giving rise to halal seafood restaurants. These halal seafood places were divided into those run completely by Chinese or Chinese-Muslims and those run by Malays.[153] From the 1990s the potential of ethnic Malays in the halal business started to be recognized, and the prime minister argued that Singapore had the "complete infrastructure" to help Malay businessmen to make the country a Muslim trading center for halal food. The backup available in Singapore should help members of the Malay Chamber of Commerce to attract importers and exporters of halal food and other items to do business.[154] The president of the Singapore Malay Chamber of Commerce (SMCC) shared this vision for Malay entrepreneurs and helped the Malays venture into the halal food business, which was estimated to have a potential turnover of about S$20 billion a year.[155] The state accorded special tribute to the SMCC for its achievements and excellence in the business world, particularly business interests in Malaysia including a supermarket across the causeway in

Johor that sells only halal food.[156] Moreover, SMCC set up a consortium to import and sell halal food as well as cooperatives.[157]

As the state halal discourse intensified, paradoxically Malay fastidiousness about halal was often seen as an ethnic problem[158] while SMCC worked to turn Singapore into the focal point and center for halal food processing technology.[159] The halal discourse from the mid-1990s is infused with business optimism, that is, a celebration of the halalization of *bak kut teh* (instead of pork ribs the soup has mutton or beef),[160] for instance.[161] The halalization of a whole range of Chinese dishes was described as recognizing the belonging of indigenous Malays.[162] That same year, the deputy prime minister argued that, on one hand, "[t]he political standing of Malays cannot be detached from their economic and social achievements" and, on the other, called on Malays to show "tolerance" and sit at "common dining tables at constituency and other public functions . . . with every care taken, of course, over halal and non-halal food, and separate utensils and crockery, so that religious injunctions are respected."[163] There seems to be ambivalence or tension involved in promoting national halal, on one hand, and concerns about ethnic cohesion, on the other, in much of this discourse.

As the market for halal globalized around 2000, Malay-Muslim companies in particular expanded their halal businesses to Australia[164] and in the national context even meals at the traditional Chinese Hungry Ghost Festival were available as halal and served at tables covered with green (considered the traditional color of Islam that signifies piety) tablecloths.[165] The state set up a center that could advice small and medium-sized enterprises on businesses related to Islam such as halal food certification, Islamic financing, and gaining access to the lucrative Middle Eastern market.[166]

SMCC launched a certificate scheme, which enabled Muslim food and beverage outlets without a proper MUIS halal license to advertise their status to the Muslim community, that is, "to flag the fact that they are wholly owned by Muslims." This would give Muslim customers reassurance that it is Muslims who prepare the halal food and drinks. Unlike the halal certification scheme developed by MUIS, ingredients and the preparation of food under this scheme did not have to be subjected to stringent inspection. The idea emerged after feedback from some Muslim companies that were unable to "reap" potential business opportunities, as they did not apply for a halal license. The new certificate would allow Muslim-owned catering companies to get the recognition that their food is also 100 percent halal when they bid for government tenders and corporate contracts that require halal food.[167]

The late 2000s witnessed even more halalization of traditional Chinese food such as mooncakes, the Chinese bakery product traditionally eaten during the Mid-Autumn Festival as we also saw it in Malaysia.[168] Reportedly, Malays also started to use traditional Chinese Medicine (TCM) as these remedies appeared as halal.[169] Last, halal wontons (a type of dumpling commonly found in a number of Chinese cuisines) at Chinese-Muslim stalls were celebrated.[170] Singapore's "double minority" setting strongly shapes the ambivalent or paradoxical role of Singaporean Malays in halal: on one hand, the "Malay problem" tends to pervade the mind of the nation, and on the other hand, Malays are seen to be patriotic and instrumental as consumers, entrepreneurs, and indigenous handlers of halal.

In the Halal Zone

In Malaysia, halal has spurred new forms of space making in the form of halal centers, areas, zones, or parks. Singapore does not in the same way as Malaysia include such zones in its halal strategies and visions and arguably the reason could be that Singapore is small in size and compared to Malaysia it is not home to many manufacturing companies. However, two localized forms of "halal zones" do exist. First, MUIS has launched a "Whole Plant Scheme" issued to manufacturing facilities and all products therein. When MUIS took steps to strengthen halal certification procedures it included this scheme meaning that manufacturers will be able to get the entire plant certified and then it will not be necessary to apply for certification for each new product.[171] Similarly, many Muslim caterers, hawkers, and restaurants have responded to the high level of halal consciousness by acquiring halal certification for an entire food court serving all sorts of halal cuisines because of the emergence of a Malay Muslim middle class with greater spending power. MUIS also offers an "Eating Establishment Scheme," issued to retail food establishments such as restaurants, school canteen stalls, snack bars, halal corners, confectioneries, bakery shops, stalls within a food court or its equivalent, temporary stalls in bazaars, flea markets, and trade fairs. Both these schemes can be seen as a form of zoning, that is, halal spaces backed by particular forms of regulation and law making in the marketplace for halal.

In 2008, a national controversy came in the wake of a Singaporean primary school insisting that only halal food could be taken into the canteen causing a stir among non-Muslim parents. The Ministry of Education declared that this decision was a mistake, and it was reversed. In a letter to all parents, the school's principal said that since the whole school canteen had been certified halal, children would not be allowed to bring non-halal food onto the premises. The school security guard and discipline master had also been checking lunch boxes to ensure that pupils complied. MUIS clarified that it "certifies only the food stalls in a school canteen, not the premises as a whole" and added that once a stallholder had obtained his halal certificate, non-halal foods cannot be brought in or out of that halal-certified stall. As for the dining area in the canteen, it is up to the school to decide whether to allow non-halal foods to be brought in.[172] This case stressed the inherent multiplicity in state regulated halal business on a national level, and Muslim community leaders, for example, spoke out against what they saw as the danger that the ban on non-halal in the school was at odds with the nation's multicultural values.[173] Soon after this incident, however, Banquet halal food courts, started by Mr. Lee, a Chinese businessman, in 1999 and certified under the "Eating Establishment Scheme," was evoked as to clearly distinguish between halal in the marketplace and the school: Banquet was a huge national business success whereas the issue of a school canteen banning non-halal food was unacceptable.[174]

Singapore does not share the Malaysian vision of designating large areas as halal zones, but zoning technologies have carved out a multitude of halal spaces to achieve strategic goals of regulation of halal in relation to market forces. In each of these zones, halal production, trade, and regulation combine and overlap in new ways.

Middle-Class Innovation

Earlier I have hinted at the role of the Malay middle class in Singaporean halal. In spite of the "Malay problem" discourses, this group is recognized not only as instrumental as proper handlers of halal but also as a growing ethnic middle-class group with increased buying power that has to be reckoned with. From the mid-1990s the halalization of fast food restaurants signified the increased strength of the Malay "purchasing power."[175] "High-quality" convenience foods such as pizza, ravioli, and dumplings were catering to changing middle-class lifestyles and households in which both partners work.[176] These increasingly affluent groups were also targeted as tourists and tours were promoted through "halal outlets."[177] Multinational fast-food chains such as Kentucky Fried Chicken and McDonald's had "gone halal of their own accord," recognizing the increasing buying power of Malays.[178] As we saw in the case of the emergence of the Malaysian middle class, this class occupies a mythical place in the advent of national development and modernity as patriotic consumers. In Singapore halal also plays into the quest for a knowledge-based economy, the cornerstones being information/communication, innovation, and creativity and halal proliferates into more and more types of products and services. From the late 1990s many articles target Malays when they promote the introduction of halal lasagna and British pie, as well as baked goods and confectioneries.[179]

Business innovation also included setting up a department with a halal supermarket and food court to "cater" for the Malays.[180] Around that time, Islamic finance in many forms gained momentum. The Takaful Fund introduced by the economic arm of the Association of Muslim Professionals, in cooperation with the NTUC income, attempted to "mobilize" Muslim funds. *Takaful* literally means shared responsibility and guarantee, collective assurance, and mutual undertakings. Thus, such "Syariah-compliant" investment is based on shared responsibility and is designed to protect the participant against a defined risk. The Takaful fund invested in halal portfolio of stocks that do not "contravene Islamic laws,"[181] and this is also the ideal for Islamic banking where *riba* (interest) is prohibited.[182] At the same time, halal unit trusts that avoid investment in stocks associated with tobacco, alcohol, gambling, and "other activities detrimental to established beliefs" emerged.[183]

Since 2004 MUIS has been certifying products such as chemical cleaning agents and health supplements—arguably due to interest from customers and companies.[184] However, some companies wanted to have not only traditional Chinese medicine but also ice, moist towelettes, and carbon dioxide halal certified. MUIS argued that some items do not need the official stamp of approval to make them acceptable for Muslim consumption. MUIS head of halal certification stated that "[i]ce and carbon dioxide are considered halal already, but some companies do it for marketing purposes and to give assurance to their customers." The number of halal-certified restaurants in Singapore grew from 533 in 2000 to 2,012 in 2009 according to MUIS. Companies such as an industrial and medical gas supplier, traditional Chinese medicine maker, and wet-wipes company producing alcohol-free moist towelettes, all reported increased sales after being halal certified.[185]

A particular case stands out: a Singaporean maker of ceramic tableware products supplying to major hotel chains and others worldwide with US$30 million (S$41 million) in global sales annually was halal certified by MUIS. This can be seen as luxury product innovation that targets more affluent middle class groups. Unlike its competitors, the company developed a clay formulation enabling the production of traditional bone china without using animal bone ash. Its investment in animal bone ash–free products led its factory to become the first of its kind in the world to be certified halal by the authorities in Singapore and Malaysia. The Malaysian authorities started to demand that food and beverage outlets or hotels have halal certification and halal-certified chinaware.[186] The Malay middle class has played a central role in the proliferation of halal in Singapore—as patriotic *dakwah* consumers who legitimize national and drastic halal transformations and push halal into more and more types of products and services, on one hand, and as well-educated indigenous bureaucrats who regulate halal, on the other.

To sum up, in this chapter I have tracked the growth of halal markets and their standardization in Malaysia and Singapore. In both zones, powerful state and market discourses thrive in the economic realm as financial nationalisms that promise future prosperity based on assumptions about statistics and probability. Thus, halal is constantly evoked as a global and growing market and this fact legitimizes state involvement and regulation. In the Malaysian halal zone the regulation of halal was part of a larger process by the Malaysian state to nationalize Islam. Fearing the implications of the reflowering of Islamic ritual life among middle-class Malays, the state began regulating halal, and from this it gradually developed the vision to become the world leader in halal production, trade, and certification. I have argued that Malaysia should be viewed as a particular halal zone in which regulatory institutions and markets meet. Halal has become entangled in complex webs of political, ethnic, and national significance in modern Malaysia and at the same time it is promoted as an example of the compatibility of the ethnicized state, modern Islam, business, and proper Islamic consumption. Forms of regulation technologies and techniques are comparable in Malaysia and Singapore, but there are also major differences. One of the main differences is that Malaysia is a leading global producer and exporter of halal products that can be found in shops around the world. Singapore is small in size; there are not many manufacturing industries in the country, and this fact limits global exports. Another reason for Malaysian dominance in halal globally is the political and institutional differences between the two countries. In Malaysia halal has been a major issue in the wake of *dakwah*, and it is inseparable from Malay privileges and rights ensured by the state and a host of Muslim interest groups. The local market for halal consumption in Malaysia is vast and growing due the buying power of large Malay middle-class groups. Other explanations for Malaysian dominance are strong trade relations between Malaysia and Britain, a center for global halal consumption, for example, and a sizable Malay Muslim diaspora around the world (Fischer 2011). In the next chapter I discuss how Malaysia plays an important role in the global halal market in London.

Even if Malaysia is dominant in halal globally, halal in the Singaporean context evolved from being a sensitive Malay minority question or classification, as it were, to becoming a major national focus of state and market. Singapore's "double minority" setting has been a driving force in the promotion of halal—Malay Muslims are simultaneously seen as a "problem" as well as instrumental to the production, promotion, regulation, and consumption of halal. The stress on Chinese ethnicity, ethics and values also embodied a powerful narrative about the hard-working and economically successful Chinese that must "tap" the global and expanding market for halal. All this takes place in the framework of Singapore's unique form of government that can be characterized as some kind of authoritarianism that allows for close networking between key organizations and institutions. Consequently, this makes policy implementation and regulation of the halal market smoother than in Malaysia, for example. MUIS as a statutory body plays a pivotal role in regulating the halal market in Singapore. Finally, Muslims show the same "level-headed" moderation as Singapore's other ethnic communities, and the country has none of the foundational divides found in Malaysia and Indonesia threatening to put the entire framework of public participation and governance in question (Hefner 2001, 44).

Interestingly, the concern over halal is more pronounced in some Southeast Asian countries such as Malaysia, Singapore, Indonesia, and Brunei than in much of the Middle East and South Asia. The reasons for this are many, but the proliferation of halal in Malaysia and Singapore cannot be divorced from the fact that over the past three decades these countries have witnessed steady economic growth, the emergence of large groups of Malay Muslim middle-class consumers as well as centralized state incentives to strengthen halal production, trade, consumption, and regulation. Europe, the United

States, Canada, and Australia, which have many South and Southeast Asian diasporas, are emerging as centers with large and growing Muslim populations and as major markets for halal but without state regulation.

NOTES

1. *New Straits Times* January 6, 2001: Malaysian Ajinomoto is halal, says JAKIM.
2. *New Straits Times* January 9, 2001: Conduct tests to confirm Ajinomoto is halal.
3. *New Straits Times* January 11, 2001: Ajinomoto reassures Muslims its product is halal. The work of the PPIM is explored in detail in Chapter 5.
4. *New Straits times* April 12, 2001: Ajinomoto is "halal."
5. *Straits times* February 11, 2001: Ajinomoto scandal.
6. In part, this chapter and Chapter 2 are based on material first published in my monograph (Fischer 2008b), *Proper Islamic Consumption*, published by NIAS Press. I am grateful for NIAS Press for giving permission to use this material.
7. This material was first published in my monograph (Fischer 2011), *The Halal Frontier*, published by and reproduced with permission of Palgrave Macmillan. I am grateful to Palgrave Macmillan for giving permission to use this material.
8. *New Straits Times* September 20, 2002: JAKIM takes over task of checking halal food.
9. *New Straits Times* February 6, 2008: Halal industry master plan to be submitted to govt this month.
10. *New Straits Times* April 5, 2008: One body now for halal industry.
11. *New Straits Times* July 10, 2009: It's JAKIM for halal certs.
12. *New Straits Times* May 25, 2010: Halal forum to push for strong masterplan.
13. *New Straits Times* May 15, 1996: Opportunities in global "halal" market.
14. *New Straits Times* September 24, 1996: Explore "halal" market, industry urged.
15. *New Straits Times* September 24, 1997: Angliss to export halal food.
16. *New Straits Times* February 7, 1998: Halal food industry merits more attention.
17. *New Straits Times* July 26, 1998: 54ha site for '"halal" food industries.
18. *New Straits Times* August 2, 1998: Strategies to capture global halal food market.
19. *New Straits Times* November 28, 1998: Halal food must be hygienic and safe, says expert.
20. *New Straits Times* December 5, 1998: Quality way to broaden market for halal goods.
21. *New Straits Times* May 30, 2001: New focus on halal concept; December 5, 2008: Uproar over non-halal hotels.
22. *New Straits Times* July 24, 2002: Ministry identifies six areas for halal food production; September 4, 2002: Bid to make Malaysia as halal food hub.
23. *New Straits Times* December 24, 2002: Imports must meet SIRIM standards.
24. *New Straits Times* June 21, 2003: Halal food industry told to go global.
25. *New Straits Times* July 19, 2004: Halal producers losing out; July 19, 2004: Halal Bonanza.
26. *New Straits Times* July 19, 2004: Hard work, funds needed to penetrate halal food market.

27. *New Straits Times* November 6, 2007: We need "glocal" Malays, says Najib.
28. *New Straits Times* April 23, 2008: Najib: Stay competitive with new strategies.
29. *New Straits Times* May 15, 2008: Standards for halal status.
30. *New Straits Times* August 29, 2008: Call to tap biodiversity.
31. *New Straits Times* May 8, 2009: Najib: Expand into the global halal industry.
32. *New Straits Times* November 20, 2009: Mukhriz: Link up globally; December 9, 2009: Halal service providers must target niche areas; May 21, 2010: Promote halal products to all.
33. *New Straits Times* May 31, 2010: Tap big halal demand.
34. *New Straits Times* May 13, 1996: Call for laws on "halal" sign.
35. *New Straits Times* July 24, 1996: Recognition for "halal" food logo; July 26, 1996: Standard logo for halal food worldwide may be used.
36. *New Straits Times* November 18, 1996: Pusat Islam's role in the "halal" food industry.
37. *New Straits Times* October 26, 1998: Certification of halal products can spur exports.
38. *New Straits Times* November 21, 1998: Need for clear policy in halal certification.
39. *New Straits Times* December 5, 1998: Certification gains wider acceptance.
40. *New Straits Times* March 2, 1999: Ilham Daya must clarify halal certs, inspections charges.
41. *New Straits Times* February 27, 2002: Honest labels.
42. *New Straits Times* July 23, 2002: More companies apply for halal certification to tap RM570b market. In January 10, 2013, one Malaysian Ringgit or RM was worth US$ 0.33.
43. *New Straits Times* September 24, 2002: Do not depend only on halal label.
44. *New Straits Times* November 18, 2002: Proposal to standardize halal certificates.
45. *New Straits Times* March 21, 2003: Company to carry out halal certification.
46. *New Straits Times* August 28, 2003: Halal labels—79 to be made enforcement officers.
47. *New Straits Times* October 1, 2003: New standardized halal certification logo for all States.
48. *New Straits Times* December 20, 2003: Don't rely solely on "halal" label to stay competitive, says PM.
49. *New Straits Times* December 21, 2004: Meat must have JAKIM "halal" logo.
50. *New Straits Times* March 30, 2005: Halal logo with microchip soon.
51. *New Straits Times* February 27, 2010: Standard halal cert, symbol to beat fakes.
52. *New Straits Times* February 17, 2010: JAKIM: Law on halal logo by year-end.
53. *New Straits Times* May 7, 2010: Stiffer penalties for using fake halal logos.
54. *New Straits Times* August 3, 2010: Stiffer fines for halal logo offences.
55. *New Straits Times* November 13, 2010: Halal certification units for all states.
56. *New Straits Times* September 29, 2011: New rules on halal certs.
57. *New Straits Times* October 8, 1996: Food seized for "halal" tag offence.
58. *New Straits Times* January 1, 1999: "Sell halal poultry at separate stalls".
59. *New Straits Times* February 20, 2004: Noodles worth RM37,400 seized.
60. *New Straits Times* June 22, 2004: Packed powdered milk seized.
61. *New Straits Times* July 27, 2004: Warning on non-halal signs.
62. *New Straits Times* March 15, 2005: JAKIM raids food outlet over sausages.
63. *New Straits Times* March 23, 2005: Halal logo: Errant firms to be blacklisted.
64. *New Straits Times* March 29, 2005: "Halal" label on pork products.

65. *New Straits Times* July 16, 2005: Malaysia may stop import of Australian beef.
66. *New Straits Times* June 26, 2008: Beef cuts' worth RM464,700 seized.
67. *New Straits Times* July 17, 2009: Raided for halal offence.
68. *New Straits Times* March 6, 2010: Dept stops six firms from issuing halal certs.
69. *New Straits Times* March 20, 2010: Report abattoir "thugs", says Ismail.
70. *New Straits Times* September 3, 2010: Ghee product loses halal stamp.
71. *New Straits Times* July 1, 2003: Don't believe rumors over "halal" cert, Muslims told.
72. *New Straits Times* June 4, 2009: Red Bull drinks sold here are safe.
73. *New Straits Times* May 8, 2010: Trusting halal certificates.
74. *New Straits Times* May 21, 2011: Muhyiddin assures 1Malaysia UHT milk is halal.
75. *New Straits Times* May 11, 2006: The halal way to free trade.
76. *New Straits Times* November 4, 2000: No compromise on halal food standards.
77. *New Straits Times* March 6, 2002: Joint venture for halal food.
78. *New Straits Times* September 24, 2002: China checking out halal products in Kedah; October 9, 2002: Dr M: We can supply halal food to China; February 26, 2004: Chua—Tap China's halal market.
79. *New Straits Times* May 31, 2004: Halal product hub for overseas markets.
80. *New Straits Times* July 16, 2004: R&D needed to improve halal food; 9 August 2004: Tapping into "halal" food business.
81. *New Straits Times* October 8, 2004: Adopt combined approach, Abdullah tells OIC.
82. *New Straits Times* March 27, 2008: Out to make Malaysia top Muslim tourist destination.
83. *New Straits Times* May 2, 2008: Unite to face challenges, PM tells Muslim nations.
84. *New Straits Times* August 1, 2008: Potential seen for corn and oil palm in Zambia; July 1, 2008: KL, Sarajevo to help tackle food crisis.
85. *New Straits Times* July 2, 2008: Exporting our halal success.
86. *New Straits Times* November 18, 2008: PM asks Uzbek scholars to study Islam Hadhari.
87. *New Straits Times* March 17, 2009: Limbang officially part of Malaysia; 5 August 2009: Talks to focus on economic cooperation; August 6, 2009: Taking ties to next level.
88. *New Straits Times* October 23, 2009: More opportunities in OIC nations now; October 24, 2009: Stable world financial system vital.
89. *New Straits Times* December 5, 1998: Halal Chinese food that's tasty, creative.
90. *New Straits Times* August 17, 2001: "Halal" mooncake offer.
91. *New Straits Times* December 10, 2010: Halal success for traditional Chinese snack.
92. *New Straits Times* December 25, 2008: Call to provide ethnic cuisine at varsities.
93. *New Straits Times* September 23, 2002: Bumi women eye halal food market; February 20, 2009: Halal products prove a big hit; March 15, 2010: Plan for more Bumi exporters.
94. *New Straits Times* June 29, 2011: Bumis only hold 30pc of halal certs.
95. In a case study on Halal Business Park Gračanica in Bosnia and Herzegovina, the focus is on financial viability of this park as a hub for halal producers in the context of the European market (Sokoloviv 2012).

96. *New Straits Times* July 24, 2003: Selangor to set up centre to produce, market halal goods; October 18, 2003: Halal food centre for Negri Sembilan; October 21, 2003: RM1.8b investments in Selangor approved from January to June; April 28, 2004: Perak to be hub for halal meat products; June 11, 2004: One-stop halal food centres set up; June 19, 2004: Pulau Indah to be a trade hub; July 16, 2004: Malaysia keen on halal centre Selangor to use Pulau Indah to penetrate halal market; December 6, 2004: Sultan: Regional growth a boost for Kelantan; December 15, 2004: Duty-free zone for halal food; January 15, 2005: Halal food hub for Selangor; October 30, 2007: Halal centre to be ready in 4 months; December 12, 2007: Malaysia eyes RM1.7b FDIs for Selangor halal park; December 22, 2007: Proposed halal park for Selangor takes off; November 20, 2008: Zahid: Opposition states not ignored in promotion of halal hub; February 19, 2009: RM9 billion pour into Halal Hub in Sarawak; March 5, 2009: Halal hub set to bolster Labuan's economy; December 10, 2009: Penang wants to be port of choice; April 16, 2010: Perak to have halal research centre; June 5, 2010: RM70m request for halal hub; June 8, 2010: Set to be largest halal meat production hub; June 8, 2010: Halal parks draw RM4.8b investments; June 25, 2010: Collaborate to develop halal parks, states told.
97. *New Straits Times* March 16, 2005: Shafie: Abuse of halal logos worrying; March 17, 2005: Credibility is everything.
98. *New Straits Times* March 18, 2005: Shafie: Ministry to check on "halal" logos.
99. *New Straits Times* March 21, 2005: Check the halal list.
100. *New Straits Times* February 18, 2003: Adabi's vision to be global manufacturer.
101. *New Straits Times* October 8, 2008: Local brands making waves at home, abroad.
102. *New Straits Times* May 17, 2010: CBS Tech to help SMEs tap huge halal market.
103. *New Straits Times* May 25, 2010: Halal agency, telco team up.
104. In January 10, 2013, one Singapore Dollar or S$ was worth US$ 0.81.
105. *Straits Times* May 31, 1991: Slaughtering of poultry to stop in more wet markets; June 17, 1991: Many Muslims avoid abattoir fowls.
106. *Straits Times* August 17, 1991: Guidelines on halal food found in MUIS handbook.
107. *Straits Times* August 21, 1991: MUIS may print halal food handbook for restaurants.
108. *Straits Times* January 25, 1992: Book tells why Muslims cannot eat certain foods.
109. *Straits Times* July 29, 1992: S'pore seeks slice of S$96b halal food market; August 21, 1992: Singapore seen as gateway to Asean halal food market; February 7, 1994: Steering Muslims past investment pitfalls.
110. *Straits Times* August 16, 1990: S'pore "the logical choice" for halal trading centre.
111. *Straits Times* September 5, 1997: 10-fold rise in number of halal food outlets.
112. *Straits Times* May 18, 1999: Next—a halal stamp on make-up?
113. *Straits Times* October 8, 2011: MUIS to build up halal brand.
114. *Straits Times* March 23, 1978: Deceptive "halal" label: council will press for prosecution.
115. *Straits Times* July 3, 1981: MUIS asks for "halal" proof.
116. *Straits Times* November 12, 1985: Signs say "halal" but food not so—MUIS.
117. *Straits Times* May 30, 1991: PAP dialogue sessions for Malay-Muslims.

118. *Straits Times* May 23, 1992: Date and "halal" marks for abattoir poultry from July 15.
119. *Straits Times* July 12, 1992: Eleven abattoirs get permit from MUIS to slaughter halal chicken.
120. *Straits Times* July 16, 1992: Labelling foul-up on start of abattoir poultry tagging.
121. *Straits Times* June 29, 1992: When is it halal?
122. *Straits Times* July 13, 1992: Sinar is Muslim-owned.
123. *Straits Times* May 13, 1994: Malay Village pulls out ads that said food is halal.
124. *Straits Times* August 17, 1995: "Get halal certification from MUIS".
125. *Straits Times* August 21, 1995: The MUIS logo.
126. *Straits Times* April 1998: Changes will benefit others; June 28, 1998: AMLA-bill—the changes it will bring about.
127. *Straits Times* September 25, 1999: Surge in shops seeking to be certified halal.
128. *Straits Times* September 13, 2006: Review law on halal cert misuse: Judge.
129. *Straits Times* November 14, 2007: Tougher certification for halal items.
130. *Straits Times* September 16, 2008: Muslim institutions to get more clout.
131. *Straits Times* August 21, 2009: Only MUIS can certify.
132. *Straits Times* March 20, 1984: Strict checks on "halal" food.
133. *Straits Times* December 23, 1990: Two fined for forging halal certificates.
134. *Straits Times* April 6, 1993: Mattar [Minister for the Environment and Minister-in-charge for Muslim Affairs] gives "non-halal warning."
135. *Straits Times* October 20, 1993: Week's jail for forging halal cert.
136. *Straits Times* September 9, 2000: CJS Catering loses its halal certificate.
137. *Straits Times* March 5, 2004: You can be fined, jailed for misusing halal mark.
138. *Straits Times* November 5, 2011: Gift shop in a fix for selling "halal" stickers.
139. *Straits Times* January 9, 2010: McDonald's pulls pig toy.
140. One of the only studies of Singaporean halal in a global perspective (Zainal 2009) argues that local Singaporean halal standards and certification should be explored in a global context beyond their territorial and political boundaries of origin; that is, companies and restaurants in Singapore mostly obtain their supplies from halal-certified suppliers in disparate places, and these are linked through MUIS halal certification (Zainal 2009, 20).
141. *Straits Times* January 17, 1983: Ban on sale of non-halal meat at government outlets.
142. *Straits Times* January 30, 1983: KL *haram* list also applies to S'pore Muslims.
143. *Straits Times* October 11, 1991: Halal food becomes big business in Malaysia.
144. *Straits Times* September 24, 1981: MUIS writes to check on Aussie beef.
145. *Straits Times* April 1, 1990: Deal with China for halal restaurant here signed; May 29, 1992: Sino-Malay chambers' joint venture to set up halal supermarket in Ningxia; February 6, 1994: Indian and Malay commerce chambers tapping China market.
146. *Straits Times* August 29, 1995: ASEAN to boost competitiveness in farm products.
147. *Straits Times* April 5, 1997: Cover-up for sexy halal diet drink ads.
148. *Straits Times* June 22, 1997: MUIS to Muslims—don't drink Jolly Shandy.
149. *Straits Times* September 5, 2004: MUIS' reach expands globally—from Australia to Europe.

150. *Straits Times* January 19, 2006: S'pore wants bigger bite of Mid-East halal trade.
151. *Straits Times* January 12, 1982: Panel to boost image of Muslims in food and drink industry.
152. *Straits Times* January 25, 1985: On the PM's remarks about the gap between Malays and other Singaporeans.
153. *Straits Times* September 9, 1989: Halal seafood, anyone?
154. *Straits Times* May 13, 1991: S'pore "has potential as trading centre for halal food".
155. *Straits Times* August 15, 1991: Into the future.
156. *Straits Times* April 29, 1992: Special tribute to 6 Malay/Muslim businessmen.
157. *Straits Times* June 14, 1993: Malay chamber going into halal food business; December 21, 1995: Halal food cooperative opens share applications to investors at official launch today; December 23, 1995: Halal food co-op "must tap non-Muslim market".
158. *Straits Times* February 13, 1994: More needs to be done to promote ethnic ties.
159. *Straits Times* August 8, 1995: Mammoth task, but he took up the challenge.
160. *Bak ku teh* literally means meat-bone-tea in Hokkien dialect. It is a thick stew of pork knuckles and ribs in a stock of Chinese herbs, garlic, and soy sauce. In Chinese culture there is the belief that food provides not only nutrition but also therapeutic values, and this pork dish has a distinct "culinary identity". *Bak ku teh* is a highly versatile dish subject to creative innovations (Yao 2000, 66), as it is the case with its halalization.
161. *Straits Times* November 16, 1995: Muslim food Chinese style—strategy is effective in drawing more customers, including non-Muslim.
162. *Straits Times* August 9, 1996: Malay Singaporeans want to belong—in all ways.
163. *Straits Times* November 14, 1996: Way ahead for Malays.
164. *Straits Times* February 17, 2002: They're small Malay/Muslim firms, but they think big.
165. *Straits Times* August 28, 2002: Hungry Ghost meal goes halal.
166. *Straits Times* October 7, 2006: New centre to help Malay enterprises.
167. *Straits Times* August 29, 2008: Boost for Muslim F&B outlets.
168. *Straits Times* September 4, 2008: Racial bonding with halal mooncakes; October 4, 2009: Mega mooncake for Mid-Autumn Festival.
169. *Straits Times* April 15, 2007: TCM goes halal; December 24, 2009: More Malays turn to TCM for treatment.
170. *Straits Times* March 21, 2010: Yummy halal wontons.
171. *Straits Times* August 22, 2009: Strengthening procedures.
172. *Straits Times* February 5, 2008: School's "halal zone" ruling causes stir; February 6, 2008: All schools must have mix of halal and non-halal food.
173. *Straits Times* February 6, 2008: "Halal zone" would've been a step backwards.
174. *Straits Times* March 1, 2008: Faith+Food=Fault line?
175. *Straits Times* August 12, 1995: Not all S'poreans and foreigners want S'pore to do well.
176. *Straits Times* April 19, 1996: Companies looking at easy to make foods.
177. *Straits Times* April 22, 1996: Package tours for Muslims take off.
178. *Straits Times* August 26, 1996: Malays here "not doing too badly".
179. *Straits Times* September 7, 1997: Head for Far East plaza for halal lasagna; 11 February 1998: Lasagne and British pie, but it's halal; June 5, 2004: BreadTalk pops new, halal bun in the oven.

180. *Straits Times* December 25, 1996: Second chance finds the Midas touch.
181. *Straits Times* February 27, 1997: "Halal" fund follows Islamic investment principles.
182. *Straits Times* July 7, 1997: Time's right for Islamic banking.
183. *Straits Times* September 6, 1997: First CPF-approved Islamic unit trust unveiled; May 13, 2000: Focus on Islamic investment.
184. *Straits Times* February 5, 2005: More firms keen on halal certification.
185. *Straits Times* April 22, 2008: Ice, CO2 . . . more products going halal.
186. *Straits Times* May 5, 2010: Luzerne serves up halal crockery.

BIBLIOGRAPHY

Ackerman, Susan E., and Lee, Raymond L. M. 1997. *Sacred Tensions: Modernity and Religious Transformation in Malaysia*. Columbia: University of South Carolina Press.

Attorney General's Chambers. 2011. *Trade Description Act 2011. (ACT 730). Trade Description (Certification and Marking of 'Halal') Order*. Kuala Lumpur: Attorney General's Chambers.

Badawi, Abdullah Ahmad. 2006. *Islam Hadhari: A Model Approach for Development and Progress*. Petaling Jaya: MPH Publishing Sdn Bhd.

Bakar, Osman. 2008. "Malaysian Islam in the Twenty-First Century: The Promise of a Democratic Transformation?" In *Asian Islam in the 21st Century*, edited by John L. Esposito, John O. Voll, and Osman Bakar, 81–108. Oxford: Oxford University Press.

Barr, Michael D. and Skrbis, Zlatko. 2008. *Constructing Singapore. Elitism, Ethnicity and the Nation-Building Project*. Copenhagen: NIAS Press.

Cheung, Anthony B. L. 2002. "The Politics of New Public Management. Some Experiences from East Asia." In *New public management: Current Trends and Future Prospects*, edited by Kata McLaughlin and Stephen P. Osborne, 243–273. London and New York: Routledge.

Chua, Beng-Huat. 1995. *Communitarian Ideology and Democracy in Singapore*. London and New York: Routledge.

Chua, Beng Huat. 2003a. "Multiculturalism in Singapore: An Instrument of Social Control." *Race & Class* 44(3): 58–77.

Chua, Beng-Huat. 2003b. *Life Is Not Complete Without Shopping. Consumption Culture in Singapore*. Singapore: Singapore University Press.

Chua, Beng-Huat and Kian-Woon, Kwok. 2001. "Social Pluralism in Singapore". In *The Politics of Multiculturalism. Pluralism and Citizenship in Malaysia, Singapore, and Indonesia*, edited by Robert W. Hefner, 86–118. Honolulu: University of Hawai'i Press.

Clammer, John. 1993. *Race and State in Independent Singapore 1965–1990*. Aldershot and Brookfield: Ashgate.

Consumers Association of Penang. 2006. *Halal Haram. A Guide by Consumers Association of Penang*. Penang: Consumers Association of Penang.

Devji, Faisal. 2005. *Landscapes of the Jihad: Militancy, Morality, Modernity*. London: Hurst & Company.

Devji, Faisal. 2008. *The Terrorist in Search of Humanity: Militant Islam and Global Politics*. London: Hurst & Company.

Embong, Abdul Rahman. 1998. "Social Transformation, the State and the Middle Classes in Post-Independence Malaysia." In *Cultural Contestations. Mediating Identities in a Changing Malaysian Society*, edited by Ibrahim Zawawi, 83–116. London: Asean Academic Press.

Firth, Raymond W. 1966. *Malay Fishermen: Their Peasant Economy*. New York: The Norton Library.

Fischer, Johan. 2007. "Boycott or Buycott? Malay Middle-Class Consumption Post-9/11." *Ethnos* 72(1): 29–50.

Fischer, Johan. 2008a. "Nationalizing Rituals? The Ritual Economy in Malaysia." *Journal of Ritual Studies* 22(2): 13–22.

Fischer, Johan. 2008b. *Proper Islamic Consumption: Shopping among the Malays in Modern Malaysia*. Copenhagen: NIAS Press.

Fischer, Johan. 2011. *The Halal Frontier: Muslim Consumers in a Globalized Market*. New York: Palgrave Macmillan.

Fischer, Johan. 2015. "Islamic Mobility: Car Culture in Modern Malaysia." *Journal of Consumer Culture*. DOI: 10.1177/1469540514531683.

Funston, John. 2006a. "Malaysia." In *Voices of Islam in Southeast Asia. A Contemporary Sourcebook*, edited by Greg Fealy and Virginia Hooker, 51–61. Singapore: Institute of Southeast Asian Studies.

Funston, John. 2006b. "Singapore." In *Voices of Islam in Southeast Asia. A Contemporary Sourcebook*, edited by Greg Fealy and Virginia Hooker, 71–75. Singapore: Institute of Southeast Asian Studies.

Gomez, Edmund T. 2012. "The Politics and Policies of Corporate Development: Race, Rents and Distribution in Malaysia." In *Malaysia's Development Challenges: Graduating from the Middle*, edited by Hal Hill, Tham Siew Yean and Ragayah Haji Mat Zin, 63–82. London and New York: Routledge.

Hefner, Robert W. 2001. "Introduction: Multiculturalism and Citizenship in Malaysia, Singapore, and Indonesia." In *The Politics of Multiculturalism: Pluralism and Citizenship in Malaysia, Singapore and Indonesia*, edited by Robert W. Hefner, 1–58. Honolulu: University of Hawai'i Press.

Henderson, Joan C. 2003. "Managing Tourism and Islam in Peninsular Malaysia." *Tourism Management* 24(4), 447–456.

Jomo, Kwame Sundaram and Cheek, Ahmad Shabery. 1992. "Malaysia's Islamic Movements." In *Fragmented Vision: Culture and Politics in Contemporary Malaysia*, edited by Joel S. Kahn and Francis Loh Kok Wah, 162–193. North Sydney: Asian Studies Association of Australia in association with Allen & Unwin.

Kadir, Suzaina. 2004. "Islam, State, and Society in Singapore." *Inter-Asia Cultural Studies* 5(3): 357–371.

Lee, Tania. 1989. *Malays in Singapore. Culture, Economy, and Ideology*. Singapore, Oxford and New York: Oxford University Press.

Majlis Ugama Islam Singapura. 2007. *MUIS-HC-S002: General Guidelines for the Development and Implementation of a Halal Quality Management System: Principle 1—Establish the Halal Team*. Singapore: Majlis Ugama Islam Singapura.

Marranci, Gabriele. 2012. "Defensive or Offensive Dining? Halal Dining Practices among Malay Muslim Singaporeans and Their Effects on Integration." *The Australian Journal of Anthropology* 23(1): 84–100.

Mauzy, Diana K. and Milne, Robert S. 2002. *Singapore Politics under the People's Action Party*. London and New York: Routledge.

Mauzy, Diane K. and Milne, Stephen R. 1999. *Malaysian Politics under Mahathir*. London: Routledge.

Mohamad, Mahathir. 1995. "Views and Thoughts of Dr Mahathir Mohamad, the Prime Minister of Malaysia." In *Malaysia's Vision 2020*, edited by Ahmad Sarji Abdul Hamid, 1–51. Kelana Jaya: Pelanduk Publications.

Mutalib, Hussin and Kua, Ee Heok. 1994. *Islam in Malaysia: From Revivalism to Islamic State*. Honolulu: University of Hawai'i Press.

Mutalib, Hussin. 2005. "Singapore Muslims: The Quest for Identity in a Modern City-State." *Journal of Muslim Minority Affairs* 25(1): 53–72.

Nagata, Judith. 1994. "How to Be Islamic Without Being an Islamic State." In *Islam, Globalization and Postmodernity*, edited by Akbar S. Ahmed and Donnan Hastings, 63–90. London: Routledge.

Nasir, Kamaludeen Bin Mohamad. 2007. "Rethinking the 'Malay problem' in Singapore: Image, Rhetoric and Social Realities." *Journal of Muslim Minority Affairs* 27(2): 309–318.

Nasir, Kamaludeen Bin Mohamad and Pereira, Alexius. 2008. "Defensive Dining: Notes on the Public Dining Experiences in Singapore." *Contemporary Islam* 2(1): 61–73.

Nasir, Kamaludeen Bin Mohamad, Pereira, Alexius A. and Turner, Bryan S. 2009. *Muslims in Singapore: Piety, Politics and Policies*. Oxon: Routledge.

Neo, Harvey, 2008. "Institutions, Cultural Politics and the Destabilizing Malaysian Pig Industry." *Geoforum* 40: 260–268.

Ong, Aihwa. 1999. *Flexible Citizenship. The Cultural Logics of Transnationality*. Durham, NC: Duke University Press.

Ong, Aihwa. 2006. *Neoliberalism as Exception. Mutations in Citizenship and Sovereignty*. Durham and London: duke university press.

Pereira, Alexius. 2005. "Religiosity and Economic Development in Singapore." *Journal of Contemporary Religion* 20(2): 161–177.

Riaz, Mian N. and Chaudry, Muhammad M. 2004. *Halal Food Production*. Boca Raton: CRC Press.

Sallah, Sheikh Mohd Saifuddeen Shaikh Mohd, and Sobrian, Azrina. 2006a. "Editor's Note." In *Food and Technological Progress. An Islamic Perspective*, edited by Sheikh Mohd Saifuddeen Shaikh Mohd Sallah and Azrina Sobrian, ix–xiv. Petaling Jaya: MPH Publishing.

Sallah, Sheikh Mohd Saifuddeen Shaikh Mohd, and Sobrian, Azrina. 2006b. *Food and Technological Progress. An Islamic Perspective*. Petaling Jaya: MPH Publishing.

Shamsul, Amri Baharuddin. 2001. "Beyond 11 September: A Malaysian Response." *Nordic Institute of Asian Studies Newsletter* No. 4, December.

Sokolovic, Dzana. 2012. Halal Business Park Gračanica. A Case Study. Saarbrücken: AV Akademikerverlag.

Stimpfl, Joseph. 2006. "Growing up Malay in Singapore." In *Ethnicity, and the State in Malaysia and Singapore*, edited by Lian Kwen Fee Race, 61–93. Leiden and Boston: Brill.

Tan, Eugene K. B. 2004. "We, the citizens of Singapore. . .: Multiethnicity, Its Evolution, and Its Aberrations." In *Beyond Rituals and Riots: Ethnic Pluralism and Social Cohesion in Singapore*, edited by Lai Ah Eng, 65–97. Singapore: Eastern Universities Press.

Yao, Souchou. 2000. "Xiao Ye: Food, Alterity and the Pleasure of Chineseness in Malaysia." *New Formations* 40 Spring: 64–79.

Yao, Souchou. 2002. *Confucian Capitalism. Discourse, Practice and the Myth of Chinese Enterprise*. London: Routledge.

Yao, Souchou. 2007. *Singapore: The State and the Culture of Excess*. Oxon: Rouledge.

Zainal, Muhammad Firduas bin. 2009. *MUIS Halal Certification: Local Causes, Global Impacts?* BA Thesis Dept. of Geography. Singapore: National University of Singapore.

Zukin, Sharon. 2004. *Point of Purchase. How Shopping Changed American Culture*. New York: Routledge.

2 Global Halal Networks

On August 16, 2004, Malaysia's prime minister, Abdullah Haji Ahmad Badawi, officially launched the first Malaysia International Halal Showcase (MIHAS) in the capital city of Kuala Lumpur. In his speech, which he titled "Window to the Global Halal Network," the prime minister boasted that MIHAS was the largest halal trade fair held anywhere in the world and that it would establish Malaysia as a "global halal hub." Indeed, he was convinced that MIHAS was merely the first step in developing a full-fledged international halal market with the potential to herald a new era in Islamic trade—an era not seen since the great days when Islamic trade routes used to stretch across the world from East to West. Key to this internationalization was the fact that halal products are increasingly recognized globally as clean and safe in an era of diseases and "health disasters" due to "unhealthy practices."

During his speech Badawi held up the United Kingdom in particular as a highly lucrative market for halal. The following year, in November 2005, the UK would host the first Halal Exhibition at the major World Food Market (WFM) in London. Although Malaysia was not represented at the event, it would not miss the opportunity again. In 2006 Malaysia's national trade promotion agency (Malaysia External Trade Development Corporation, or MATRADE) had a booth at the WFM Halal Exhibition for the first time. MIHAS and the WFM are significant examples of what I call halal network events—that is, major public events or "stages" where the corporate sector, academia, nongovernmental organizations (NGOs), Islamic organizations, halal certifiers, and governments from around the world come together to promote and spread the sale of halal commodities globally. In this chapter, I focus specifically on Malaysia's role in developing this global halal market, that is, how halal as a global assemblage is given shape at these network events. In other words, networking is an important technique that help format the global halal market. Moreover, these halal events have themselves been standardized in not only Malaysia and Singapore, but also globally. Prime Minister Badawi's use of the word *network* in his speech is not a coincidence. As I show, the Malaysian state strategically employs the metaphor of "network" or "networking" in an effort to propagate the notion that

Malaysia is the dominant player in this market and that halal consumption of Muslim consumers is an expression of proper and patriotic practice (Fischer 2008, 2011, 2015). The state evokes the global halal network to include all the central actors of this book that have a particular function in the network: Malay(sian) activist and interest groups; science and research institutions; local and multinational companies; as well as halal certifying bodies recognized by JAKIM. Each of these actors is seen to have particular functions in this network vision.

The main motive for focusing on London in this chapter is, first, that the Malaysian state's vision of and commitment to promoting halal specifically identifies London as a center for halal production, trade, and consumption. Many states, companies, and entrepreneurs see the increasing Muslim population in the UK and Europe as encouragement to invest in such businesses and industries. Second, London is home to a substantial number of Malays and Malaysian organizations such as the United Malays National Organisation (UMNO) and (MATRADE), Malaysia's national trade promotion agency. There have been intimate connections and exchanges between the two countries since Britain's colonization of Malaysia. What is more, Commonwealth migrants from Malaysia could legally settle in Britain. In contemporary Britain, Malays are, in most cases, in the country to study and/or work.

In the ethnographic[1] portion of this chapter I shall explore an example of a recognized body in the global halal network—the Islamic Cultural Centre (ICC) in Denmark. JAKIM has "outsourced" local regulation and inspection of halal to ICC. JAKIM not only recognizes a body such as ICC but also "inspects" or "audits" such organizations in their local setting. As we shall see, halal network events in Malaysia and beyond play an essential part in the way in which the Malaysian state has encouraged the growth of a global halal network.

HALAL NETWORKS

Before moving to the ethnography, I want to explain the key theoretical concept I use in this chapter, "network." Caliskan (2010, 192) rightfully argues that nothing is as central to a successful trading relationship as networking and nothing is as effective for networking as learning about and meeting people and exchanging gifts with them. Regularly organized business meetings provide traders with opportunities to establish new relations and renew older and I shall show how networking techniques take on particular significance in the global halal market. My understanding of halal networks in Malaysia is informed by academic theories of network, especially as articulated by Manuel Castells. Castells sets out to show how the new information technology paradigm provides the material basis for the expansion of the networking form in the entire social structure locally, nationally, and globally (Castells 2000, 469). That is, networks and networking are essential tools, technologies, or techniques for individuals, social groups, organizations, states, and nations. The importance of "hubs" is to produce the strategic functions of the network. Hence, "communication hubs" are "exchangers" that play "a role of coordination for the smooth interaction of all the elements integrated into the network" (Castells 2000, 443).

The halal vision of the Malaysian state is infused with such ideas about network society and hubs. For example, in the Ninth Malaysia Plan 2006–2010, *Together Towards Excellence, Glory and Distinction* (Economic Planning Unit 2006), which outlines the country's development strategy, the strategic uses of the terms network and networking seem to be inspired by Castells's idea that networking expands in the entire social structure. Strategically, these terms are employed as part of an effort to target specific priority areas of the UMNO-led government, such as communications and internationalization. They are also evoked in the context of Malaysia as an emerging "global halal hub." Another critical influence on my work is Annelise Riles, whose book *The Network Inside Out* examines the participation of Fijian women in the United Nations' fourth global forum. One of Riles's (2000, 172) central insights is that the effectiveness of networks is generated by its self-description. A similar observation can be made about the halal network in Malaysia. The network is also an example of "institutionalized utopianism" (Riles 2000, 3), that is, idealization rather than an actually existing or complete social form. Hence, networks cannot be free from the ties that imagined them (Green, Harvey, and Knox 2005, 807).

To sum up, the Malaysian state evokes the halal network as a metaphor through which technical systems and institutions (hubs) and bodily processes and techniques (proper halal handling by Muslims) are imagined and made to stand for each other (Otis 2001). Halal networks are linked to the state and are accompanied by a set of stories and imperatives to connect, and together, these aspects give shape to halal as a global assemblage.

HALAL ENTANGLEMENTS IN MALAYSIA AND BEYOND

At MIHAS 2004,[2] Badawi proudly announced that "[t]oday we will mark the unveiling of a new standard for Malaysia—a Muslim standard for the world." The prime minister was referring to the launch by SIRIM of a Malaysian Standard MS 1500, *General Guidelines on the Production, Preparation, Handling, and Storage of Halal Foods*. Ideally, this new standard should further strengthen Malaysian state halal certification in its efforts to cooperate with multinational companies (www.pmo.gov.my).

Halal in Malaysia is intricately linked to a powerful UMNO-driven ethnic state nationalism. The channeling of privileges and funds through ethnic

UMNO corporatism has been systematically institutionalized in Malaysia, and this has led to a form of party political capitalism controlled by the Malay elite (Gomez 1994). In public, as we saw in the case of the media halal discourse in Chapter 1, this type of capitalism is effectively promoted as a capitalism that adheres to Islamic standards. The economy thus fused with a politics of ethnicity that in itself was defined in terms of religion (Shamsul 1999, 43).

Groups of Malay entrepreneurs in Kuala Lumpur and beyond are actively engaged in strategic brainstorming sessions about who they could access in their multiplex networks for support (Sloane 1999, 22), and in many cases, connections to important people in the network went through UMNO contacts. These entrepreneurs used the English words for network and networking. In the mother tongue of the Malays, Bahasa Malaysia, "network" is translated as *rangkaian* (cluster). Government ministers use this term to establish a Malay language for business and to encourage Malays to create Chinese-like business societies (Sloane 1999, 21). Now the state encourages these Malay entrepreneurs to network in global halal zones, that is, strategically promote halal in the global market with state backing.

These points are important in order to understand how the UMNO-led state promotes the halal network as pure and proper in public while ongoing rumors evoke how the halal industry in Malaysia is inseparable from UMNO links and covert networks. Companies controlled by the government, government-linked companies (GLCs), figure prominently in the Malaysian halal business, and these GLCs are entangled in a web of UMNO and personal linkages. Another example of these powerful rumors evoking ethnicized politics is the following. The owner of a Malaysian restaurant in London, Hamza, was extremely alert to halal requirements and only employed Malays. This restaurant advertises itself as "Malaysian (halal) cuisine." He complained about one of the other Malaysian restaurants in London owned by a Chinese. It is often rumored among Malays that, despite Malay requirements and sensitivity, the Chinese use lard in food production and cooking. Even though the restaurant displayed a halal sign, alcohol was available in the restaurant's bar. Moreover, no Malays, but mostly Chinese, were employed there, and most important, on several occasions Malaysian ministers, even the prime minister, were said to have frequented this establishment on their visits to London. As a consequence, the immoral practices of the political elite are seen as undermining the state discourse on halal. Moreover, employing Chinese and not Malays is unpatriotic and unsupportive of the vision to create a global halal network.

Historically Malaysia has played a central role in arguing for an indigenous origin of the Southeast Asian idea. This self-conscious centrality is based on communications and Islamic trade networks, and the Malacca Straits area has always been a meeting place of ports and portages making Malaysia a booster of Southeast Asian unity (Reid 1999, 7).

Powerful Chinese networks divided into linguistic tribes organized the trade of commodities across Southeast Asia (Reid 1999, 11). Malaysian leaders have been very interested in building regional organizations such as the Association of Southeast Asian Nations (ASEAN). Today, there is strong cooperation and competition on halal among many of the ASEAN countries. The Malaysian halal network gives rise to aspirations of Malay Muslim networks to signify the connectedness and prescriptions of organizations vis-à-vis more deep-rooted networks such as historical Islamic trade networks or Chinese networks.

"Networking, Consolidating and Energising": Halal Network Events in Malaysia

This section explores Malaysian halal networking at two major halal events in Malaysia, namely, the Malaysia International Halal Showcase (MIHAS) and the World Halal Forum (WHF), a gathering of Islamic, political, and commercial notables in Kuala Lumpur that the state promotes as the premier halal network event. These network events are products of concerted efforts by Malaysian state institutions to include organizations from around the world. However, before doing so, I briefly look at the history of comparable halal network events in Singapore.

Arguably, the world's first international Muslim food and technology exhibition was held in Singapore in 1990 by SMCC and the MUIS.[3] Not until the mid-1990s did these events specifically started to promote halal on a global scale.[4] This became an annual halal event, and it was later called Singapore International Halal Showcase (SIHAS). In both Malaysia and Singapore the state calls on Malay entrepreneurs and businessmen to widen their global networks and "include non-Malay/Muslim businessmen."[5] An important point here is the inclusion of non-Muslim investors and companies seen to have an essential function in the otherwise Muslim-dominated network, that is, as non-Muslim investors. In 2004 the chairman of Islamic Food Council of Europe (IFCE), which arranged the 4th International Halal Food Conference in Brussels, as already shown and as I return to in greater detail later, invited MUIS to Brussels to benefit from MUIS "halal know-how."[6]

Now back to the ethnography. Since its start in 2004, MIHAS has developed into an annual halal network event. However, the Muslim Trade Exhibition and Conference (IMTEC) held in Kuala Lumpur in 1998 was one of the first halal events in Malaysia. The theme was "Positioning Islamic Trade in the Next Millennium" and was aimed at globalizing the market for Islamic trading by recognizing the potential of relations between Muslim and non-Muslim countries based on Islamic principles and standards. In the eyes of the Malaysian state, the halal producers and traders, and a plethora of Islamic organizations, the increase in network events indicates the emergence of a global halal network. MIHAS 2006, "themed" as "Networking, Consolidating and Energising," was held at the massive Malaysian International Exhibition & Convention Centre ("the Jewel at the Southern Metropolitan Hub," as this convention center is dubbed). MIHAS consisted of three main activities, first, seminars held by companies such as Tesco and Malaysian state organizations, for example, MATRADE and JAKIM. Participation in these seminars provided me with an insight into the halal vision in the interfaces or gray zones between the state, business, and religious revivalism. It struck me that this was the first time I witnessed such a determined, smooth, and direct commercialization of halal and Islam in Malaysia. We learned that Malaysia should be alert to competition from skilled "networking nations" such as Brunei, Singapore, Thailand, and Indonesia. Consequently, the government has established 32 MATRADE offices worldwide, an "overseas network," including an office in London. When I discussed Malaysian challenges with "networking nations" with MATRADE's trade commissioner in London he explained that the dominance of Thai ethnic cuisine was a particular concern and that the Thai state's subsidizing and "financial assistance" is taking place "subtly" and "not openly." To illustrate this point, the state and the media in Malaysia often call on entrepreneurs and companies to catch up with competing countries such as Thailand. Thailand successfully set up a Halal Science Center in 2003 at the country's largest university, Chulalongkorn University, and has created its own national procedure for halal certification (www.halalscience.org). Thailand has made a major advance in the halal market, as it has a globally recognized ethnic cuisine and is a world-renowned tourist destination, and ingredients for Thai cooking are widely available.

Second, MIHAS included "trade-matching programs" and "networking sessions" in which producers, traders, and buyers could come together. During this event, the deputy minister for Entrepreneurial and Cooperative Development was quoted as stating that Malay entrepreneurs at MIHAS especially should "grab this opportunity to enhance their business networking at the international level."[7] After MIHAS, another article concluded that this halal event was a "huge success" and that it had proved to be the most "cost effective platform" for halal world players to promote their products and widen their business networking and trade activities globally.[8]

Third, MIHAS included a large number of product demonstrations and samples. These product demonstrations testified to the fact that, in Malaysia, halal has also proliferated into a wide range of nonfood products (toiletries, medication, and health products) and services such as banking, insurance, and education. The global trend in recent years has been to see that a thriving business in Islamic goods has emerged. Everything from stickers, rugs, holiday cards, and plaques with Islamic calligraphy to special types of holidays aimed at Muslim audiences, watches displaying *salat* (prayer times) and other features, logos and ringtones on mobile phones, clothes, and so on touch on and "Islamicize" virtually every aspect of life (D'Alisera

2001, 97). At the same time, there has been a marked change from craft production to mass production of religious commodities (Starrett 1995).

As one would expect, MIHAS was an essential arena for networking, in particular with respect to exchanging business cards, and I was soon receiving e-mails advertising new products and announcing new halal trade fairs around the world. Among the entrepreneurs I met at MIHAS, Altaf, a Malay woman, in many respects reflected the ways in which networking is practiced in Malaysian halal. She holds degrees in accounting and business studies from the UK and was at the time involved in promoting halal for the Malaysian state by organizing trade promotions, as well as with her private company. Of particular interest to Altaf was the promising UK market, which she knew from her studies here and which figures so prominently in the Malaysian state's halal vision. I also had the opportunity to meet Altaf at the Halal Exhibition at the WFM held in London in November 2006, which had developed into a significant network event in which a MATRADE delegation also participated. In 2010 her company had a booth at MIHAS.

At the Halal Exhibition, Altaf envisaged halal as giving Malaysia an edge and a "niche trade network," whereas Europe and the US otherwise dominate global trade. The news that Nestlé had entered into a halal business deal with Malaysia was proof to Altaf that it was only in cooperating with multinationals and using their existing trade networks that a country such as Malaysia could succeed. Altaf was confident that the emerging halal trade was forging new Malay "community networks" on a global scale. Unlike the Chinese, Malays were traditionally "confined" to Malaysia. Now there was the political will to promote Malaysia in terms of halal internationally, and this was indicative of a major shift toward a more global attitude. In essence, these last points reflect the materialization of an entrepreneurial New Malay mentality that, to a large extent, is a product of the New Economic Policy as a sort of an ethnic network policy of the Malaysian state. In many ways, Altaf is the quintessential Malaysian halal networker: she is a young socially and physically mobile Malay woman that practices networking between state institutions, Islamic organizations, and companies; she possesses extensive knowledge of proper halal production, trade, regulation, and consumption and uses products and communication technologies such as websites as network tools. Interestingly, Altaf was not herself very particular about halal in her everyday life, and she was not wearing the *tudung* (long headscarf) on any of the occasions I met her. Like many of the other entrepreneurs involved in the halal network she is not a *dakwah* activist but, rather, a modern entrepreneur that tries to optimize Malaysian and personal halal performance on the global scale.

In 2006 the WHF, a gathering of Islamic, political, and commercial notables arranged by KasehDia, was held for the first time in Kuala Lumpur. The establishment of this network event signifies the diversification and multiplication of halal network events in Malaysia. In 2010, Halal Malaysia Week included World Islamic Economic Forum, WHF, World Halal Research (an event with the heading "Inspiring Innovation through Research"), MIHAS (now mainly a halal trade fair), as well as a Workshop on the Halal Awareness Programme (training on halal production and logistics). At each of these events, politicians, company representatives, entrepreneurs such as Altaf discussed earlier, and scientists actively network to promote halal. After having done fieldwork at these network events since 2006 I have become part of this halal network, that is, networking at halal events and through mailing lists and social media. An example of this is the way in which Malaysian state representatives and companies are interested in my research results on halal while as a researcher I am considering access to interesting data that these actors can provide.

I was at WHF 2010 held at the luxurious Kuala Lumpur Convention Centre in central Kuala Lumpur. This network event is now the major event for the halal industry globally. In his opening speech at WHF Malaysia's prime minister Najib Abdul Razak, who succeeded Badawi in 2009, explained to the more than 800 delegates that the gathering of halal industry stakeholders (the corporate sector, academia, NGOs, Islamic organizations, and governments from around the world) provided the best "platform for networking among those interested in the halal industry." The audience learned from organizers that the WHF was established to be an arena for discussion, networking, and collaboration to stimulate the growth and development of the halal market. In the WHF program booklet, breaks were designated for "networking and refreshments" as well as for *salat* (prayer). The entrepreneur Altaf, discussed earlier, together with other participants explained to me that Najib's "political goodwill" toward supporting halal was considered lower than that of his predecessors and that his speech as WHF 2010 was anxiously anticipated.

At WHF, KasehDia's founder specifically addressed the confusion caused among companies and certifying bodies by the friction between JAKIM and HDC, calling for a strong "masterplan" and "leadership" applicable to all stakeholders in the industry to address the inability of government agencies to work together. This plea was also reported in the Malaysian media.[9] At the end of WHF delegates were given a questionnaire and were asked to evaluate the networking performance of WHF. In 2010, WHF Europe was held in Earl's Court Conference Centre in London for the first time.

The halal network is intimately tied to Malaysian network events. The Malaysian halal network is, to a large extent, evoked through and at these halal network events and this has taken place since 2004. Today, there are halal network events every week around the world, and these actively shape halal as a global assemblage. In Malaysia, imagined halal networks always involve some form of location and are thus both political and moral constructions of space and place that are never free from the political and religious ties that imagined them. MIHAS, the WHF, and other national halal events are part of more global halal networks, and to this point I now turn.

NETWORKING ENTREPRENEURS

This section explores the work and role of entrepreneurs such as Altaf in London. Altaf runs several consultancy firms that help Malaysian companies with the process of halal certification and regulation in Malaysia and globally, especially in London where she lives for extended periods. Altaf works with companies that produce sauces, pastes, herbal products, baby food, and dried fruit, among other things. She takes on clients and products to "tap into the global halal market" and "pushes" them to become "fully certified." As a consultant she determines when a company is ready for certification: "Business development with a focus on getting the product ready for the world market," she explains.

In the local market in Malaysia certification does not hold the same importance, that is, as long as products, such as Ramadan cookies, which are sold for the feast marking the end of the fast of Ramadan, are produced by Malays certification is not essential, Altaf explains. This is an example of the way in which the powerful ethnic state nationalism works in Malaysia. However, if these cookies are exported to the UK, "[t]hat's where I come in," she explains. This difference between the local and the global market with different standards is essential and somewhat ambivalent: Malaysia is one of, if not the, strictest countries when it comes to halal globally, but at the same time because of the way in which halal is linked to Malay ethnicity, privilege, and political dominance, certification of Malay-produced commodities is often seen to be unnecessary. However, outside Malaysia these products following the global proliferation and regulation of halal commodities do need certification. So for these goods to enter European supermarkets and hypermarkets they must be certified and as a consultant Altaf helps companies in the UK with this process. When considering the advantages of Malaysian companies in the global market for halal, Altaf argues that these "[r]eally understand what halal is and they can answer any question to ensure the halalness throughout the supply chain and this is a comfort to consumers." However, these companies need the global marketing, investments, and distribution networks of multinationals such as Tesco to export their products.

A study of halal food and nonfood products in the UK by MATRADE maps the potential of this market. Owing to European Union (EU) regulations, Malaysia is not allowed to export meat products to the EU. Hence, the Malaysian bid to enter the EU market targets nonmeat halal products. The study states that "Malaysia's international image is that of a modern, progressive Muslim nation" and that the Malaysian halal logo and certification system is recognized in the UK because no single body in this market officially acts as a halal certifier (MATRADE 2006). Because of these regulations, Altaf advises companies on which halal products that can be exported into the EU. To my knowledge, these companies were owned by Malays. These products can now be found in stores in London and elsewhere.

Because these products are "all plant-based" it is relatively easy to have them halal certified by JAKIM.

Another aspect of her work focuses on assisting Malaysian companies to ensure halal certification by local halal certifiers in the UK such as the Halal Monitoring Committee (HMC; www.halalmc.co.uk). In so doing, Altaf draws on her experiences with strict and highly regulated halal certification in Malaysia. For example, Altaf put a Malaysian company in contact with HMC and a Malay-owned restaurant in London that specializes in Malaysian halal food. These local halal certification bodies play an important role as they are leading halal organizations in the UK, where JAKIM has no authority. Hence, cooperation between these certifiers and Malay entrepreneurs is important for the Malaysian state to establish and expand the halal market.

Compared to JAKIM certification, these local types of certification she considers "much easier, but also more doubtful because you just register online and they scan in the certificate and email it to the company." JAKIM is also far more particular about lists of approved ingredients compared to the non-state-certifying bodies. An essential part of Altaf's work consists of cooperating with JAKIM and MATRADE. She advises these and 'gives them feedback on what's happening out there' building on her extensive experience with halal in the European market and the UK, in particular—for example, the workings of the local halal certifiers in Britain. Even if some of these nonstate certifiers are recognized by JAKIM, an entrepreneur such as Altaf is more in touch with the everyday working of these organizations.

The Halal Act should ensure that halal certification was not abused and that sanctions against halal offenses were far more heavily enforced. This strengthens JAKIM's legal status and thus, the regulation of halal and should have a positive effect on Altaf's work: a stronger emphasis on enforcing certification as a "point of reference that stresses that you are accountable. Logos are not just something you print out. Soon we will have a halal barcode to avoid forgery." Entrepreneurs such as Altaf play an essential role in the Malaysian halal network: they promote Malaysian halal and push standardization in markets where the Malaysian state has little or no authority.

HALAL NETWORKS ON THE GLOBAL STAGE

I now explore the Malaysian halal network on the global stage, that is, how halal as a global assemblage is given shape at international halal events. At the 4th International Halal Food Conference held at Sheraton Hotel in Brussels, Belgium, all the players in the global halal network were present: Islamic organizations from around the world, state Islamic councils (Malaysia, Singapore, and Indonesia), and nonstate halal-certifying bodies such as Islamic Food Council of Europe (IFCE) that arranged the conference, as well as local and multinational companies had come to attend this conference.

The chairman of this halal certification is also vice president of the influential halal-certification body International Food and Nutritional Council of America (IFANCA) based in Chicago. JAKIM recognizes IFANCA and IFCE as halal-certifying bodies. He was born in Malaysia, where he worked with JAKIM, and has been involved in setting up Malaysia's state regulated form of halal certification since the early 1980s. The chairman said he hoped that the conference would open up opportunities for market access and the establishing of "networking" for the various players in the halal food industry worldwide.

During breaks and lunch everybody was encouraged to, and did, exchange business cards and "networked." The Malaysian ambassador to Belgium was present, and he drew attention to Malaysia's role in setting global standards in halal production and exports as well as establishing "opportunities for market access establishing networking for players worldwide"—especially at halal events such as MIHAS and WHF held in Malaysia. Then a JAKIM representative made the case that to enhance market competitiveness mechanisms to monitor and audit halal must be in place. Nestlé Malaysia's representative explained that as Malaysia aspires to be a halal hub Nestlé willingly shares its expertise and global networking with relevant halal authorities as the company has done since 1992 when its halal policy was formulated. I explore these aspects further in Chapter 6.

I now turn to another halal event that links the Malaysian halal network to the global stage. In November 2005, the first Halal Exhibition at the major WFM was held. The venue was ExCeL London, a major exhibition and conference center in Docklands, an area in the southeastern part of the city that has been redeveloped principally for commercial and residential use. In 2006, a delegation from MATRADE, Malaysia's national trade promotion agency, had a booth at the Halal Exhibition for the first time. A large number of booths sold a wide variety of fresh, chilled, and frozen halal food products such as meat/poultry, sausages, samosas, kebabs, bread, fast food, baby food, nuts, and dry fruits. Candy in these booths included fruit gum made with fish gelatin and chocolate bars. Halal drinks were also displayed—fruit drinks, Mecca-Cola (promoted as an Islamically correct cola that is an alternative to the imperialist megabrands), and what appeared to be Zamzam water that can also be found in Kuala Lumpur, as we shall see. Zamzam water is marketed as a sacred source of water from God coming from the Well of Zamzam located near the holiest place in Mecca, the Kaaba (the square building inside the great mosque in Mecca, containing a sacred black stone). Nonfood halal products were also displayed, for example, NewGenn cleaning and disinfection for use especially in food preparation. As we shall see, some of these products are certified with logos displaying and identifying the certifier, but many are not. Besides the Halal Exhibition, the WFM also included a Kosher Exhibition and an Ethnic & Speciality Food Exhibition. The Ethnic & Specialty section is placed in a middle position separating the halal and kosher sections. These different zones are clearly marked on the map of the WFM one receives before entering. Hence, halal is marked on the map of the exhibition. In many cases halal marks the single booths, and is written on products (in Arabic and/or Roman characters). Many companies and Islamic organizations were represented at the Halal Exhibition, including the Malay entrepreneur Altaf.

Another halal event reflects forms of Malay(sian) social, political, and economic organization in a diasporic context. In August 2006, the Malaysian High Commission arranged a Malaysia Day Carnival and UMNO branches from all over the UK gathered at a Malaysian research center outside London. Each UMNO branch is in charge of a food stall selling (halal) food to a large number of guests. In his opening speech, the high commissioner of Malaysia to the UK declared that to achieve Vision 2020, imagining Malaysia as a fully developed nation by 2020, exchanges between the UK and Malaysia are essential. In the foreword to the *Programme Book* of this event, the high commissioner argues that Malaysia Day Carnival has been an event that strengthens the bond of friendship and "networking" among Malaysians in the UK providing an opportunity for the High Commission, Malaysian private sector, and various organizations in the UK to promote Malaysia. This network event also involved the Malaysian Business Forum, as well as the Overseas Malaysian Executive Council and several producers of Malaysian halal products.

On November 11, 2006, I was at Malaysia Hall in Bayswater, an area of west London that is one of the city's most cosmopolitan areas, for a talk by the managing director of Khazanah Nasional, the Malaysian government's strategic investor in new industries and markets. Its main objective is to promote economic growth and make strategic investments on behalf of the government, which would contribute towards nation building.

The setting in which this played out was a highly formal and "national" conference room with pictures of the Malaysian king, queen, and the present and former UMNO prime ministers, as well as the Malaysian national flag. Participants explained to me that the speaker was a very important person who "controls" a lot of funds in the interfaces between the Malaysian state and GLCs worldwide. When the speaker entered the room, the organizers humbly bowed, and as the talk was about to start, a few of the participants returned from praying in the prayer room next door.

Convincingly, the managing director discussed visions and initiatives the Malaysian state together with the GLC were, and still are, putting in place to make the best of globalized markets and business opportunities. "Inshallah" (God willing) was added when hopes for a bright economic future for Malaysian national capitalism were expressed. The speaker explained to the audience about how foreign direct investment, human capital, networking, sustainability, and transparency are all essential in the global world of business today. Most of all, it is important to locate strategic "niches in value chains" for Malay(sian) entrepreneurs to exploit, and this is particularly so within information and communication technologies (ICTs), tourism and Islamic finance, and halal. After this talk, Malaysian halal food was served in the adjoining canteen.

In July 2010 the Inaugural Oxford Global Islamic Branding and Marketing Forum held the conference "The Rise of Global Islamic Business: Muslim Market Opportunities and Challenges." The poster for the conference argued that the while the market for Syariah compliant products is worth more than US$2 trillion, this market is not well understood (www.sbs.oxford.edu/islamicmarketing). Halal played a key role at the conference and state representatives from Malaysia under headings such as "Building a City's Islamic Brand and the Marketing Challenges Faced" together with company representatives and academics discussed the future of the global halal industry with respect to food, cosmetics, pharmaceuticals, and logistics. These discussions were intersected by "networking lunches" and "networking breaks." Obviously, this conference qualifies as a halal network event in which the Malaysian state, companies, and academia together network, but it also signifies the importance of education, research, and science in the global market for halal. Interestingly, none of the nonstate halal certifiers were present. I cannot help wondering if this high-profile event held in Oxford was considered too formal or even "academic" for these nonstate certifiers.

The preceding network events testify to the way in which the Malaysian state plays an important role in the global halal network, and thus the shaping of halal as a global assemblage was composed of technoscience, certification, and standardization. Halal events help standardize halal with particular reference to the role of powerful certifiers such as JAKIM and MUIS. These halal network events on the global stage are inseparable from Malaysian national networks. In a way, all these halal network events have become "standardized" within the last decade or so; that is, these events are arranged to confirm the existence of a global halal network to generate global order. The different actors in this network are seen to possess certain types of qualifications, knowledge, or skills.

AT THE ISLAMIC CULTURAL CENTRE—A HALAL BODY RECOGNIZED BY JAKIM

The ICC was founded in 1976 and is housed in a villa in the northwestern suburbs of Copenhagen, Denmark. ICC is privately run and houses a mosque, has a Koran school, and arranges courses for local Danish Muslims who for the most part are of Arab and Pakistani origin. ICC is the largest halal certifier of meat, as well as nonmeat, products in Denmark. Denmark is a major exporter of both food and nonfood products, and thus, halal is an important question for the state and companies. The Danish embassy (as shown in Chapter 6) in Malaysia and other markets in which halal is important try to help Danish companies with their export and local manufacturing of products that must live up to halal requirements. Delegations from countries where halal is important come to Denmark to inspect abattoirs and other types of production.

ICC has been recognized by JAKIM since 1997 when the globalization of the halal market gained impetus. Similarly, but on a much larger scale, the IFCE, which arranged the conference in Belgium, is recognized by JAKIM, and these organizations have important network functions, that is, to ensure that halal is properly handled in a Muslim minority context in Europe. ICC's imam has lived in Denmark since 2001 and is the organization's "halal supervisor," he explained. He is also involved in halal with companies in Germany, Sweden, Poland, and the UK. The imam receives delegations from countries where halal is important, and his function is also important as meat and poultry for the most part is stunned before slaughter. In the eyes of many Muslims and Islamic organizations that prefer unstunned meat, this is a controversial question, and it seems to reinforce the need for proper Islamic handling of such products: a JAKIM-recognized local halal-certifying body such as ICC is responsible for ensuring that slaughtering follows proper Islamic procedure and keeping records of this, including the appointment of the Muslim slaughterer to certify that this has been carried out according to the Malaysian standard for slaughtering and handling of meat production, as well as in accordance with the Malaysian Protocol for Halal Meat and Poultry Production.

In Denmark it is mandatory that a state veterinarian and a Muslim abattoir employee control the ritual slaughter process. ICC must approve the Muslim abattoir employee. He pronounces the prayer *Allah Akhbar* (God Is Great) at the start of the slaughter process and after each break. Denmark also exports a wide range of nonmeat food products such as cake, chocolate, chips, and even enzyme production as we have seen. So for Danish companies to export to Malaysia these products must come with a certificate stating that no prohibited ingredients are involved in the production process. The imam recalled an episode where a Danish company called him and asked for halal certification. He replied why the company would want certification for its nonmeat products and that that this was surely not necessary. The company representative said that this was because JAKIM wanted halal certification for this particular product.

The imam asks companies to send him samples he can submit to laboratory testing for alcohol and pork gelatin. Symptomatically of what we have seen, the interest in halal and its regulation is, to a large extent, generated from Southeast Asian countries such as Malaysia, Singapore, and Indonesia. Following the tightened regulation and legislation on halal in Malaysia, JAKIM has stepped up halal requirements and enforcement. JAKIM asks the imam to look into "everything" that is exported to Malaysia.

ICC educates butchers employed at abattoirs across Denmark in the meaning of halal and in how to practice halal requirements. ICC also looks into the question of the halalness of raw materials sent to laboratories for testing. However, the imam stresses that companies are "honest" and send all the requested information needed to verify production, and much of this information is readily available on company websites that the imam can refer to when dealing with JAKIM. Generally, JAKIM "trusts" the information given by ICC. In 2011 JAKIM paid ICC an announced visit and was happy with ICC's "procedure," and I could not help think of this as a part of halal audit culture; that is, auditing is, to large extent, about cultural and economic authority granted to auditors and their activities. Thus, in and between divergent halal zones, institutionalized pressures exist for audit and inspection systems to generate comfort and reassurance. The imam does not think of the relation between ICC and JAKIM to be "cooperation" but, rather, as characterized by a "responsibility" to exchange "Islamic information." Even if halal requirements set by JAKIM and other certifiers are strict and tend to increase this always has to be in accordance with Danish law, the imam explains.

ICC does not work in accordance with standards set by JAKIM but, rather, more universal "Islamic standards." The imam stresses that there are many standards in the global market for halal and that ICC has to adapt to and be flexible about this kind of diversity. However, Islam is the same all over the world in spite of this variety of halal standards, he concludes. The knows this because he often attends halal events in countries such as Saudi Arabia and Kuwait, but he had not yet been to Malaysia—JAKIM, instead, goes to him, and this point stresses the importance of the ICC as a recognized halal body in the global halal network.

I have shown how the Malaysian state promotes its vision of a halal network enabling Malaysia to sell halal commodities through the business of ethnic Malay Muslim entrepreneurs globally, but the network also guarantees the halalness of imports from around the world. Today, modern halal is part of a huge and expanding globalized market in which Islam, standards, and technoscience are keywords. The halal network is fueled by the revival and expansion of ancient Islamic trade networks vis-à-vis powerful Chinese networks organizing the trade of different commodities. The halal network is intimately tied to Malaysian and global network events; that is, the Malaysian halal network is, to a large extent, practiced as a technique through and at these halal network events. Within the last decade or so, these developments have given shape to halal as a global assemblage. The emergence of more and more different types of halal network events signifies the standardization and globalization of these events. From my participation in these events I have learned that diverse halal classifications across global halal zones increasingly are becoming standardized. Thus, the global halal network evokes shared standards and interests among its actors. Imagined halal networks always involve some form of location and are thus both political and moral constructions of space and place that are never free from the political and religious ties that imagined them. Bureaucratically certified halal by the ethnicized state fuels visions and efforts to develop and control the halal market as an economic, religious, and political network. The earlier discussions also show how the participation of various types of organizations in halal events gives shape to halal as a global assemblage. Hence, from their origin in Malaysian and Singaporean halal zones these events have proliferated throughout global halal zones.

NOTES

1. In ethnographic studies, the position of networks tends to have shifted from being a specific tool of methodology to become a "metaphorical device" or cultural form in and through itself focusing on the art, activities, stories, aesthetics, and performance of networking (Knox et al. 2006, 125).
2. This halal network event for one was arranged by KasehDia—a communication and consulting company formed in 1999 that stresses Islamic values. The company engages in publication, events, branding, and consultancy, and I discuss this company in greater detail in Chapter 5.
3. *Straits Times* September 28, 1989: Malay chamber to stage world's first Muslim food and technology show.
4. *Straits Times* June 30, 1994: Plan to help supply of halal food worldwide; August 15, 1995: Toehold in global halal market—fair seen as big tapping ASEAN business.
5. *Straits Times* January 8, 1995: Malay businessmen urged to widen network; April 1, 1995: Use unique strengths with Muslim markets, Malay entrepreneurs told.
6. *Straits Times* April 22, 2004: MUIS to help Europe set halal standards.
7. *New Straits Times* May 13, 2006: SMEs Urged to Boost Networking at International Halal Event.
8. *New Straits Times* on May 18, 2006, wrote that "Halal Showcase Rakes in Deals Worth RM168m."
9. *New Straits Times* May 25, 2010: Halal forum to push for strong masterplan.

BIBLIOGRAPHY

Caliskan, Koray. 2010. *Market Threads: How Cotton Farmers and Traders Create a Global Economy*. Princeton and Oxford: Princeton University Press.

Castells, Manuel. 2000. *The Rise of Network Society*. Malden, Oxford and Carlton: Berg Publishers.

D'Alisera, Joann. 2001. "I Love Islam. Popular Religious Commodities, Sites of Inscription, and Transnational Sierra Leonean Identity." *Journal of Material Culture* 6(1): 91–110.

Economic Planning Unit, 2006. Ninth Malaysia Plan, 2006–2010. Prime Minister's Office, Putrajaya.

Fischer, Johan. 2008. *Proper Islamic Consumption: Shopping among the Malays in Modern Malaysia*. Copenhagen: NIAS Press.

Fischer, Johan. 2011. *The Halal Frontier: Muslim Consumers in a Globalized Market*. New York: Palgrave Macmillan.

Fischer, Johan. 2015. "Malaysian Diaspora Strategies in a Globalized Muslim Market." *Geoforum* 59: 169–177.

Gomez, Edmund Terence. 1994. *Political Business: Corporate Involvement of Malaysian Political Parties*. Townsville: Centre for South-East Asian Studies, James Cook University of North Queensland.

Green, Sarah, Harvey, Penny and Knox, Hannah. 2005. "Scales of Place and Networks: An Ethnography of the Imperative to Connect through Information and Communications Technologies." *Current Anthropology* 46(5): 805–826.

Knox, Hannah et al. 2006. "Social Networks and the Study of Relations: Networks as Method, Metaphor and Form." *Economy and Society* 35(1): 113–140.

MATRADE. 2006. *Malaysia. Exporters of Halal Products*. Kuala Lumpur: MATRADE.

Otis, Laura. 2001. *Networking: Communicating with Bodies and Machines in the Nineteenth Century*. Ann Arbor, MI: The University of Michigan Press.

Reid, Anthony. 1999. "A Saucer Model of Southeast Asian Identity." *Southeast Asian Journal of Social Science* 27(1): 7–23.

Riles, Annelise. 2000. *The Network Inside Out*. Ann Arbor: The University of Michigan Press.

Shamsul, A. B. 1999. "Consuming Islam and Containing the Crisis. Religion, Ethnicity, and the Economy in Malaysia." In *Economies or Economics*, edited by Mason Hoadley, 43–61. Copenhagen: Nordic Institute of Asian Studies.

Sloane, Patricia. 1999. *Islam, Modernity and Entrepreneurship among the Malays*. Houndmills, Basingstoke. Hampshire: Macmillan Press.

Starrett, Gregory. 1995. "The Political Economy of Religious Commodities in Cairo." *American Anthropologist* 97(1): 51–68.

3 Halal Training[1]

This chapter discusses the workings of Islamic bureaucracies with a particular focus on the MUIS halal training. The fact that Malaysia and Singapore have become increasingly and explicitly committed to an indirect supervisory role in halal and Islamic audits is both a solution to a technical problem as well as ways of redesigning the practice of government. Staff policies such as setting up a Halal Committee or Halal Team to handle halal properly as well as the establishment of sections in companies that specialize in halal compliance are examples of the increasingly prominent role of internal control systems that can be audited. Both audits and inspections take the form of bargaining within the context of a license or permit in morally uncertain territory in which values, technology, and business intersect. Based on participation in MUIS halal training that is mandatory for relevant companies and institutions in Singapore, I explore how this particular form of training works as a technology or technique that tries to standardize halal understanding and practice. As we shall see, halal regulation plays an essential role in these processes and training, to a large extent, focuses on developing proper halal skills among employees.

In the neoliberal imaginary of contemporary capitalism, workers' employment value depends on their skills. Skills terms, especially *communication*, *team*, and *leadership*, formulate aspects of personhood and modes of sociality as productive labor. All skills are assumed to be commensurable and readily available for inculcation into workers (Urciuoli 2008). Discourses of communication, team, and leadership skills all come together in halal training, as we shall see. Ideally, team members complement each other's capacities, they should be productive and high functioning, make great decisions, resolve conflict, gain consensus, and communicate/collaborate fluidly. Team training is about the ideal flexible worker who is seen as self-monitoring, self-assessing, continuously self-improving, and internalizing the organization's key interests (Urciuoli 2008, 216). Thus, the team as a paradigm of productivity and organizational control is internalized through the reconstitution of expertise and redistribution of worker responsibility in small, impermanent teams (Urciuoli 2008, 219). Team training is seen to promise optimal labor coordination resulting in higher productivity and personal transformation (Urciuoli 2008, 222).

Rudnycky's (2010) research conducted in Krakatau Steel, a state-owned steel enterprise in Java, Indonesia, explores training sessions and the methods known as "Emotional and Spiritual Quotient" developed by spiritual reformers. These motivational speakers fuse economic progress with spiritual reform. In this case training is a powerful tool in shaping and guiding individual ethical comportment in line with national interests and strategies. In the Indonesian case, Microsoft PowerPoint was the preferred technology through which a rapidly growing movement for spiritual reform was mediated. Narrating PowerPoint presentations indicates the ability to participate in circuits of transnational business that combine corporate matters and Islam. This technology or technique is powerful in producing representations of the world and truth about the world (Rudnyckyj 2010), and the same can be said about halal training in Singapore.

Before moving to my participant observations at MUIS halal training in Singapore, I consider Halal Industry Development Corporation (HDC) halal training in Malaysia. The main difference between these two types of halal training is that while halal training at the time of my fieldwork in 2009–2010 was mandatory for companies in Singapore this was not the case in Malaysia. HDC's offer of halal training is argued to increase halal awareness through "halal-oriented custom training modules, certification guidelines, and technical advisory services." The concept of halal training aims to promote further knowledge and increase human development on all halal matters based on "standardized" training modules. The ultimate goal of halal training is to make Malaysia the Global Halal Hub. The training takes place in a "fully equipped, conducive" training center of "international standard" that "features all the essential facilities from the prayer room, spacious dining area and cozy lounge, to the comfortable, hi-tech training areas and resource outlets" (http://www.hdcglobal.com/publisher/bi_halal_training).

Halal training courses are often advertised in e-mails as well as at halal network events. A particular course advertised in an e-mail was titled "JAKIM E-Halal and Malaysia Halal Certification & Its Applications." This course was held in MATRADE (Malaysia External Trade Development Corporation) Exhibition and Convention Centre, Kuala Lumpur in December 2010. A certificate of attendance was provided to all participants. The course was to prepare companies for the Halal Act. The course methodology rested on a "complete learning system with defined objectives" through lectures, discussions, and case studies. A comparable course was held in March 2011, and although it was focused on similar issues as the course discussed earlier, it stressed the changed legal context of halal regulation in Malaysia, that is, the introduction of the state halal logo and certification. Thus, halal training is inseparable from the changing legal landscape in Malaysia. This is also the case in Singapore, and to this aspect I now turn.

HALAL TRAINING AT MUIS ACADEMY

In 2009 I participated in MUIS's halal training held at MUIS Academy, Singapore, that develops and conducts courses on Islam. MUIS Academy "serves as a conduit for MUIS to share Singapore's model of religious administration and service, expertise and technology" (MUIS Academy folder, n.d). This training consisted of two courses: "Level 1: Halal Foundation Programme with an Introduction to the Singapore MUIS Halal Quality Management System" (HalalMQ) and "Level 2: Halal Training Programme. Developing & Implementing Halal Quality Management System" (HalMQ). The objective of Level 1 is to be able to understand the definition and basic concepts of halal certification, to be better prepared to comply with MUIS halal requirements, and to gain an overview of the principles of HalMQ (The Singapore MUIS Halal Quality Management System). The course is mandatory for one Muslim member of staff and one other staff member in the Halal Team (http://www.muis.gov.sg/cms/services/hal.aspx?id=7156).

MUIS Academy is a modern type of conference facility equipped with all the latest teaching equipment. It is part of Singapore Islamic Hub (SIH) that comprises the Muhajirin Mosque, Madrasah Al-Irsyad Al-Islamiah (Islamic school), and MUIS headquarters. About 30 participants are in the Level 1 class, and it is important to sign in before the course starts. The basic structure of the training is a series of Microsoft PowerPoint slides narrated by the Malay teacher. He explains about the day's program, which runs from 9 a.m. to 5 p.m. and consists of lectures, team exercises, problem solving, and case studies, as well as questions and answers. The course is aimed at Halal Team members, Halal Liaison Officers, and managers and supervisors from companies and state institutions who are responsible for halal certification, as well as Muslim employees.

The atmosphere is relaxed among the mainly Malay and Chinese participants. The teacher writes his name on the whiteboard and explains his relationship with MUIS. He recognizes several of the participants from his earlier role as an MUIS inspector in companies and institutions. Hence, these participants know that the teacher also represents the audit/inspection authority. He has worked in the civil service for some years and has been involved in business so his knowledge of halal is extensive. He now works for Warees Halal Division, a subsidiary of MUIS, which helps firms attain MUIS halal certification through the process of consultation. Once companies are certified, Warees Halal undertakes the task of ensuring that firms comply with requirements of the halal certification, that is, conducting site audits, engaging local Muslim organizations abroad to conduct regular periodic audits, and sending halal-certified products for laboratory tests on an annual basis.

The course starts with a round of introductions focused on participants' type of organization and business, the role halal plays in their working life, and course expectations. For example, one participant is from Singapore General Hospital. In Singapore there is an increasing focus on public institutions such as hospitals and halal because Muslims from the Middle East, in particular, have become medical tourists, she explains. Between introductions the teacher jokingly asks why participants attend this mandatory course. A man working as a lawyer representing a local company is interested in some "basic knowledge" on halal. Yet another participant is employed by an enterprise that is implementing the HalMQ system, and she hopes to be better equipped to do this after the course. A man who works as a manager wants to improve halal management in his canteen. When all participants have introduced themselves, the teacher explains that all questions and critique relating to MUIS halal regulation are welcome—the system cannot be improved without critique, he says. The training is not about "right and wrong" but about "interaction and discussion," so participants should come forward with all inquiries and not be shy.

Quiz 1 was on "What is halal?" This question is discussed in groups for a while. A woman is the first to give her opinion, and she thinks that pork and lard avoidance and proper ritual slaughter essentially define halal. A man adds that alcohol should be avoided, and another man argues that carnivores are haram. The teacher nods approvingly and asks if any other participants have additional ideas. Because there were not, he poses a question about the halal status of amphibians such as frogs that are a delicacy among some Chinese in Singapore. The teacher repeats that participants should be "brave in your answers" and that "no one is punished for wrong answers." When participants offer no further explanations five slides with definitions of halal from the Koran are shown. The teacher adds that in principle, everything is halal except for what is mentioned as haram in the Koran and ruled as haram by *ulama* (Islamic functionaries). He describes the Koran as a "manual" of "religious aspects" Muslims live by.

Quiz 2 was on "What Is Halal Certification?" Groups again discuss, and the accompanying slides, to a large extent, are focused on MUIS's role in halal certification and its accompanying legislation. Thus, in Singapore, only MUIS can certify halal and other types of halal certification must be approved by MUIS. Halal certification by JAKIM in Malaysia and by MUI in Indonesia is an example of bodies that are also approved elsewhere in the region. The teacher poses a question about what certification is. This seems to be a challenging question among participants who speculate whether halal certification could be compared to nonreligious certification. The teacher clarifies that in order to understand halal certification it is imperative to understand halal. One thing is clear: a proper halal mark "sells."

This is certainly not the case if you go to China or the Netherlands, for example. In these countries there is no centralized state authority that can define and certify halal and certification is carried out by competing Muslim organizations. This means that where there is no clear halal certification in the form of logos, consumers and companies must be on their guard and critically ask about the halalness of products, raw materials, and services. "Is it enough to build trust in food on race?" the teacher asks. In multiethnic Singapore, trust in food cannot be based on race, he reasons, and to ensure halalness, state-regulated certification provided by MUIS is efficient. Halal certification is by far the most reliable indicator of halal assurance, the teacher concludes.

The course then moves to discussing the origin of MUIS in 1968, the fact that in Singapore it is only MUIS that can certify halal, that MUIS as a statutory board "exists because of law," and that there is "a law behind it", that is, the AMLA. Warees Halal, the company that employs the teacher, is an expression of the way in which MUIS and halal in Singapore have global aspirations: Warees is now handling halal globally because this is not within the jurisdiction of MUIS. As halal is lifted out of its local context to become a global assemblage MUIS and Warees Halal are differentiated, systematized, specialized, and bureaucratized to promote and regulate it. The Halal Certification Strategic Unit of MUIS is ISO 9001 certified (deals with the requirements that organizations wishing to meet the standard have to fulfill) and provides a range of "personalized" services for companies, and there is an E-Halal Kiosk in MUIS Halal Consultation Room within the Singapore Islamic Hub. Even if Singapore's halal vision, to a large extent, focuses on global Muslim markets because the local market is limited, halal promotion and regulation in Singapore itself is extensive to demonstrate national dedication to tapping this lucrative market.

Before moving to "Team Exercise 1: What Are Your Benefits to Halal Certification?" the fees for the different number of MUIS halal certification schemes are outlined. The different schemes are as follows: Products Scheme, Food Preparation Area Scheme, Storage Facility Scheme, Poultry Abattoir Scheme, and Endorsement Scheme. When asked about benefits of halal certification to their organizations, participants mainly give economic reasons such as expanding markets. However, benefits of halal certification also generate questions among participants about challenges posed by such certification, questions relate to halal and ethnicity, for example. A man asks why he has to take this mandatory course when he is a Muslim who is supposed to be knowledgeable about halal. A supermarket director of food safety and quality from the largest supermarket chain in Singapore, NTUC FairPrice Co-operative LTD, has logistic challenges marking the separation of halal and non-halal products in her store. The supermarket received complaints from Muslim consumers that frogs were placed next to halal crabs in the supermarket. Consumers wanted to know what MUIS's position on this issue was. I return to these issues in Chapter 7. Yet other questions related to announced/unannounced inspections, their frequency, and their nature. The teacher answers to the best of his ability, and most of his answers tend to rely on the way in which halal is legally regulated in Singapore; that is, MUIS as a statutory body in Singapore regulates halal, and it has employed a number of contact officers that deal with particular challenges participants may experience.

The teacher then asks about disadvantages of certification and participants argued that the cost, time, "restrictions," "hassle," and audits can be considered disadvantages. The teacher draws attention to a case of a primary school canteen with which he was involved. In 2008, a Singaporean primary school (discussed in Chapter 1) insisted that only halal food could be taken into the canteen, causing a stir among non-Muslim parents. The Ministry of Education declared that this decision was a mistake, and it was reversed. In a letter to all parents, the school's principal said that since the whole school canteen had been certified halal, children would not be allowed to bring non-halal food onto the premises. The school security guard and discipline master had also been checking lunch boxes to ensure that pupils complied. MUIS clarified that it certifies only the food stalls in a school canteen, not the premises as a whole, and added that once a stallholder has obtained his halal certificate, non-halal foods cannot be brought in or out of that halal-certified stall. The teacher stressed that this story exemplifies the importance of knowing what kind of halal scheme to apply for.

During the coffee and lunch breaks, I had the opportunity to discuss halal with some of the participants. The director from the large Singaporean supermarket, NTUC FairPrice Co-operative LTD discussed earlier, explains to me that there is an increased focus on halal in Singapore and thus the need for halal training has risen. The other representative from FairPrice present at the training was the Malay Muslim man who earlier wondered why he as a Muslim had to take this course. The director was handling Muslim complaints about frogs' legs placed next to crabs and finds that translating halal into actual corporate practice in the supermarket has been resource demanding but that rules and regulations are becoming clearer. Separating halal and non-halal products in supermarket outlets, for example, that are not designed for this poses a challenge. For a time, a "green mark" on the floor signified this separation, before halal and non-halal were separated in different sections of the supermarket. These are some of the issues on which a company such as this one consults MUIS. Other aspects brought up during the break concern the role of law in halal in Singapore and, more broadly, the transformation halal is undergoing in the local setting and how this affects participants' organizations.

Even though the teacher emphasized that it is preferable to have questions asked during class, a number of queries relating to the individual participants' situations surfaced during breaks. These take many forms and include very mundane issues such as who can one contact in MUIS. The teacher recommends e-mailing MUIS for answers to questions. Another aspect he introduces is that while auditors audit differently, there is no question about the legal background and enforcement of halal in Singapore; that is, MUIS is a statutory body inseparable from AMLA and ensures that his advice has a firm legal foundation.

The training then moved to a discussion about the different halal schemes MUIS offers. Participants are advised to carefully consider the characteristics and relevance of these schemes. A man argues that selecting the most appropriate scheme can be complicated, and this question leads to a discussion of more general points relating to submitting applications. The teacher offers an example of the importance of certification: at a dinner with guests from Malaysia and Brunei there was a discussion about where the duck on the plates was from. Uncertainty can easily arise when meat or other products do not carry a logo with a recognizable certifier such as MUIS. While Malaysia and Brunei are recognized as countries with stringent halal certification, China, for example, does not have the same kind of state halal system. The teacher stresses that more and more consumers are accustomed to identifiable and reliable halal logos, and certification helps create confidence in the expanding market for halal in which gray zones are common—can artificial pork flavor be halal certified, the teacher jokingly asks to the amusement of participants, as well as the researcher.

A woman asks if other types of halal certification have to go through MUIS. The teacher replies that MUIS has a list of recognized halal-certifying bodies worldwide, including JAKIM, and that this ensures the integrity of halal regulation. This point clarifies the relationship between MUIS and other certifying bodies among participants, and more broadly, this is an example of the kind of clarity that this training can offer participants.

The discussion then centers on a case of alleged halal-certified pork in the FairPrice supermarket discussed earlier. Of course, pork cannot be halal certified, everybody agreed, but somehow a MUIS halal logo ended up on pork in the supermarket. FairPrice and MUIS systematically explored the case, and it was concluded that the incident referred to arose because of a rumor in an e-mail that halal pork was on sale in Singapore. MUIS inspectors did not find any halal pork when investigating the matter, and it was referred to as a case of "sabotage," but a police investigation could not place responsibility. This case increased the call for fixed halal standards and guidelines among companies such as FairPrice.

Next, Singapore's role in an international halal network is presented, that is, Singapore's formal international network within ASEAN and Unofficial Meetings of Religious Ministers in Brunei, Indonesia, Malaysia, and Singapore, on one hand, and "informal" overseas networks of bilateral meetings, exchange visits as well as international conferences and seminars on the other. All this testifies to the global scope of Singapore's halal recognition.

After a brief question-and-answer session, the basic concept of halal food is discussed. Special dietary requirements of different "belief systems" such as halal, kosher, and "vegetarian"; general criteria of halal food; and halal slaughtering inform discussions. A video on slaughter processes in Australia raises ethical questions about meat eating in general. The question of stunning is also discussed, and the teacher explains that after stunning the animal must show signs of life. In Brunei, for example, stunning is not allowed.

Then the question of halal status verification is on the agenda. The main point is that halal status verification can take three forms: halal certificates; halal certification labels, such as the MUIS logo on products; and food labels and ingredient lists. The teacher provides examples of rumors about the questionable halalness of products and of how halal status verification can address such issues. In Singapore, halal status verification is inseparable from AMLA; that is, halal status verification is solely handled by MUIS.

Types of halal offenses include misuse of the MUIS mark, and thus AMLA, false or misleading claims about halalness in violation of the Sales of Food Act and Sedition Act, and forgery related to the penal code. The Singaporean Parliament enacted a law giving MUIS sole certification rights and legislation was tightened. A number of specific halal offences are discussed, and after a couple of questions from participants on the aspect of offenses, the teacher looks into the Singapore MUIS Halal Quality Management System (HalMQ). The teacher shows that the benefits of HalMQ increased the competitive advantage of certified companies, halal compliance through a more structured and systematic approach, credibility of Singapore halal certification, and international recognition of Singapore halal certification.

Afterward HalMQ implementation plans for new and existing halal certificate holders are discussed as well as 10 detailed HalMQ principles, for example, establishing the Halal Team. After a discussion of the application process, Team Exercise 2 deals with the issues touched on in groups. After group work, the groups presented their discussions and findings, and there is also time for queries. A woman asks how large the MUIS halal logo on products can be, and the teacher replied that this depends on the size of products; that is, there has to be fair relationship between the size of the logo and the product surface. Finally, the teacher issued certificates to participants.

LEVEL 2: DEVELOPING AND IMPLEMENTING THE HALAL QUALITY MANAGEMENT SYSTEM (HALMQ)

The objective of MUIS's Level 2 training is that participants understand the basic concepts & requirements of HalMQ, learn how to prepare and document HalMQ procedures, and gain an overview of internal audit and assessment techniques. This training is strongly recommended for Halal Team leaders/members within halal-certified premises (http://www.muis.gov.sg/cms/services/hal.aspx?id=7156). The teacher who taught Level 1 is also responsible for Level 2, and the basic structure of the course is the same. Compared to Level 1 fewer participants attended Level 2. The two-day course takes place in the same room as Level 1. The teacher starts out by explaining how this Level 2 course continues some of the points raised in Level 1 and could be seen to lead to a Level 3 course, "Conducting Halal Internal Audits." After introducing himself, the teacher outlines the course objectives. Participants should be able to understand MUIS general halal certification requirements, identify basic concepts of HalMQ, comprehend the benefits and rationale for HalMQ, learn how to prepare the documentations for HalMQ, and gain an overview of internal audit and assessment techniques.

The teacher asks participants why they spend time and money on Level 2 and what their expectations are before a round of introductions starts. A Pizza Hut representative, who also attended Level 1, explains that she is there to deepen her halal knowledge. Another representative from a local company says that she wants to "merge halal and management systems together." A woman from Singapore General Hospital, also present at Level 1, has the same aim. A man from Brunei explains that he is there because Brunei does not offer such a course even if the Brunei government encourages institutionalization of halal. A chef at the NUS (National University of Singapore) Cultural Centre (a venue for events that reflect the cultural heritage of Singapore and international arts and entertainment) wants to learn more about halal management in his canteen. The NTUC FairPrice representative is also present and so are representatives from about 15 other state institutions and companies.

The basic structure of the course is General Halal Certification Requirements, an introduction to HalMQ, the 10 principles of HalMQ, and a maintenance program, in other words, keys to maintaining a good halal system. In terms of the General Halal Certification Requirements three areas are essential: halal basic requirements (documentation for raw materials), staffing (mandatory participation in halal courses for and establishing the Halal Team), and systems with particular reference to tightened legislation and complying with HalMQ principles. In all this, the teacher explains, logos and certificates are essential. A man asks if it would be possible to have mandatory and recognized certificates for imported raw materials, and the teacher replies that this would be desirable but that unlike Singapore, most countries do not have a state certification body like MUIS that can issue reliable certificates. What is more, the teacher makes clear that even if imported raw materials come with a logo, the certifier and, thus, the logo are not necessarily recognized by MUIS. A man asks about the role of the Muslim staff or Halal Team. The teacher reasons that the mandatory Muslim staff and Halal Team play an "advisory role" to give "public assurance."

In the Group Exercise 1 participants listed the benefits of implementing HalMQ. After discussing this question in groups, the following arguments are presented: increased sales, standardization, confidence, "HalMQ is good for Singapore," and increased recognition, that is, "a good system that can be recognized abroad. Singapore is positioning itself globally and is recognized for technology," as a man put it. A woman from a multinational fast-food chain tells the class that the company had to undergo *sertu* (ritual cleansing) by MUIS in 1998 when the restaurant was first halal certified. She likes this kind of standardization "because then it's the same for all companies." The teacher adds that actually demands to standardize and proliferate halal in Singapore also came from companies and not only from MUIS and the state. Each of the chain's outlets has a MUIS halal logo on the door and a certificate behind the counter, but she would prefer that all outlets could be certified together and not on an individual basis, as is the case.

The teacher then moves on to Principle 1 of HalMQ—establishing the Halal Team. This team should include a team leader, at least one Muslim staff, and "relevant personnel from multi-disciplinary backgrounds." What is more, Terms of Reference (TOR), as well as roles and responsibilities of individual members, should be established. Team members should be sent for halal training. The "team approach," the teacher explains is central when dealing with halal. A couple participants ask about the ideal size of the Halal Team in their particular workplace; this varies according to the number of employees, the teacher explains. Another question is, How many employees must complete MUIS halal training? The teacher replies that Level 1 is compulsory and that every employee on the Halal Team must go, whereas Level 2 is optional and "recommended" because then companies will be better equipped to work with auditors. In any case, if problems arise they will be settled by MUIS.

Principle 2 of HalMQ has to do with the definition of the product or nature of business and the teacher makes clear that MUIS has a helpline that can always assist in case of questions. It is important that applicants carefully consider the particular scheme or product they apply for. In Group Exercise 2 participants should imagine that they are Halal Team members and document the profile of the team and the nature of products and business. The teacher explains that it is important that the whole group support the individual group member presenting findings in the form of posters on the wall. In its presentation, the first group goes over the different group members' experiences relating to the task at hand. The teacher praises the presentation and poster but also asks about possible improvements. A man answers that the certification process could perhaps be spelled out, and the teacher nods. Another participant adds that in his company the Halal Team is appointed by the company management. A central concern is to make sure that certified products have logos and noncertified products do not, he makes clear.

In general, the atmosphere is relaxed, and many jokes are blended in with the course content. When presenting its poster a group explains that when applying for halal certification, the Muslim staff on the Halal Team should endorse incoming raw materials. The Halal Team's TOR is to satisfy such halal requirements, and all members should have completed MUIS training. The teacher says that the exercise is there for participants to know what to do, for example, to appoint a Halal Team leader. The group should remember that each team member should have different roles and at least one Muslim staff member should be on the Halal Team to comply with HalMQ requirements. What is more, the "halal file should be signed by Muslim staff," as a man from the group makes clear.

The teacher stresses that if one Halal Team member fails, the whole team fails. A couple of questions concern the relationship between halal legislation and how companies should live up to this. Many questions relating to the particular situations of participants surface during the break—for example, one question concerns the process of tightened legislation taking place in Singapore and how this relates to legislation and regulation of halal more globally. Another question focuses on sentencing in connection with different types of halal offences and how companies can ensure that they are not punished for using raw materials with fake halal logos.

Principle 3 concerns the construction of a flow chart, and Principle 4 is to identify halal threats and control measures. In Group Exercise 3 groups now developed the flow chart for business operation and identify possible threats and control measures. Both the teacher and participants think that the poster presented after the group work should read more like a "real" flow chart, and the group presenting takes this advice into consideration. The teacher stresses that it is important that group work flowcharts on posters are depicted as realistically as possible in order for groups to receive the most accurate comments. Groups gather around the poster again to go over it and learn how the teacher would "monitor" this particular flow chart as in real life. A man from a local company has a specific question: Does a truck have to be halal for transport? The teacher explained that the driver has to know about transporting halal and that if the truck has been carrying any *najis* (filth), such as pork, it must be ritually cleansed. In case of "heavy pork pollution several ritual washings" carried out by MUIS are necessary.

In connection with Principle 5 on Halal Assurance Points (HAPs), Group Exercise 4 is to identify the HAPs including allowable limits and prescribed practices. During group work the teacher circulates among groups and discusses and answers questions before the first day of the course ends. The second day of the course starts with a discussion of Principles 6 and 7 on the establishment of a monitoring system and corrective action for each HAP, followed by Group Exercise 5 on these topics. During the first group's presentation the question of controlling suppliers is brought out: How can companies and restaurants control raw materials from suppliers?

During the break the teacher explains about the confusion in Malaysia in the wake of the tension between JAKIM and HDC and that halal is more tightly regulated in Singapore. He brings up the issue that essentially, halal is an Islamic injunction and that quite of number of questions about halal is for religious scholars to answer. For example, for fish to be halal they must have scales and Imams determined this in a *fatwa* (opinion concerning Islamic law issued by an Islamic scholar). Another issue is that these interpretations and rulings differ between the different schools of Islamic jurisprudence. The teacher contends that halal is not exact science but is open to interpretation and that MUIS plays a central role in this type of interpretation and regulation. A couple of Chinese participants argued that halal is mainly important in Singapore because of business because Chinese do not really observe any kind of religious food taboos. After discussing Principles 8 (establishing documentation and record keeping), 9 (verifying the halal system), and 10 (reviewing the halal system), the teacher issues certificates to all participants, and this concludes the course.

To conclude, halal training plays an essential role in Malaysia and Singapore—especially in the context of changing landscapes of halal legality and standardization. Moreover, as halal is lifted out of its local context to become a global assemblage, MUIS and Warees Halal are differentiated, systematized, specialized, and bureaucratized to promote and regulate it. The training structured around Microsoft PowerPoint slides pushes halal control and self-control into companies and state institutions such as universities and hospitals to satisfy the need to connect internal organizational arrangements to national visions and strategies. Most important, perhaps, training instills or disciplines a form of common managerial model that emphasizes the encouragement of internal compliance systems. In other words, training technologies and techniques discipline halal understanding and practice in employees and institutions. Moreover, halal training also signifies standards and standardization, that is, the design and qualities of products as well as proper conduct of companies, for example, with regard to the production, preparation, handling, and storage of halal. Training is aimed at enhancing skills in terms of communication, team, and leadership and it is in itself a form of skills-related product that offers workers advice or exhortation about acquiring, assessing, and enhancing their own skills. In Singapore halal training is mandatory for companies and so is the setting up of the Halal Team, and these points reflect how standards can also refer to persons or teams, as it were, with certain qualifications, knowledge, or skills. Halal training can also be seen as Islamization of knowledge central to the relationship between Islam, standards, and technoscience, and to that aspect I now turn.

NOTE

1. This chapter partly builds on material first published in Johan Fischer, "Halal Training in Singapore," in *Halal Matters: Islam, Politics and Markets in Global Perspective*, ed. Florence Bergeaud-Blackler, John Lever, and Johan Fischer (Abingdon, UK: Routledge, 2015), 175–191.

BIBLIOGRAPHY

Rudnyckyj, Daromir. 2010. *Spiritual Economies: Islam, Globalization and the Afterlife of Development*. Ithaca: Cornell University Press.

Urciuoli, Bonnie. 2008. "Skills and Selves in the New Workplace." *American Ethnologist* 35(21): 211–228.

4 In the Halal Lab

During my fieldwork in 2010 I attended a World Halal Forum Delegation trip to the Islamic Science University of Malaysia (USIM). The World Halal Forum is the leading global halal network event and brings together Islamic organizations, halal certifiers, politicians, scientists, and companies. This event testifies to Malaysia's leading global position as a laboratory for the setting of new standards for halal production, preparation, handling, storage, regulation, and science. The state of Malaysia has effectively driven these halal standards since the early 1980s, but it is only within the last decade or so that halal has been fully integrated with a localized form of Islamic technoscience, that is, the Islamization of material technology, techniques, and specialized social expertise.

At USIM we visited the Institute of Property Management & Islamic Finance, the Institute of International Fatwa Management & Research, and the Faculty of Syariah & Law, as well as the Institute of Halal Research & Management (IHRAM),[1] which is a center of excellence in USIM for Islamic-based education, research, training, services, consultation, and laboratory analyses with issues regarding halal. IHRAM's brand new laboratory makes use of technology and techniques to locate alcohol, pork, and other types of contamination in food and drink, for example.

In this chapter I explore halal in the context of Islamic technoscience. To do so it is necessary to look at a particular form of Malaysian Islamization of knowledge that exists in the interfaces between Islamic revivalism, state regulation, and secular sentiments. Before moving to the Malaysia ethnography, I briefly consider how these issues play out in Singapore. Here, "healthy" chocolates developed by Singapore Polytechnic (the first polytechnic in Singapore with about 15,000 enrolled students) students under the supervision of a senior lecturer from Chemical and Life Sciences had been certified as halal by the MUIS: chocolates are infused with inulin, a dietary fiber that promotes the growth of good bacteria in the large intestine and helps in the absorption of nutrients. Inulin is found in wheat, onions, and garlic.[2] Several lecturers from USIMs IHRAM, including its director as we shall see, visited Singapore Polytechnic to learn more about its halal research.

THE ISLAMIZATION OF KNOWLEDGE

In this section I discuss studies that explore the relationship between Islam/religion and technology, with a particular focus on the Islamization of knowledge. There is a growing interest in the relationship between Islam and science, as reflected for example, in the book series *Islam and Science: Historic and Contemporary Perspectives* (Iqbal 2012). Much of this research is theological, philosophical, and ethical in orientation. Often arguments tend to revolve around the compatibility of Islam and science. To my knowledge, however, the question of how halal fits into a whole range of modern Islamic technoscientific and secular processes and discourses has not been explored empirically. Existing scholarship on Islamic technoscience (Furlow 2009; Lotfalian 2004) does not in any systematic manner explore halal production, trade, and regulation. Scholars who advocate for the Islamization of knowledge tend to argue that while science is neutral in itself, it is the attitude by which we approach science that makes it secular or Islamic. Thus, science is intricately linked to ideology, scales of priorities, and control/direction of research (Iqbal 2012, xv), as is the case with halal and Islamic technoscience.

The interfaces between Islam and science/technology/techniques can also be explored as an expression of post-Islamism, that is, an endeavor to fuse religiosity/rights, faith/freedom, and Islam/liberty while acknowledging secular exigencies and breaking down the monopoly of religious truth (Bayat 2007, 11). Post-Islamism stresses religious ethics in society and ambiguity, multiplicity, inclusion, and compromise (Bayat 2007, 12–13). An ethnographic study explores why and how transplant medicine surfaced as a topic of much social and ethical debate in Egypt. Amidst dramatic political and economic change, debates over transplant medicine in Egypt reflected and shaped crises in medical and religious authority, dissent toward the regime, the privatization of health care, advances in science, and the Islamic revival (Hamdy 2012, 1). Throughout the world each introduction of new technology provokes rehearsal and debate in spaces between biotechnology and ethics (Hamdy 2012, 250). As in the case of halal, the Islamization of knowledge is essential in coming to terms with new forms of technoscience.

Some studies explore debates at the religious, scientific, legal, and political level, sparked by the introduction of new biomedical technologies (Atighetchi 2007), while others argue that Islamic orthodoxy impedes scientific inquiry in the Muslim world (Hoodbhoy 1991). An interesting study (Prakash 1999) analyzes the intimate relationship between science, colonialism, and the modern Indian nation. Similar to Malaysia, in India, science was a symbol of both empire and freedom, on one hand, and progress and universal reason, on the other. Nationalists sought for parallels and precedents for scientific thought in India's own intellectual history creating a hybrid form of knowledge that combined Western ideas with local cultural and religious understanding, molding a modernity that was both Western and indigenous. This is comparable to the emergence of Islamic technoscience that is the product of tensions between Islamic revivalism and the secular, which is also anti-/postcolonial in nature. In the same vein, a historical study (Mrázek 2002) draws attention to an important shift that took place in the technological culture of the late-colonial Indies and the way in which the trajectory of change in technological culture had important consequences for Indonesian nationalism associated with handling these technologies and creating a common modern social space.

I consider Geertz's (1968) seminal text on Islam in Morocco and Indonesia important. The power of Islam in Indonesia, and other parts of Southeast Asia more generally, Geertz writes, is based on an inclination toward absorbing all styles of thought into one broad stream. This tradition is generally receptive to the argument that "Islamic doctrine and scientific discovery are really not conflicting but complementary forms of belief" (1968, 106) so that the "secular" and the "scientific" are merely practical and useful expressions of Islamic knowledge (1968, 112).

I end this section with an example of the way in which scientific knowledge and practices were Islamized in Malaysia. Syed Muhammad Naquib al-Attas is a Malaysian Muslim philosopher. He is an important proponent of the Islamization of knowledge/science in a context of Islamic revivalism or *dakwah* in Malaysia and globally. He argues for the Islamization of the mind, body, and soul and reacts against "secular" Western values, knowledge, and science. From this perspective, one of the main points of divergence between "true religion" and secular philosophy and science is the way in which the sources and methods of knowledge are understood (al-Attas 1989, 3); that is, al-Attas reacts against philosophical and secular rationalism, which depends on reason alone and "denies authority and intuition and rejects revelation and religion as sources of true knowledge" (al-Attas 1989, 5). In the eyes of al-Attas, knowledge comes from God and is acquired through the channels of the sound senses (al-Attas 1989, 9). Arguably, science according to Islam is ultimately a kind of "allegorical interpretation of the empirical things that constitute the world of nature." (al-Attas 1989, 31). The acquisition of modern science and scientific techniques must be recast into the Islamic metaphysical framework (Al-Attas 1995, 38).

In sum, the Islamization of knowledge impacts on emergent technologies and techniques across Asia and Malaysia is at the forefront of this transformation. Technologies/techniques are linked to state power, markets, forms of religious revivalism and post-Islamism. While the compatibility of religion/Islam and science is well documented in both academic arguments and empirical studies, the question of how halal fits into a whole range of modern Islamic technoscientific and secular processes and discourses has not been explored empirically.

ISLAMIC TECHNOSCIENCE IN MALAYSIA

With the revival of interest in Islam from the 1970s onward, the Malaysian state's Islamization efforts included Islamic religious education and research. The unprecedented boosting of Islamic education and research led to increased numbers of government-funded primary and secondary religious schools and tertiary Islamic education also expanded. Islamic faculties in local public universities were enlarged and new Islamic university colleges were established to cater for the student population specializing in Islamic education. An example of this was establishing the International Islamic University (IIU) to implement the concept of integrating knowledge with morals. The state continues its Islamization efforts by initiating the setting up of Islamic educational institutions of various kinds (Aziz and Shamsul 2004), and it is in this context Islamic science and halal in the Islamic Science University should be seen.

One of the Mahathir administration's most significant and controversial efforts was to make religious knowledge an examinable subject in the mainstream curriculum to ensure the Malay community adhered to Islamic teachings. In the 1980s, increased emphasis on Islamic studies in the curriculums of secular institutions was initiated around the same time halal became regulated by the state. In addition to Islamic studies, curriculums in tertiary education included engineering, economics, management, and political science (Liow 2009, 54).

In his ethnographic exploration of Islamic courts in Malaysia, Peletz (2002) sees rationalization as forms of cultural/religious changes (e.g., the proliferation of halal) and rethinking to make these compatible with modern institutions and organizations (e.g., JAKIM and USIM). Political variables shape the direction and content of cultural changes and legal rationalization in Malaysia (Peletz 2002, 17–18), and there are striking similarities between the way in which Islamic courts, state halal certification, Islamic technoscience, and education have been rationalized. In much the same vein, Maznah (2010) argues that instead of the idea that Malaysia is only moving toward desecularization, there is an equal movement toward a secularized and rationalized Syariah bureaucracy. The hegemony of the Syariah bureaucracy is based on its power as arbiter of a legal and official form of Islam in Islamic public institutions. In sum, the Malaysian state is not desecularized, but rather, Islamic technoscientific institutions are transformed through a secularized mode of rationalization.

HALAL AND ISLAMIC TECHNOSCIENCE IN EVERYDAY LIFE

The question I pose before moving to the study from IHRAM is, How do Malay Muslim middle-class consumers, who are often evoked as highly particular about halal in powerful discourses in Malaysia, understand the role of science and research in halal consumption? My study on halal consumption among middle-class Malays (Fischer 2011) explored how these consumers made sense of discourses in Malaysia that promote halal as healthy, pure, and "scientific" in an age of food scares and uncertainty. A running theme through much of this type of discourse in Malaysia is the notion that food is literally transformed and becomes part of human bodies.

Several of my informants referred to arguments and "evidence" from various sources, mostly from the Internet, that pigs are more prone to carrying a range of diseases and parasites. These arguments often build on "scientific" evidence that extends and elaborates the traditional taboo on pork in Islam. What is more, pigs are often associated with *najis* (filth). For most informants, pig avoidance makes your diet healthier; for example, you will avoid "bad" bacteria. Informants who believed that halal was healthier listed the following reasons: the method of slaughtering, emphasizing that the animal should not be stunned and the draining of the blood removes diseases; halal is a religious injunction put in place by God; and halal is not open to human interpretation.

One register of middle-class Malays was convinced that halal is healthier. Arguments supporting this sentiment were that halal, in the form of a food prohibition, came into existence because draining the blood, for example, was healthy as it cleaned out "germs." Such narratives tend to circle around health as one of the main reasons behind food taboos in Judaism and Islam, but these are being sanitized; that is, they are being subjected to demands for verification and substantiation that are not necessarily of a religious nature. Another narrative was that halal is healthier because it is a way of killing an animal that ensures that the meat is fresh.

Another register of Malays referred to sources claiming that halal is healthier, but these studies are not always convincing because they are seen to lack backing by proper scientific evidence based on laboratory research. Thus, these middle-class Malays were skeptical about the source of these claims as well as their validity in the modern scientific world. However, some Malays believe that if an animal has not been slaughtered properly and the blood drained as fully as possible, the dried blood can actually "mutate" with human blood and cause diseases. Therefore, these Muslims strive to demonstrate how such rules conform to modern reason and the findings of scientific research. For example, a woman informant explained to me that she was not entirely convinced about the claim that dried blood can mutate with human blood, but in general, she adhered to the idea that all the "reasons" in Islam could be backed by scientific evidence.

This call for a scientific substantiation of halal as a healthy alternative evokes the problem of religious institutions that claim authority in an expanding religious market, as in the case of certification. Even if some imam or *ustaz* (religious teacher) contends that halal is healthier, these claims must undergo some form of scientific verification. Hence, religious discourse and authority are not in themselves enough to convince skeptical Muslim consumers who explained to me that they need scientific evidence to be convinced about the relationship between halal and health. Thus, the issue of whether halal is healthier is contested among middle-class Malays; that is, my informants do not uncritically accept the powerful discourses that claim halal to be healthy and pure in an age of food scares.

The more halal proliferates as a globalized religious market, the more "scientific" modes and methods of production and traceability become important for producers, traders, and consumers, and this is inseparable from halal science and research in Malaysia. The increased focus on such methods to verify commodities as halal based on science constantly expands the requirements to cover new types of commodities and practice, including cosmetics, pharmaceuticals, and hygiene products. Science in a variety of forms was a significant topic in the lives of my informants. A central question, for example, was why and to what extent informants avoid genetically modified (GM) foods. My survey data showed that among respondents, two equally large groups of modern Muslim consumers would avoid and/or buy GM food, respectively.

Informants linked science and halal in divergent ways. In the eyes of some informants, technoscience and halal were inseparable. Among other Malays, this point was more linked to broader questions of food safety and health. The ambiguous question of authority between science/technology, secular government, the marketplace, and religious institutions in modern societies, run through these discussions. For example, the question of whether halal is or should be linked to health and nutrition was contested. Most of my Malay middle-class informants acquired their basic knowledge of halal within the school system in Malaysia, including tertiary education that is essential for the conditioning of middle-class identities, and this nationalized and Islamized type of knowledge conditioned their halal understanding and practice. Informants would refer to this type of knowledge as a natural part of "a national curriculum," "common understanding," "general knowledge," or "a syllabus."

HALAL INSCRIPTIONS

The classic study *Laboratory Life* (Latour and Woolgar, 1979) shows that scientific laboratories and the devices they contain exist to produce "inscriptions," that is, laboratory equipment work as "inscription devices" that can transform a material substance into a figure, text, or diagram (Latour and Woolgar 1979, 51), a "system of literary inscription" (Latour and Woolgar 1979, 52). An effect of such literary inscription is that the "material elements" of the laboratory are inscribed with outcomes of past controversies available in the published literature (Latour and Woolgar 1979, 87). Debates over Islam, science, education, economy, everyday life, and the secular in Malaysia all qualify as historical and localized types of inscriptions that condition Islamic technoscience and thus halal research.

Before moving to the empirical exploration of halal laboratories, I discuss two journal articles that address the technoscientific aspects of halal. The first of these articles is written by scholars from the Faculty of Biotechnology and Biomolecular Sciences, Faculty of Food Science and Technology, and Institute of Halal Food from Universiti Putra Malaysia. University Putra Malaysia is one of the leading universities in halal research in Malaysia and beyond. It cooperates with the Islamic Science University of Malaysia, although these institutions simultaneously compete over state funding for halal research. These scholars developed a method for species identification from pork and lard samples; that is, genomic DNA of pork and lard was extracted and was found to be of good quality, producing a clear distinction between species. They concluded that the method is a reliable technique for detection of pig meat and fat (Aida et al. 2005, 47). The authors argue that in most countries food manufacturers choose to use lard as a substitute ingredient for oil because it is cheaper and easily available. This has generated increased awareness regarding the composition of food products, and hence, it is the task of food-control laboratories to be able to carry out species differentiation of raw materials to be used for industrial food preparation and the detection of animal species in food products (Aida et al. 2005, 47).

Another article by the same authors presents research on a method for detection of the presence of pig derivatives in three types of food products—sausages and casings, bread, and biscuits; that is, genomic DNA of these food products was extracted. The researchers conclude that the identification assay gave excellent results for the detection of pork adulteration in food products, and it is a reliable technique to avoid species adulteration or fraudulent species substitution for halal authentication (Aida et al. 2007, 569). Thus, within the last decade or so this area of scientific research has emerged and attracted scholars and resources in Malaysia and beyond. The authors contend that there is an increasing trend in some countries to mix pork and lard in food products for the purposes of "adulteration to gain extra profit" and that "[c]onsumers nowadays demand higher protection from falsely labeled food products for economic, ethical or religious and public health reasons" (Aida et al. 2007, 569). The authors argue that this is the sociological background for the development of the extraction of genomic DNA from processed food.

In these articles, research carried out in Malaysian biotech laboratories is essential. "Asian biotech" refers to an assemblage of science, politics, and collective concerns that configure a realm of transcendent imagery in which science, in tandem with ethics, shape political identities. A strong sovereign impulse runs through biotech projects in Asia shaping political meanings of biological problems made visible and solvable by the new sciences (Ong 2010, 21). Asian biotech reflects the way in which state entrepreneurialism makes biotechnological innovations the new model for cutting-edge capitalism. Halal material elements, research and the articles themselves are thus inscribed with a whole range of religious, political, social, and economic discourses.

IN THE HALAL LAB

Based on research carried out in hospital clinical pathology labs and blood banks in Malaysia, an interesting study shows how blood samples may accrue layers of meaning as they travel round the lab through the special properties of blood and the socially embedded interventions of laboratory staff (Carsten 2013). It is possible to find political, national, and economic interests inscribed in laboratory life. Similar to blood, the effect of the work that goes on in laboratories transforms halal into a laboratory object with detached personal or moral attributes generated in the spaces laboratories constitute (Carsten 2013, 134).

Halal Products Research Institute (HPRI) at Universiti Putra Malaysia was established in 2006 to undertake research and development in the halal products industry based on a "comprehensive, balanced and multifaceted" approach to study "all aspects" of halal products at national and global levels. The institute aims to be a center of excellence in halal products research, as well as providing professional services in realizing the aim of developing the field of agriculture and make Malaysia a global halal hub, which is a major vision of the Malaysian state (www.halal.upm.edu.my).

In 2009, the Halal Products Institute held a Symposium on Halal Science and Management focusing on the analysis and management of halal products. The 34 contributions to the proceedings from this conference testify to the massive focus on halal in the context of Islamic technoscience and education in Malaysia and included papers titled "Volatile Profiling of Alcoholic Food and Beverages and Industrial Alcohol," "Rapid Detection of Pork in Food Products by Electronic Nose for Halal," "Potential Use of Amino Acids Analysis for Distinguishing Bovine And Porcine Gelatines," "Detection of Pork in Pastry Products for Halal Verification via Polymerase Chain Reaction (PCR) Techniques," and "Fourier Transform Infrared (FTIR) Spectroscopy Profiling of Lard and Other Shortening in Puff Pastry," to name a few (Hashim et al. 2009). Several presenters of these papers were from USIM's IHRAM, and I now explore the workings of IHRAM, with a particular focus on how Islamic technoscience and halal are combined in terms of education and research, cooperation or networking among universities, and the writing of research proposals.

On IHRAM's website the Institute is described as follows: IHRAM is a main Centre of Knowledge on "Syariah-compliant" Islamic management and "Islamic-based education, research, training, services, consultation and laboratory analyses with issues regarding halal and haram" (http://www.usim.edu.my/usimweb/en/index.php?option=com_content&view=article&id=214:institute-of-halal-research-and-managementihram&catid=62:center-of-excellent&Itemid=204). USIM is in many ways the basis for and comparable to "Syariah-compliant" companies, that is, ways in which Malaysia's Islamic economy has emerged in some Malaysian businesses as a form of corporate culture reconfiguring workplace identities and social relations based on the rules for commerce and management contained within the Qur'an and Hadith (traditions concerning the life and works of the Prophet Muhammad (Sloane-White 2011).

During the World Halal Forum Delegation trip to USIM and IHRAM, participants were invited to cooperate on halal research and dissemination of knowledge. The female director of IHRAM, who was educated in food science and nutrition, explains about the institute's focus and activities—for example, halal services and Islamic finance that seek to avoid *riba* (interest) are part of ongoing halal research that supports the national vision to make Malaysia a Halal Hub.

The director argues that several areas of research and planning are important for realizing this halal vision: government halal standards, Islamic finance, the development of Syariah audit procedures and services monitored by a Syariah committee that looks into whether institutions are Syariah compliant, social security to increase the "Muslim economy," and marketing and traceability, as well as "extension of reach," for example, through publications to the *ummah* (community of Muslims), cooperation with industry players, and *fiqh* (the human attempt to understand Syariah) issues. More specifically, *fiqh*, in the director's understanding, is the code of conduct from the Koran and Hadith based on God's laws that determine what is *wajib* (mandatory), halal (acceptable), haram (prohibited and sinful), *sunat* (encouraged), *makruh* (discouraged), and *mubah* (neutral).

In the eyes of the director, all these issues seem to have taken on increased actuality in the context of the global financial crisis and overconsumption of limited natural/man-made resources that are unevenly distributed in a world characterized by immorality and greed. She stresses that the core values and objectives of IHRAM build on the compatibility of science and technology on the one hand and Islamic knowledge on the other. This combination will create an integrated "holistic mainstream knowledge" for the *ummah* and produce future responsible Muslim leaders who will serve all alike. She reasons that science, technology, and Islamic values meet in the education of BAs, MAs, and PhDs with critical knowledge generated in IHRAM's brand-new laboratory that makes use of haram detection technology and techniques to locate alcohol, pork, and "minerals contamination such as lead and mercury" in food and drink. Thus, the research in IHRAM and its laboratory also focuses on broader issues or inscriptions as it were such as health and hygiene, contaminants, heavy metals, cholesterol, and edible products, which can cause allergies. The director reasons that fraud through deliberate adulteration of high-quality food ingredients with inferior, cheap, or harmful substances is also haram and thus not necessarily only related to Muslims.

This type of research has been undertaken at the Universiti Putra Malaysia for some years, but now USIM and IHRAM are also involved. Traceability is a key issue in much of this research, and as halal proliferates, more and more areas are subsumed under IHRAMs expertise. Another research focus is on food texture—for example creating "fluffy" textures in particular kinds of foods. Foods such as cakes, confectionaries, and ice cream are avoiding haram gelatin by substituting this with halal alternatives. To do so, this research carefully explores amino acid, fat, starch, and protein in food and drink processing, as well as in particular processes such as emulsion.

The development and refinement of plant gel, which can substitute animal-based gelatin, is a central issue in much of this research that moves beyond the stable taxonomy of halal and haram. In addition to halal and haram, doubtful substances should be avoided; that is, there is a gray area between the clearly lawful and the unlawful, expressed in the word *mashbooh*. The director elaborates on this issue, referring to a Hadith that defines the concept of *Mutasyabihat*—when halal and haram status is unclear or uncertain and that, thus, such "in-between" things should be avoided. In this way, differences in understanding, interpretation, and approaches result in complexity of context and handling when determining the halalness of a product causing confusion in the industry and for consumers and monitoring agencies alike. One of the key tasks of halal science and research is to reestablish halal and haram as a stable taxonomy based on Islamic science and knowledge, as well as the application of modern technology.

My fieldwork at USIM for the most part took place in laboratory facilities. I met BA, MA, and PhD students and lecturers, many of whom had come from other Muslim countries, doing research on halal. As a sign of IHRAM's international outlook, the institute receives visitors from various national and international laboratories, universities, and trade organizations wishing to learn about the halal research activities at USIM. When researchers explained about the technical details of their research it was mostly about the usage of particular types of technology and methods—for example, the use of gas chromatography–mass spectrometry using triple quadrupole and Fourier transform infrared spectroscopy (FTIR) that can detect the sensitivity of haram materials such as alcohol and lard. These materials can be traced as parts per million. This means, forensic-wise, that many irregularities in the food industry can be exposed.

Thus, technology and sensitive methods used in IHRAM and similar laboratories in Malaysia can measure very low detection limits of haram contaminants. Two issues stood out in all of this research: first, the possibility of using high-end laboratory equipment for halal traceability purposes, that is, tracing haram pollutants in a variety of forms in often minuscule quantities. The results, the director explains, can be used in court cases, as evidence by the Ministry of Health, for instance, and in companies that do not carry out routine quality control analysis on products. Companies that claim to produce halal but, in reality, do not cannot easily mislead consumers with the availability of the state-of-the-art laboratory equipment sensitive enough to detect adulteration at the molecular level. In several cases, not unlike that which we saw in the case of the food scandal in Indonesia, these exposures caused "regional anger" in Southeast Asian countries such as Malaysia, Indonesia, Brunei, and Singapore.

Another important issue for IHRAM and USIM is the usage of technology in Muslim education, that is, problem solving and improvement of the quality of life. In a wider perspective, the director reasons that technology is only valuable as long as it is backed by "Islamic knowledge," which must not be in conflict with the Koran and Sunna. Islamic knowledge covers all areas of research and education in USIM, and this is the case with halal.

The large bakery laboratory is full of new equipment and students are carrying out "quality tests" on bakery ingredients. As we move through the laboratories, the director explains that an essential aspect of this research is applying for funding to cover research, academic positions, education, and laboratory equipment. The technology and procedures for detecting DNA are expensive, and there are more affordable alternatives in existence for the screening of doubtful substances. For instance, a halal protein-based test kit for personal use is being developed, and this can reveal pork content within minutes. IHRAM is an example of how a rationalized Syariah-compliant science department inscribes Islamized knowledge into education, research, training, services, consultation, and laboratory analyses.

THE SECULAR IN TECHNOLOGY, TEXTS, AND FUNDING

During my research, in the context of the economic crisis, I often heard the argument that halal and Islamic finance could be seen as potential remedies against predatory global capitalism. From an "Islamic holistic perspective" the focus on halal production, trade, consumption and regulation was an antidote to such secular capitalism. Hence, in times of crisis, funding for a variety of forms of halal research, including Islamic finance, can prove attractive to the state as well as to investors that look for "pure" alternatives to runaway capitalism.

Laboratory equipment is also used for "secular" basic scientific research on a wide range of topics that are not necessarily related to halal, such as the development of a new form of yeast and sourdough from plantains as a biotech food ingredient. In a way, secular technology and techniques can be seen as a kind of inscription or knowledge that resists Islamization. This point evokes understandings of "the secular" that explore what people do with, and to, secular ideas and practices in different times and places (Asad 2003, 194).

Similarly, the textbooks used at USIM follow the secular syllabus based on the Ministry of Higher Education, Malaysian Quality Assurance

Framework Guidelines. In general, USIM stresses the history and philosophy of science from an Islamic viewpoint. The director explains to me that Islamic education does not "segregate" science, social science, and fundamental and applied science, in the way "secular science" does. Simultaneously, Islamic education allows for multidisciplinary approaches.

IHRAM had arranged a meeting including representatives from University Putra Malaysia and myself to look into possible cooperation between our three universities on halal. The scholars representing Universiti Putra Malaysia start out by explaining their backgrounds in research on Muslim consumption in Saudi Arabia. In Malaysia, Saudi Arabia and the Middle East, in general, are often seen as highly lucrative, but also undeveloped or underdeveloped markets in which halal is traditionally limited to ritually slaughtered meat and pork/alcohol avoidance. Researchers from USIM and University Putra Malaysia were interested in learning more about the European market for halal and increased access to this: what was the state of JAKIM certification in a country such as Denmark?

I explained that in much of Europe and in the welfare states of the Nordic countries, in particular, the state plays a major role in certifying organic products that are regulated in much the same way as halal (without the spiritual content halal can be said to signify). This means that in the European market the state plays an essential regulatory role between consumers and the market. Hence, state certification of halal, as is found in Malaysia, is unfamiliar to the state in Europe, but state involvement, per se, is not. In turn, we discussed tightened legislation on halal in Malaysia. Within the last couple of years, Malaysia has passed laws that enforce halal, and as such, forging logos, for example, is a now major criminal offense that carries fines and imprisonment. All these legislative measures, the scholars contend, aimed at protecting and promoting national halal as a brand of the state. Tightened halal legislation evokes Islamic technoscience as an important inscription in halal research because evidence of fraud from halal laboratories are now used in court cases.

One of the essential activities of research is drawing up (successful) applications for funding. Therefore, I discuss a proposal for funding that I was asked to comment on during my fieldwork. This research proposal was for funding from The Ministry of Higher Education in Malaysia, and it focused on developing halal traceability procedures for local Malaysian and export markets. In many ways it was similar to research proposals elsewhere. The proposal must have an identifiable Project Leader and in this case this person was from *Muamalat* (commercial and civil acts or dealings under Islamic law) Administration, Faculty of Economics and Muamalat, USIM.

The research area should be clearly defined. The "location of research" was outlined as being all regulatory bodies of "halal fatwa" in Malaysia, such as JAKIM and selected state Islamic councils. The proposed project would have a duration of two years and included seven other researchers, and these had to detail research projects that had been completed within the last three years: title of research, duration, and year commenced/ending. One of the involved researchers, for example, developed a database of halal chocolates and pastries in Malaysia. Moreover, they must include information about academic publications that had been published by the researchers for the last five years.

The research proposal explores the "legality" and "traceability" of producing and manufacturing halal products in order to inform Muslim consumers and to develop Malaysia as a halal hub. The focus was limited to processed halal food and beverages and focused on regulators and authorities building on a qualitative interview methodology. The output of the research was outlined to be a complete list of halal certified products including the mapping of the "flow of halal certification and its legality." A couple of research questions and hypotheses were included in the proposal including a literature review. The proposal argues the central task at hand was this: to study the development of halal, traceability, and *fatwa* management. The proposed study continues the state's policy to explore the current status of halal *fatwa* traceability. The problem statement summarizes the main approach: in halal business and networking, traceability of halal procedures are significant because the process of halal certification and integrity depends on the identification of ingredients, flows of processes, packaging, transportation, and financing of halal products. Regulatory agencies such as JAKIM and state religious councils together with stakeholder groups such as Muslim Consumers Association of Malaysia (PPIM) are to supervise this research. An important question in the proposal is to develop the integrity of JAKIM in issuing halal certification because "society always argue and question the credibility of JAKIM." Finally, the budget, including funding for one MA student, is detailed.

Islamic technoscience and modern halal are inseparable from some broader issues all related to the Malaysian state: bureaucratic workings; secular syllabuses required by the Ministry of Higher Education and the imperative question of attracting external funding for halal research. All these issues testify to the way in which halal research institutions have been rationalized and standardized in Malaysia. The more halal proliferates as a globalized religious market, the more Islamic technoscientific modes and methods of production and traceability become important for producers, traders, the state, researchers, and consumers. The increased focus on such methods to verify commodities as halal based on Islamic technoscience, and the Islamization of knowledge more broadly constantly expands the requirements to cover new types of commodities and practices. At the same time, the fusion of religion, science, and technology is inseparable from state support and funding. Modern forms of halal research in Malaysia challenges and reconfigures what are often considered separate secular realms of the state and politics, on one hand, and the intimacy of religious life and expression, on the other. A central theme is claims for authority through halal both articulated by the state and Islamic technoscience in the interfaces between expanding markets, the secular and the rights of Muslim consumers. Rationalized Islamic authorities are increasingly relying on science and scientific evidence in the regulation, innovation, and proliferation of halal. During my work with scientists in Muslim universities, Islamic organizations, certifiers, and companies, I gained insight that religion, science, and technology are fully compatible in the market for a wide range of halal products and services. My study from the Islamic Science University of Malaysia demonstrates how science and research, also in terms of allocating research funding, are a major focus area for the state, on one hand, and halal science institutions cooperate with companies in terms of product development, innovation, and testing, on the other hand. In the nationalized halal laboratory of Malaysia, scientists make use of haram-detection technology and techniques to locate alcohol and pork but also focus on broader issues of health, hygiene, and contaminants. This point shows that modern halal research is also inscribed with a whole range of "secular" issues. More and more types of technologies and techniques can verify and thus move beyond the symbolic approach to determining whether a substance is "religious." The food scandal in Indonesia helped condition a form of global capitalism in which halal standards and regulation became inseparable from Islamic technoscience.

NOTES

1. In Arabic *ihram* signifies a state of purity necessary to perform pilgrimage achieved through ritual cleansing and symbolized by a seamless two-piece white garment covering the upper and lower parts of the body for males and modest clothing for women.
2. *Straits Times* October 5, 2006: Sweet and halal.

BIBLIOGRAPHY

Aida, Azrina Azmi et al. 2005. "Analysis of Raw Meats and Fats of Pigs Using Polymerase Chain Reaction for Halal Authentication." *Meat Science* 69(1): 47–52.

Aida, Azrina Azmi et al. 2007. "Detection of Pig Derivatives in Food Products for Halal Authentication by Polymerase Chain Reaction-Restriction Fragment Length Polymorphism." *Journal of the Science of Food and Agriculture* 87(4): 569–572.

al-Attas, Syed Muhammad Naquib. 1989. *Islam and the Philosophy of Science*. Kuala Lumpur: International Institute of Islamic Thought and Civilization.

al-Attas, Syed Muhammad Naquib. 1995. *Prolegomena to the Metaphysics of Islam: An Exposition of the fundamental elements of the worldview of Islam*. Kuala Lumpur: International Institute of Islamic Thought and Civilization.

Asad, Talal. 2003. *Formations of the Secular: Christianity, Islam, Modernity*. Stanford, CA: Stanford University Press.

Atighetchi, Dariusch. 2007. *Islamic Bioethics: Problems and Perspectives*. New York: Springer.

Aziz, Aziz and Shamsul Amri Baharuddin. 2004. "The Religious, the Plural, the Secular and the Modern: A Brief Critical Survey on Islam in Malaysia." *Inter-Asia Cultural Studies* 5(3): 341–356.

Bayat, Asef. 2007. *Making Islam Democratic: Social Movements and the Post-Islamist Turn*. Stanford, CA: Stanford University Press.

Carsten, Janet. 2013. "'Searching for the Truth': Tracing the Moral Properties of Blood in Malaysian Clinical Pathology Labs." *Journal of the Royal Anthropological Institute* (N.S.): 130–148.

Fischer, Johan. 2011. *The Halal Frontier: Muslim Consumers in a Globalized Market*. New York: Palgrave Macmillan.

Furlow, Christopher A. 2009. "Malaysian Modernities: Cultural Politics and the Construction of Muslim Technoscientific Identities." *Anthropological Quarterly* 82(1): 197–228.

Geertz, Clifford. 1968. *Islam Observed. Religious Development in Morocco and Indonesia*. Chicago: University of Chicago Press.

Hamdy, Sherine. 2012. *Our Bodies Belong to God: Organ Transplants, Islam, and the Struggle for Human Dignity in Egypt*. Berkeley, CA and London: University of California Press.

Hashim, Puziah (Ed) et al. 2009. *Proceedings of the 3rd IMT-GT International Symposium on Halal Science and Management*. Serdang: Universiti Putra Malaysia.

Hoodbhoy, Pervez. 1991. *Islam and Science: Religious Orthodoxy and the Struggle for Rationality*. London: Zed.

Iqbal, M. (Ed) (2012). *Islam and Science: Historic and Contemporary Perspectives*. Farnham: Ashgate.

Latour, Bruno and Woolgar, Steve. 1979. *Laboratory Life: The Social Construction of Scientific Facts*. Beverly Hills, CA and London: Sage.

Liow, Joseph C. 2009. *Piety and Politics: Islamism in Contemporary Malaysia*. Oxford: Oxford University Press.

Lotfalian, Mazyar. 2004. *Islam, Technoscientific Identities, and the Culture of Curiosity*. Lanham: University Press of America.

Mohamad, Maznah. 2010. "The Ascendance of Bureaucratic Islam and the Secularization of the Sharia in Malaysia." *Pacific Affairs* 83(3): 505–524.

Mrázek, Rudolf. 2002. *Engineers of Happy Land: Technology and Nationalism in a Colony*. Princeton, NJ: Princeton University Press.

Ong, Aihwa. 2010. "Introduction: An analytics of biotechnology and ethic at multiple scales." In *Asian Biotech: Ethics and Communities of Fate*, edited by Aihwa Ong, 1–54. Durham and London: Duke University Press.

Peletz, Michael G. 2002. *Islamic Modern: Religious Courts and Cultural Politics in Malaysia*. Princeton, NJ: Princeton University Press.

Prakash, Gyan. 1999. *Another Reason: Science and the Imagination of Modern India*. Princeton, NJ: Princeton University Press.

Sloane-White, P. 2011. "Working in the Islamic Economy: Sharia-ization and the Malaysian Workplace." SOJOURN: *Journal of Social Issues in Southeast Asia* 26(2): 304–334.

5 Halal Activism

On June 2, 2014, BBC reported that JAKIM declared Cadbury chocolate free from pork DNA. Earlier government tests on two Cadbury products had suggested they might not have been suitable for Muslims. Persatuan Pengguna Islam Malaysia or in English the Muslim Consumers Association of Malaysia (PPIM) said it would maintain its call for a boycott of Cadbury chocolate and the boycott would only be lifted should the earlier health ministry tests be acknowledged as wrong (http://www.bbc.com/news/business-27663857). This incident shows that Islamic technoscience is central to modern halal understandings and practices, but it also highlights the role of Muslim consumer activism, and to this point I now turn.

I am in the SembangSembang Café[1] in The Mall in central Kuala Lumpur. The Mall is comparable to the multitude of other shopping malls in Kuala Lumpur, but it also stands out by housing the SembangSembang Café. This café is run by PPIM, an organization that protects the interests of Muslim consumers and entrepreneurs. The café provides shelf space for PPIM members' (halal) products, and PPIM and its café are an essential space for Malay Muslim entrepreneurial networking. Thus, this chapter continues my exploration of halal networking started in Chapter 2 with a specific focus on halal activism.

This chapter examines how halal activists in Malaysia try to expand halal requirements to cover more and more products and processes and lobby for the state to incorporate these requirements into halal production, trade, consumption, and standardization. An important question here is how these activists work in the interface zones between new forms of Islamic revivalism, the ethnicized state, and Muslim consumer culture, and protection. Networking is an important skill practiced in and between these interface zones. Halal activism has a long history in Malaysia, as we have already seen, and it is a driving force behind the way in which halal has developed into a global assemblage, but empirically this is not well understood. I show that national halal standardization hinges on a particular form of activist halal classification.

I am discussing halal with PPIM's executive secretary and a friend of mine, the Malay entrepreneur Altaf, whom I have known from halal network events since 2006. It is through this entrepreneur that I have come into contact with the PPIM, and she is why I was in the SembangSembang Café that day. Both Altaf and the PPIM executive secretary are part of the halal network, and the café plays an important role in the way in which this activist and entrepreneurial networking is practiced. The networking and activities of PPIM and its members that take place in the café do not directly involve the state, but PPIM's role is essential to understanding the proliferation of halal in Malaysia and beyond: ways in which Malay Muslim interest groups network and protect Malay Muslim rights through promoting Muslim products and businesses, and halal in particular. In other words, groups such as PPIM and its network constantly push for increased Muslim consumer protection and rights. In the eyes of these groups, the state is unable or reluctant to deliver enough support for these demands.

In Singapore by comparison, modern *dakwah* or Muslim activist groups do not to the same extent place great emphasis on halal vis-à-vis the state. However, Malay Muslim interest groups, such as SMCC, try to promote halal, but such interest organizations are regulated by the Chinese-dominated state that uses SMCC in an instrumental way in order to handle halal properly.

Before engaging in the ethnography, I consider the relationship between the Malaysian state and Malay Muslim interest groups. In Chapter 1 I briefly discussed the *dakwah* group Darul Arqam, or the House of Arqam, that was an Islamic group whose believers sought to follow the behavior of the Prophet Muhammad in everyday life. Arqam cultivated and marketed an Islamic vision of Malay independence and prosperity through the production of a wide range of halal food products. Ideally, this vision was to ensure the group full independence from any kind of non-Muslim control. Arqam successfully promoted this vision of communal self-sufficiency, and their halal goods were traded throughout peninsular Malaysia. However, the state effectively curbed Arqam as the vanguard of halalization, nationalized the proliferation of halal, and concentrated its certification in the realm of the state where it has remained. However, there are still many alternative halal logos in existence in Malaysia. As we shall see, many of these can be found in the SembangSembang Café, and ironically they are a product of halal activism that pushes for the support of and legal protection of national halal in Malaysia.

To preempt *dakwah* groups such as Darul Arqam and Parti Islam SeMalaysia (PAS), the state started to "nationalize" Islam, as we have seen earlier, and Malaysian Islam may be the most monolithic and most state regulated in the Muslim world. Ever since foundation of the UNMO, the party has insisted on the inescapable bonds among nation, state, Islam, and Malayness, on one hand, and an ideology built on Malay privileges and domination on the other. These tendencies are reinforced by Malay Muslim interest groups that push for Malay rights and the promotion, as well as tighter regulation, of halal.

The New Economic Policy (NEP) has brought about a marked propensity of the *bumiputera* electorate to lean heavily towards the state for solutions to their problems (Gomez 1994, 290). In line with this, Malay Muslim consumer groups and activists constantly push for support and privileges and the proliferation of halal reinforces this tendency. These groups have to a large extent replaced, reformed, professionalized, and modernized traditional *dakwah* thinking and practice in the field of proper Islamic consumption (Fischer 2007, 2008). Islamic consumption in Malaysia has been subjected to state and business intervention in the form of extensive market research and the political institutionalization of consumption, for example the setting up of the Ministry of Domestic Trade and Consumer Affairs in 1990. Clearly, this is a sign of the state's bid to protect the entitlements of Malay(sian) consumers against what the state and consumers increasingly see as confusing, globalized, and excessive consumer culture. Consumers' trust in and dependence on the state as an honest broker in consumption legitimates state intervention regarding the right ways to shop as well as guidance in terms of public debates about value. However, in multiethnic Malaysia the state cannot solely promote and protect Malay Muslim consumer interests and this is why Muslim consumer organizations such as PPIM and others play a major role in safeguarding the rights of Malays. I now turn to a discussion of three activist organizations, namely, KasehDia, Yayasan Ekonomi Sejagat (Foundation for Global Economics), and PPIM that all each in their own way work in the interface zones between Islam, standards, and technoscience to promote halal as a global assemblage.

KASEHDIA: COMMERCIAL ACTIVISM

KasehDia was formed in 1999 as a communication and consulting company stressing Islamic values. The company engages in publication, events, branding, and consultancy. Arguably, it is the world's first company of its kind in the halal industry: KasehDia is the creator and organizer of the World Halal Forum (WHF), and many of the halal network events discussed earlier. Being the organizer of WHF KasehDia is central to the way in which the Malaysian halal network is practiced at major halal events or stages where the corporate sector, academia, nongovernmental organizations (NGOs), Islamic organizations, halal certifiers, and governments from around the world convene. At WHF 2010 KasehDia's founder, Jumaatun Azmi, specifically addressed the confusion caused among companies and certifying bodies by the friction between the JAKIM and the HDC. She called for a strong "masterplan" and "leadership" applicable to all stakeholders in the industry to address the inability of government agencies to work together. More specifically, she took comfort in the move to corporatize HDC as an agency under the Ministry of International Trade and Industry (MITI) to prepare and implement an action plan for the development of the Halal Act. This move would hopefully ensure "proper coordination" when all the "key" agencies under MITI could be "streamlined."

The company publishes the *Guide to Good Eating* book series by Jumaatun Azmi, which are handbooks to halal food in Kuala Lumpur, Thailand, Australia, and London. The multiplicity and ambiguity involved in the processes of halal production, certification, marketing, and consumption is addressed in the handbook *Halal Food: A Guide to Good Eating—Kuala Lumpur* (Azmi 2003). In the book, more than a hundred restaurants, takeaway counters, and cafés in Kuala Lumpur are listed and reviewed. Much more than strictly traditional halal requirements are involved in guiding Muslim consumers: the spatial context (atmosphere/feel/ambience) of food consumption as practice may be just as significant as the intrinsic qualities of the food and its ingredients. The various establishments are classified according to their halalness, for example, whether alcohol is sold or food is produced and served by Muslims or non-Muslims. In the introduction the authors explicitly state that they are referring to and relying on the official channels of Malaysian halal certification and not on their personal preferences (Azmi 2003, IX). All of this is expressive of new formations of meta-industries that are beyond the strictly religious focus on halal/haram dichotomies and halal certification, but instead target the marketing, pluralization, and promotion of halal as a brand or logo of the Malaysian state.

KasehDia also publishes *The Halal Journal: Business, Lifestyle, Trends.* In May 2006, I met the director of KasehDia at the luxurious Palace of the Golden Horses outside Kuala Lumpur, where he was giving a talk on the activities of KasehDia. The director argues that the Malaysian state's focus on halal is finally being acknowledged by "industry giants" confirming their positions in the halal market, with Nestlé, Tesco (a UK-based international grocery and merchandising retail chain). *The Halal Journal* (2006, 25) reported that in June 2006, Tesco, one of the world's leading inter-national retailers, announced that it would be sourcing 1 billion Ringgit of certified halal products over the next five years to service selected UK stores. He explained that halal in Malaysia was not only about state certification but also that halal was now understood as a "business" and had become "value-added marketing" on products. Now, producers suddenly saw themselves as an industry or network in their own right that could realize the global potential of halal. Malaysia is set apart, as the director explained, by the "political goodwill" behind the promotion of Malaysia's "tradition" of halal on a global scale, that is, a type of network in which the state and companies have come together.

During my research I have been in contact with KasehDia many times; for example, KasehDia representatives have attended a talk I gave at University Kebangsaan Malaysia or in English the Malaysian National University in 2010. That same year during fieldwork in Malaysia I visited KasehDia in Kuala Lumpur. The first of the two representatives I met with came from Australia. He has a technical background and holds a BA in environmental management with as specialization in technology foresighting. Previously, he worked with marketing for research and development companies and SIRIM. The other representative present is a Malay man that is educated in international business at Nottingham University, Malaysia Campus. He worked for a transnational accountancy firm with special emphasis on advisory corporate governance.

In 2010 KasehDia had grown to have more than 30 employees since its founding by Jumaatun Azmi in 1999. Her main motivation for starting KasehDia was dissatisfaction with the availability of halal in Australia and elsewhere and a more general wish to expand the market for Islamic products. Thus, what started as a kind of consumer activism transformed into entrepreneurship and close cooperation with the state. In 2004, KasehDia started Malaysia International Halal Showcase (MIHAS) and subsequently *The Halal Journal*, the Guide to Good Eating book series, as well as a more general focus on communication, products, values, events, and research based on an Islamic perspective.

The majority of the staff are Muslim while two senior members are not. Even if this is not central to the organization, the representatives call this a "sensitivity issue." The main philosophy is that activities have to be based on "good Islamic values," and it is often an advantage that Muslim employees deal with Muslim customers. Similarly, the representatives find that hiring Muslim employees with "Syariah knowledge" is an advantage in the everyday working life of KasehDia. The company also does consulting in Singapore, Thailand, and in Indonesia in connection with the palm oil industry, for example. KasehDia is not financially supported by the Malaysian state, but it carries out a variety of services for state institutions; that is, the company is not formally government-linked.

KasehDia also undertakes training of employees and the company for example arranged a workshop for Néstle on halal awareness. As we have seen, the general tendency is that the more halal proliferates, the more the need to outsource areas such as training becomes imminent. KasehDia undertakes such training for companies that wish to "penetrate" the European Union (EU), the Middle East, and other markets and "provides support" for JAKIM and HDC. KasehDia employees have not themselves received halal training by JAKIM or HDC, and this point reflects the broader tendency that halal training was not mandatory in Malaysia in 2010. The representatives stress that it is important for companies to build relationships with JAKIM and HDC trainers/auditors and that training plays an important role in this respect. This is especially important as regulation in the form of inspections and audits to some extent can be premised on the "interpretation" of the inspector/auditor. As we saw in the case of training in

Singapore, the teacher/trainer can also be inspector/auditor and building personal relationships is important in this respect. KasehDia cannot issue certificates of participation in training in contradistinction to JAKIM/HDC, so this type of "outsourced" training is not standardized or certified by the state.

An important question stood out during my discussions with the KasehDia representatives, namely, that "[i]f you're Muslim you don't really need halal certification"; that is, as long as halal is handled by Muslims it is seen to be proper in itself. However, in a globalized market non-Muslims will always be involved somehow, and this is where halal regulation comes in, and especially the tightening of regulation in the form of the Halal Act. The dilemma is that in Malaysia Muslims are conventionally seen to embody proper halal handling, skills, or qualifications. This, however, is changing as halal increasingly is regulated and legally enforced. Thus, individualized Malay Muslim classifications of halal are being subjected to more formally and legally backed forms of standardization.

One of the KasehDia representatives wrote an article in *The Halal Journal* on the need for tightened legislation that was to become the Halal Act. This piece of legislation would centralize certification procedures with the Malaysian state to avoid a mix of all kinds of certifications. Hopefully, the Halal Act would remove the confusion caused by the struggle over authority between JAKIM and HDC. In the eyes of the KasehDia representatives, JAKIM is the traditional authority in halal regulation in Malaysia that embodies the Islamic ethos whereas HDC was supposed to be the modern coordination body that unfortunately "tried to do too much and not lived up to what they claimed they would do." In any case, HDC would function as a "reference center" in the future halal market in Malaysia.

During my fieldwork in 2010 the Halal Act was yet to be passed, and the KasehDia representatives speculated about the exact contents of the act and how this would affect the relationship between halal markets and regulatory institutions, halal zones, as it were, and KasehDia's role in this. Representatives agreed that the Halal Act was long overdue and that "it could only be a good thing" when considering the state of confusion of the global and local markets for halal. They hoped for increased halal "accreditation" by the Malaysian state so that more halal certification bodies, based on Malaysian International Organization for Standardization (ISO) halal standards, would be recognized by the Malaysian state. Many of the expectations to tightened halal regulation in AMLA in Singapore had been fulfilled and the representatives wished that similar developments would follow in Malaysia. However, there was concern that, with such tightened legislation in the future form it would take, JAKIM would be "overloaded" and thus had to outsource regulation and inspections/audits, which would again cause confusion. For example, many restaurants run by Muslims were not halal certified, and if they were to be so as part of the Halal Act this would necessitate that a lot of resources were put into regulating this. One of the critiques of JAKIM coming from companies KasehDia works with was that the certification procedure was too long, and subsequently this was cut down from three months to one month. In the wake of tightened legislation and regulation, the representatives feared that it would be difficult to maintain such efficiency in the future. Hence, one thing is the need for tightened legislation and regulation and quite another matter is allocating sufficient resources for enforcing this.

KasehDia is a good example of a halal organization that is both a company and an interest group simultaneously. The organization cooperates with the state while pushing this same state to proliferate and regulate halal stringently. Simultaneously, the company offers consultancy services in Malaysia and elsewhere. KasehDia has been instrumental in establishing a halal network in Malaysia and beyond.

YES:[2] STATE ACTIVISM

YES is a nonprofit organization established in 2006 under the Companies Act of 1965 that regulates the behavior of companies in Malaysia. According to YES (n.d) the organization is entrusted with implementing economic development programs based on Halalan-Toyyiban Principles, that is, halal and pure principles. However, these principles are not enough. The Halalan-Toyyiban Program serves as a platform for the socioeconomic development of the community and it uses Halal-Toyyiban standards as the base to enhance the capacity and capability of participants in the food production and product handling areas. Enhanced capacity and capability are translated into local and global "trade facilitation" as a network for producers, buyers, consumers, and other related parties in the halal food industry. YES facilitates the collaboration and self-reliance of the *ummah* to "stimulate, inculcate, promote, motivate and coordinate social economic and economic development."

The Koran and Hadith (traditions concerning the life and works of the Prophet Muhammad) "provide the main source of reference and enabler to achieve synergy and consistency." Compared to KasehDia, YES shares more of the traditional aims of *dakwah*, that is, the aim on fusing Islamic, political, social, and economic issues to ensure Malay Muslim rights. Another difference is that while KasehDia also employs non-Muslims YES is overwhelmingly a Malay Muslim organization. Although YES formally is set up by the state, it has the status of a company and this multiplicity allows it to articulate strong Malay Muslim views that are not directly coming from the state. Partners and sponsors of YES are the Malaysian state, the Malaysian Islamic Chamber of Commerce, the Muslim Consumers Association of Malaysia, and the Research Institute of Standards in Islam, as well as various NGOs, government-linked companies (GLCs), and financial institutions.

The woman entrepreneur, Altaf, put me in contact with YES. I first met with a leading representative of YES at the organization's headquarters in the lush greenery of Bukit Persekutuan[3] at the outskirts of Kuala Lumpur. The taxi driver jokingly told me that Bukit Persekutuan is also called Bukit Tunku because Malaysia's first prime minister Tunku Abdul Rahman's house was located here, and more generally this is an elite residential area. The YES representative knew about my work on halal and was most accommodating during my extended period of fieldwork. He was educated as an architectural engineer in the US in the 1980s and now worked with project management for companies such as YES. At the same time, he sat on several JAKIM committees and other committees, for example working on certification authority and "who gets halal certified and not." The YES representative was also involved in the work of PPIM and vice versa. He has been involved in Muslim consumer activism since the 1980s and has "pushed" for standards since that time.

In the eyes of YES, the formulation and passing of the Halal Act had been an essential issue for a long time and he was confident that it would be passed. The purpose of the Halal Act was to "position" Malaysia in the global halal trade. Historically, the Malaysian background for this was distrust by Muslim consumers prompting the state to regulate halal from the 1980s onward. However, to the YES representative Malaysia was still caught in the trap of excessive focus on individual and group consumer sensitivities that blocked Malaysian halal for "going global." Lobbying for the Halal Act had been going on for decades, and now everyone realized that the Trade Description Act was no longer enough to regulate halal national and globally. "More law and standards," the YES representative explained to me, were needed to move Malaysian halal to a "mandatory" level. In practice, all Islamic councils in Malaysian states had made a federal agreement that involved to "synchronize, standardize a uniform logo." This process was based on MS 1500 (General Guidelines on the Production, Preparation, Handling, and Storage of Halal Foods) as well as other types of standards that had been launched recently.

To YES, halal had yet to "deliver the desired result for Muslims and Muslim entrepreneurs" such as Altaf. To do so, legal backing, focused branding, and "moving beyond products towards larger issues of sustainability and environment" in not only Malaysia but also globally were crucial. Moreover, halal is much more than a religious injunction it also has to do with dietary requirements, the environment, hygiene, organic production, and animal welfare in the modern world, the YES representative asserted. This is an important issue because one of YES's aims is to expand halal into larger global issues and away from the narrow interests of individual Malay Muslim interests. It was undesirable that the halal industry was "controlled" by non-Muslims and this industry should be "participative." An expected 8,000 people were needed in the halal industry to expand halal into these new fields meaning that the current number of 200 to 250 inspectors would have to be vastly expanded. However, the government, JAKIM, and HDC did not currently have the capacity to train so many inspectors.

The novel and much more ambitious approach to halal would take halal "beyond Syariah standards" and this approach was shared by PPIM, as we shall see. In all this the passing of the Halal Act was essential and the legal backing for setting up a Muslim committee in non-Muslim companies would ensure adherence to new standards in halal production and handling. In sum, the new initiatives underway would "move the halal paradigm to be as broad as possible." Then, before the law was passed, there was no formal JAKIM requirement to display a halal logo in Malaysian restaurants and corporations, for example. Ideally, certification should be applied systematically "all along the supply chain beyond product certification." The YES representative explained that even the muftis in the many Malaysian states, as well as the Islamic opposition party Parti Islam SeMalaysia (PAS) supported the halal vision, and in this way the whole Malaysian halal project had become a national one: "The whole country is now united in global halal trade backed by consolidated state authority," the YES representative argued.

The political backing for halal in Malaysia had undergone a series of phases: Mahathir's preemption of *dakwah* through consumer protection often focused on individual states, Badawi's halal vision of Malaysia was that the country become a halal hub (even if this perspective was not clearly defined), and the current administration led by Prime Minister Najib continued these initiatives but also focused on a strong local market in Malaysia for the country to participate in the global market for halal. Reforms under Prime Minister Badawi, who succeeded Mahathir and was in office from 2003 to 2009, focused on nurturing smaller *bumiputera* enterprises. This included encouragement of competitive advantage in Malaysian economy by developing niche markets for halal and Islamic products through a vendor system in which companies were tied to government-linked companies (GLCs), companies controlled by the government, and multinationals such as Carrefour and Tesco (Gomez 2012, 68).

Halal had become part of the New Economic Model—an economic plan Najib launched in March 2010 just as my fieldwork was starting. The New Economic Model aimed at doubling the per capita income in Malaysia by 2020 and to move away from affirmative action based on Malay Muslim ethnicity toward a more competitive and investor friendly market. The New Economic Model, thus, framed halal as more "global," "standardized," and "innovative" lifting it out of being limited to questions of local products and consumer protection. The current government had demonstrated its commitment to halal by allocating large sums for this purpose. Prime Minister Najib seemed to be focused on these initiatives and this was critical to realize the halal vision.

The controversy between HDC and JAKIM was an important question for YES. Now that JAKIM was the authority in charge the task at hand was to systematize the endorsement of halal certification bodies globally. "HDC did not deliver, flip-flop," he explained. The uncertainty arising from this controversy undermined Malaysian halal authority and competitive performance among certifiers in Indonesia, Singapore, and Thailand. In short, the political project of promoting halal in Malaysia was "paralyzed."

When we discussed if halal was "boundless," that is, should crockery for example ideally be halal certified, YES's position was clear: there is no limit to halal, and it could and should expand into all areas of business, but also a sustained environment and business in contradistinction to the immoral ways of the West that had generated the current economic crisis affecting the whole globe. Hence, it was only a matter of time before crockery required certification adhering to the defined Halalan-Toyyiban Principles of YES, that is, halal and pure principles in the "entire supply chain where standards mean a sustainable situation and certification is a way of life." That would, for example, remove heavy metal from food products. Several production standards stipulate that Muslims must be involved in production, but of course in many cases halal cannot be produced by Muslims alone.

We also discussed the political project of setting up halal parks across Malaysia and beyond. Since 1997 the representative was a consultant to federal marketing agencies entrusted to develop a national food terminal for food security. He was involved in formulating the idea to set up halal parks in the first place, but this plan was "hijacked" by developers that did not fully comprehend this vision and thus could not translate it into practice—to these developers halal parks were merely "real estate." Halal parks in Malaysia, he summarized, "never got off the ground." The only noticeable success was the Halal Park in Pulau Indah that was "picked up by the HDC" in an unfocused way.

In sum, YES aims at promoting and expanding halal into as many products and services as possible, that is, taking halal to a "mandatory" and "global" level, as it were. During my fieldwork with YES I was introduced to the executive secretary of PPIM, which runs the SembangSembang Café, and to the work of PPIM I now turn.

PPIM: MUSLIM CONSUMER ACTIVISM

PPIM focuses on business development and social responsibility but also works to assist small and medium-sized Muslim enterprises that do not have the working capital required to have their products placed on shelves of supermarkets and hypermarkets. Moreover, the SembangSembang Café provides shelf space for PPIM members' products free of charge. PPIM also consults with members on their goals and ways to actively promote products and business. The SembangSembang Café is used as a focal point "to encourage Muslim Consumers to support Muslim businesses as well as to actively promote products which are certified halal." Second, the café offers "a range of business and personal enhancement classes and lectures" on themes such as strategic partnerships for women, in particular, that provide the resources for the PPIM's members to secure the finances they require to start businesses. An event coordinator is responsible for this training and several classes consisting of women are to graduate from this program. Third, networking and business facilitation are essential for PPIM. The organization argues that many people come to the café to meet friends, potential business partners, or "those who can nexus business with opportunities!" (http://sembangcafeppim.blogspot.dk/p/aktiviti.html).

Besides PPIM and its executive secretary's involvement in halal, the organization has been active in calling for boycotts of Coca-Cola in 2002, among other similar calls to boycott. As we saw in Chapter 1, PPIM's executive secretary called on authorities to conduct scientific tests on the food seasoning products from Ajinomoto to confirm products were actually halal, and this was also the case with Cadbury. The call to boycott Coca-Cola post 9/11 under the heading "Our program will hurt Coca-Cola" was a protest against American interference in Muslim affairs. PPIM's executive secretary said, "The boycott is in response to Western interference in the internal affairs of Muslim countries in the guise of fighting terrorism" (http://news.bbc.co.uk/2/hi/asia-pacific/2542517.stm). In spite of these calls to boycott Coca-Cola and similar products, Coca-Cola is of course widely available in Malaysia (Figure 5.1).

Figure 5.1 JAKIM halal-certified Coca-Cola on the shelf in a supermarket in central Kuala Lumpur

In a broader perspective, much current anticonsumerist and antiglobalization discourse identifies boycotting as an immensely powerful force. Religious and secular activists alike promote consumer boycotts as a type of practiced resistance that promises to break US economic, military, and cultural hegemony. I have explored the political and cultural effects of the Malaysian Islamic opposition's call to boycott US goods in Malaysia in the wake of 9/11 (Fischer 2007). This issue evokes a wide range of contestations and paradoxes in the everyday lives of Malay Muslim middle-class families. Most of all, the boycott confronts divergent Malay middle-class groups with the problem of how to translate intentionality into practice. However, parallel to these calls for boycotts are calls to buycotts that encourage Muslim consumers to buy locally manufactured and state-certified halal products for example.

In Malaysia, Coca-Cola is fully halal certified by JAKIM. On Coca-Cola's Malaysian website (www.coke.com.my) the company deals with a plethora of rumors about its products—for example, denying constant rumors that its beverages contain alcohol and "ingredients extracted from the stomachs of pigs. . . . All our soft drinks are non-alcoholic and they don't contain any ingredients from mammals and poultry." As early as 1998, PPIM pushed for a halal standard because the organization was concerned with the religious principles in management practices. It was timely for such a standard to be developed because Muslims worldwide had been dependent on standards set by the West, which might not necessarily comply with Islamic teachings, the executive secretary explains. The times I met with PPIM's executive secretary in the SembangSembang Café in the Mall in central Kuala Lumpur, we discussed many of the preceding issues. As we have seen, the café provides shelf space for PPIM members' (halal) products, and PPIM and its café is an essential space for Malay Muslim entrepreneurial networking.

In May 2010 I discussed halal with Altaf and PPIM's executive secretary in the SembangSembang Café. Altaf explained to me that even if she was not very strict about halal in her personal life, halal was extremely important in contemporary Malaysia with respect to the state and companies and in the eyes of consumer groups such as PPIM, and this was the reason we were there that day. In the SembangSembang Café an abundance of material on Islamic and current topics of interest to Muslims, including courses and training, are on display and the products on the shelves are produced by Muslims and aimed at a Muslim audience. Two issues were central in our discussions: the need for and expectations to tightened halal laws and the way in which halal is inseparable from Malay rights in Malaysia.

Networking is ubiquitous in the café: the executive secretary's phone constantly rings and texts are received, and many people ask his advice on issues related to the main functions of the café—the business interests of Malay Muslims. Small groups of members sit around the café with mobile phones and laptops and used the free Wi-Fi connection. The executive secretary explains to me that he has been involved in the Muslim consumer movement for more than 30 years. Similar to what we saw earlier in the case of boycotting, PPIM encouraged JAKIM to "withdraw" halal logos of Coca-Cola, Starbucks, and Colgate "because of support of the Zionist government, illegal money, oppression, but JAKIM will not do it." This is an example of the way in which PPIM in the interface zones between Islam and regulation evokes halal to pressure the government to acknowledge that halal is also premised on global questions such as the oppression of Muslims. These points are symptomatic of the "bigger picture" these activist groups promote against a more reluctant and pragmatic state that considers diplomatic relations and "moderate Islam" essential.

The executive secretary explains to me that the reason to form PPIM in the first place was to establish a platform for addressing "unfair treatment" of Muslims and their culture. PPIM has supported a "clear direction" in Malaysian halal for many years both with the government and with "Muslim consumers uncritically feeding the system." An important PPIM critique of the state in Malaysia is that this is not sufficiently involved in acknowledging and supporting Muslim consumption and halal. Hence, because of lack of state support, Muslims are still "backward" in terms of entrepreneurial possibilities—in the eyes of PPIM, it is unsatisfactory that so little of halal production, trade, and regulation on a global scale and in Malaysia is in "Muslim hands," and PPIM's work aims at addressing exactly this aspect. However, the last 500 years of Western and colonial oppression has instilled a kind of inferiority in many Muslims, and this is not easily changed.

The main objective is no longer to provide proper halal food to Muslims, this objective has, to a large extent, been met in Malaysia, but to make Muslims see that halal is an "asset" similar to kosher that should be on Muslim hands. PPIM works "actively and proactively" toward these aims, for instance by setting up the SembangSembang Café in which all products and activities contribute toward this aim. Ideally, 90 percent of employees in the halal industry should be Muslim. Right now, big companies operating in Malaysia often would not even let their Muslim employees go for Friday prayer.

The SembangSembang Café is not directly financially supported by the Malaysian state but through Muslim companies and individual members' support. Conversely, the products displayed support Muslims and Muslim interests in Malaysia, the executive secretary explained. He made clear that the organization has been "pushing" for the Halal Act for a long time and that it was long overdue. This law would also once and for all demonstrate that halal was being regulated by JAKIM as the central state institution in Malaysia erasing the confusion and uncertainty following in the wake of the JAKIM–HDC controversies.

The executive secretary was quite "liberal" when it came to the plethora of halal logos to be found on the products on the shelves of the Sembang-Sembang Café. He used the word *liberal* when referring to Prime Minister

Badawi's approach to halal. The prime minister would eat anywhere as long as the food was halal and, in the eyes of the executive secretary, disregard the many larger issues involved in halal such as Muslim ownership and interests. This liberal approach undermined the Malaysian halal "territory" and allowed foreign interests to dominate the halal industry. The government at the time, under Prime Minister Najib, however, was willing to correct some of the errors of the past and was focused in its approach to regulating halal, and the Halal Act that was hopefully passed as soon as possible was a testimony to that.

At SembangSembang, I found a wide variety of halal and "Muslim" logos on products. I examined some of the products found on the shelves of SembangSembang and discussed with PPIM's executive secretary. The first product found in the café is Fortune Minuman Coco A+ (Figure 5.2). It is a coco powder to be mixed with milk or water. The bag displays four logos. The first logo from the left is a "Muslim Product" and "Usahawan (literally, entrepreneur) Muslim" logo with no identifiable organization/certifier behind it. It is the first time the executive secretary notices this logo. The second from the left says UsahaOne (literally, one effort), but it is not clear what this logo signifies, and the executive secretary guesses this has to do with "green" production, but it is difficult to guess when there is no identifiable certifier or organization shown. Next is a "Buatan Malaysia" or

Figure 5.2 Logos found on Fortune Minuman Coco A+

"Made in Malaysia" logo. Then there is an IMP (Islamic Manufacturing Practice) logo, but neither the executive secretary nor the researcher is sure what the logo or the organization behind it, more specifically, represents. The executive secretary argues that even when the Halal Act is passed these "Islamic" logos may be placed on products and elsewhere because most of them reflect Muslim entrepreneurial interests and "wholesomeness" more generally, and they do not directly interfere with state halal regulation. Last, JAKIM's logo is on display. It is, however, an older version that includes "H–2," a code that signifies that the product is certified in a particular Malaysian state, Kedah, by the Islamic Council of Kedah. In addition, there is a "Visit Kedah. Heritage, Nature, and Adventure" advertisement on the front of the pack that displays pictures of a traditional Malay house (heritage), a fishing village (nature), and rafting (adventure). This advertisement is part of the "Visit Malaysia" tourist campaign. Moreover, a "1 Malaysia best" logo showing a picture of the Petronas Towers and Suria Kuala Lumpur City Centre, once arguably the highest buildings in the world with Kuala Lumpur's most luxurious mall below them, accompanies the Kedah advertisement on the front of the pack.

We then look at a Tunjuk Langit Swietenia Body Scrub made from the mahogany fruit that is also literally called sky fruit. Logos from left to right include Buatan Malaysia, Good Manufacturing Practice Compliance, PPIM's logo, the JAKIM logo, and a round yellow logo with leaves and a trademark that I could not identify. Another product by the same company is "health capsules" containing the same fruit, but this only carries the PPIM and JAKIM logos. PPIM's logo, the executive secretary explains to me, signifies that "you're from our community," and the JAKIM logo that the product if properly certified by the state. More generally, an increasing number of health products are halal certified.

We looked at a jar of Mango Jam. Logos top to bottom are "Buatan Malaysia," JAKIM H–2 Kedah (which will be removed in the future when halal cannot be certified by individual Islamic councils in individual states) and an MADA Premium Product logo that we could not identify. Then we looked at a glass of Halagel Extra Virgin Olive Oil capsules, marketed as a health supplement. The outer shell of each Halagel Softgel is made from Halagel Gelatin certified as halal by JAKIM. Halagel is a company that since 1997 has imported and distributed halal food and pharmaceutical grade gelatin and empty hard gelatin capsules for Malaysia and the Southeast Asian markets. The company produces industrial products (Halagel® Pharmaceutical Gelatin), consumer products (many types of toothpaste and salts) as well as Neutraceuticals (different kinds of oils such as olive oil). Supported by the Malaysian state and research institutions, Halagel has "embarked on an extensive research" in the production of halal gelatin, halal empty hard gelatin capsules, and halal soft gels by using only confirmed halal sources to fulfill the niche market in Southeast Asia and worldwide (www.halagel.com). The company also produces a toothbrush, but this cannot formally be certified and its production context audited under the current legislation, the executive secretary explains.

Then we look at *nasi briyani*, a rice-based dish made with spices, rice, and meat, fish, eggs, or vegetables. This product is described as "produk usahawan iks bimbangan fama," meaning that it is a product manufactured by entrepreneurs that have been supervised by Federal Agricultural Marketing Authority (FAMA), a marketing agency under the Ministry of Agriculture and Agro-Based Industry set up to monitor, coordinate, control, and develop product marketing of Malaysian agriculture. The executive secretary is unsatisfied with these claims that are not backed by proper certification and logos. The fact that this product still carries an old halal logo that says Malaysia in Arabic and Roman characters in the middle and "Bahagian hal ehwal Islam, Jabatan Perdana Menteri" (Islamic Affair's Division under the prime minister's department) add to his dissatisfaction. This product, he complains, is "not properly certified," carrying uncertified claims and a dated logo.

A Coco V chocolate milk spread is produced in Malaysia but without any recognizable certifier. The halal logo on the jar simply states in Arabic that this product is halal. The executive secretary admits that this is not the best possible type of certification, but he knows that this is a Muslim-manufactured product that lives up to halal requirements. Another type of product we look at is Sos Cili Pedas, chili sauce by the company Mudim. This sauce is certified by JAKIM, carrying the older version of the logo we saw earlier that includes "H–2"—a code that signifies that the product is certified by the Islamic Council in the Malaysian state of Kedah. A "Buatan Malaysia" or "Made in Malaysia" logo is placed next to the JAKIM logo. It is also stated on this product that it is a "Muslim Product," but it does not carry a logo. Another chili sauce, Sos Cili Padi, carries the JAKIM logo, "Made in Malaysia" logo, and FAMA's logo.

Last, I found Zamzam water in the café. Zamzam water is marketed as a sacred source of water from God coming from the Well of Zamzam located near the holiest place in Mecca, the *Kaaba* (the square building inside the great mosque in Mecca, containing a sacred black stone). Interestingly, this water, the executive secretary explains, contrary to the other products in the café, did not need any of the halal logos on it I noticed on the other products in the café. Conversely, in Malaysia most brands of bottled mineral water are JAKIM certified.

The products discussed earlier display and combine a wide range of information in formal logos or simply by putting bits of text on the surface of the packaging. These types of information can be formalized, as in the case of the most recent JAKIM logos at one end of the spectrum to rather cryptic logos without text or messages that are not easily comprehensible at the other end. Thus, a wide range of institutions (state) and organizations (interest groups/companies) try to instill in consumers ideas about what proper Islamic consumption is or should be or attempt to sacralize commodities in a religious market as it were. Many of the preceding products are located somewhere in the grey zone between formal certification, national sentiments ("Made in Malaysia"), and fuzzy forms of Muslim interests.

To my mind, a central point of tension is that an organization such as PPIM pushes for state or national formalization of the halal market in terms of certification and regulation in general while recognizing a product as halal as long as it is produced by Muslims—either members of PPIM or not. Thus, in this market, the trade relation is as much premised on proper Muslim or ethnic handling as a kind of uncertified standard as it is on the products, per se. Marking or tagging commodities with logos or other types of information is a technology or technique that help personalize this form of exchange or transaction; that is, ideally the producer, the trader, and the consumer all share the symbolic content of the halal logo. Information on products, as we have seen contains religious and totemic dimensions and evokes culturally potent forces such as religion and ethnicity. Advertising certified and uncertified halal products works as a kind of "logo logic" by attaching political and moral messages to products.

AT JAKIM

YES and PPIM were interested in my research with companies in Malaysia and beyond. They encouraged me to make a research proposal and present this at a meeting with JAKIM. Both organizations are closely linked to JAKIM and are part of the halal network. Hence, I was invited to present my proposal at a meeting with JAKIM's head of halal certification in Cyberjaya.[4] Present at the meeting were JAKIM's head of halal certification, a couple of company representatives, the representative from YES and the PPIM, as well as myself. Two things were on the agenda: first, a Malay woman from a company that manufactures Islamic food and health products similar to those mentioned earlier asked the JAKIM head of halal certification for support and advice for improving her business. The JAKIM head of certification is a woman who is also an *ustaz* (religious teacher). A Malay man had similar difficulties and sought the same kind of advice. The JAKIM representative agreed to look into these cases.

The last issue on the agenda was my presentation of a research proposal for JAKIM. At this point in time, I had progressed with my research in Malaysia and Singapore in companies, shops, and restaurants and it was this knowledge that I proposed JAKIM take into consideration when cooperating with multinationals in particular. Based on my ethnographic data with these companies I suggested that JAKIM would be interested in how these understood the benefits as well as challenges involved in JAKIM halal certification. I argued that existing consultancy studies mainly focused on how the Malaysian state and companies brand and market halal on a global scale while there were few empirically substantiated studies of modern forms of halal certification seen from the perspectives. In the car on our way back to Kuala Lumpur, the YES representative explained to me that the issues presented by the two company representatives reflected the problems of "globalizing" Malaysian halal, that is, in his eyes Malaysian halal was often stock in disputes about petty Malay Muslim issues blocking for the "bigger picture, visions."

In this chapter I have shown halal activists or organizations promote halal on a big scale in the interface zones between new forms of Islamic revivalism, the ethnicized state, and Muslim consumer culture and protection. Even if the state in Malaysia has preempted earlier and competing forms of *dakwah* halal understanding there are still many alternative halal logos in existence in Malaysia. While halal activists constantly call on the ethnicized state to tighten halal regulation, some of these organizations simultaneously promote a range of alternative halal logos that seems to challenge efforts to centralize and standardize national Malaysian halal. These alternative logos can work to personalize or ethnicize the otherwise impersonal trade relation; that is, they signify proper Muslim or ethnic handling of production and products, but they are not expressions of any kind of legally backed certification, which is a key objective of the state and activist organizations alike. Many of these products could be classified as "boundary objects"; that is, they are subjected to entangled and crisscrossing classifications schemes of bureaucracies and interest organizations.

NOTES

1. In Bahasa Malaysia, *sembang-sembang* means "casual conversation" or "chatting."
2. Yayasan Ekonomi Sejagat (YES) or in English Foundation for Global Economics.
3. Literally, Bukit Persekutuan means "Federal Hill," and it has its name because Kuala Lumpur has the status of Wilayah Persekutuan or Federal Territory.
4. Cyberjaya is a town with a science park as the core that forms a key part of the Multimedia Super Corridor in Malaysia. This zone stretches southward from Kuala Lumpur for "high-tech" development to turn the nation's main metropolitan area into a "nod"' or "hub," in transnational social and economic networks.

BIBLIOGRAPHY

Azmi, Jumaatun. 2003. *Halal Food: A Guide to Good Eating—Kuala Lumpur*. Kuala Lumpur: KasehDia Sdn. Bhd.

Evans, Hajj Abdalhamid. 2006. "Looking Forward with Hindsight." *The Halal Journal: Business, Lifestyle, Trends*, November–December: 24–25.

Fischer, Johan. 2007. "Boycott or Buycott? Malay Middle-Class Consumption Post-9/11." *Ethnos* 72(1): 29–50.

Fischer, Johan. 2008. *Proper Islamic Consumption: Shopping among the Malays in Modern Malaysia*. Copenhagen: NIAS Press.

Gomez, Edmund Terence. 1994. *Political Business: Corporate Involvement of Malaysian Political Parties*. Townsville: Centre for South-East Asian Studies, James Cook University of North Queensland.
Gomez, Edmund Terence. 2012. "The Politics and Policies of Corporate Development: Race, Rents and Distribution in Malaysia." In *Malaysia's Development Challenges: Graduating from the Middle*, edited by Hal Hill, Tham Siew Yean and Ragayah Haji Mat Sin, 63–82. Routledge, London.
Yayasan Ekonomi Sejagat (n.d.). *Yayasan Ekonomi Sejagat*. Kuala Lumpur: Yayasan Ekonomi Sejagat.

6 Manufacturing Companies[1]

This chapter is an ethnography of how halal certified manufacturing companies comply with rising halal requirements in respect to issues such as certification, staff policies, technoscience, and innovation, for example. I understand companies or corporations to be types of sociological laboratories with histories, cultures, structures, hierarchies, and values to observe and analyze (Mitchell 1998, 34). These business organizations possess shared characteristics such as explicit rules, division of labor, and aims that involve acting on or changing everyday life and have governing ethos (e.g., making money or a management principle) (Gellner and Hirsch 2001). My ethnography recognizes that companies are composed of (Malay) individuals who are themselves the products of the state nationalization of Islam. My study on halal in manufacturing companies is comparable to ethnographies that explore the complexities of bureaucratic practice and corporate practitioners in China (Kipnis 2008) and Japan (Miyasaki 2013). Moreover, Mazzarella (2003, 4) shows how the people who create advertising in Indian advertising agencies adapt to complex cultural politics of mass consumerism in a globalized marketplace. However, corporate employees are to a large extent part of teams—for example, Halal Committees, as we shall see. Ideally, team members complement each other's capacities; they should be productive and high functioning, make great decisions, resolve conflict, gain consensus, and communicate/collaborate fluidly. Thus, the team as a paradigm of productivity, and organizational control is internalized through the reconstitution of expertise and redistribution of worker responsibility in small teams (Urciuoli 2008, 219).

I study companies with a particular interest in standards and their stories. The chapter consists of two parts: the first deals with companies in Malaysia that are certified by Jabatan Kemajuan Islam Malaysia (JAKIM). Thus, I discuss how companies that manufacture products in the Malaysian halal zone comply with direct state regulation and legislation. For example, companies in this zone are legally required to set up a Halal Committee comprised by Muslims and follow specific national standards for allowed ingredients.

The second part explores the same issues, but in the context of companies that are certified by halal-certification bodies that are recognized by JAKIM in Malaysia and Europe. I explore how companies that operate in the European halal zone characterized by weak forms of halal regulation are faced with multiplicity and ambiguity—especially in the context of being certified by JAKIM-recognized organizations. More specifically, an important issue in this chapter is how companies that manufacture their products in Europe operate in a "gray" halal zone between secular government (e.g., in Europe it is not allowed to have a Halal Committee composed of Muslims) and rising halal requirements in the highly regulated Malaysian halal zone into which these products are imported (Fischer 2011). Thus, the move from the first to the second part shows how halal regulation in the Southeast Asian halal zone has a major bearing across global halal zones and, thus, on the emergence of halal as a truly global assemblage. In other words, in this chapter, I analyze differences in and between divergent halal zones and how this shape and reshape halal as a global assemblage. The interface zones between Islamic standardization and technoscience are of particular relevance in this chapter.

These processes really took off in the wake of the Ajinomoto scandal, and they have accelerated ever since, as we shall see. The globalization of the market for halal and its regulation within the last decade or so has necessitated that JAKIM and MUI "outsource" inspection/audit responsibilities to International Food and Nutritional Council of America (IFANCA) and Halal Food Council of Europe (HFCE), for instance. A particular focus is on the social organization of business, that is, how companies as social organizations think about and practice halal requirements and the shift from divergent forms of halal classification toward standardization. The multinational companies I explore are, for the most part, based in Europe—for example, Nestlé in Belgium and Novozymes in Denmark. Outside Southeast Asian nations such as Malaysia, Singapore, and Indonesia, states around the world including that of Denmark do not really interfere with or regulate halal production, trade, and consumption. However, in Malaysia, the Danish state, along with other states through embassy representation, is involved in assisting home country companies in halal matters.

The commercial section of the Danish embassy in Kuala Lumpur, for example, offers its services to Danish companies that operate or want to operate in Malaysia. I discuss the involvement of embassies in halal because it shows how the state is engaged in this market. The embassy has employed a local Malaysian advisor responsible for agro-based industries, halal food, and consumer/retail products. When we discuss the embassy's involvement in halal in the summer of 2010, the advisor explained to me that she had 10 years of experience working with trade matters including halal issues in connection with her position. In that period the market for halal in Malaysia, regulated by JAKIM, had become far more "structured"; that is, more and more halal network events are taking place in Malaysia arranged by JAKIM and Halal Industry Development Corporation (HDC), for example.

At the same time, Malaysia's halal certification and logo are not only important for companies operating in Malaysia, it is also recognized within the Association of Southeast Asian Nations (ASEAN) and globally, and this poses challenges for Danish companies and Denmark more generally as a country that has a large export of agro-based products. Denmark recognizes the importance of deepening halal understanding and practice—especially in connection with abattoirs and the export of food products for Muslim countries and groups.

The advisor explains that abattoirs in Denmark have halal inspections every two to three years by Department of Veterinary Services in Malaysia together with JAKIM. These bodies send officers to Denmark to check that poultry, for example, are slaughtered properly according to Islamic principles. The embassy tries to assist Danish companies as these often consider Malaysian halal requirements complex. In addition to the processing fee imposed by Department of Veterinary Services, the companies inspected in Denmark must cover the travel expenses when these agencies visit Denmark. Similarly, but at a lower cost, Danish companies must pay JAKIM accredited Islamic Cultural Centre (ICC) in Denmark (discussed in Chapter 2) for certification, labeling of products with logos, and inspections. Thus, there are powerful linkages in and between global halal zones and simultaneously halal as a global assemblage moves across these zones.

The division of labor between JAKIM and an accredited certifying body such as ICC is that formally the recognized certifying body cannot do the inspections for JAKIM, so these are carried out by JAKIM and Department of Veterinary Services in Malaysia together with the Danish Veterinary and Food Administration. The responsibility of the recognized certifying body is to ensure that slaughtering follows proper Islamic procedure and keeping records of this including the appointment of the Muslim slaughterer, to certify that this has been carried out according to the Malaysian standard for slaughtering and handling of meat production, and in accordance with the Malaysian Protocol for Halal Meat and Poultry Production. Hence, the aspect of legal transactions and rules are essential to the way in which state institutions in Malaysia and Denmark understand and practice halal regulation of companies.

The European Union (EU), the advisor explains, has argued that the high cost of inspection and travel fees imposed for inspection is a kind of trade hindrance and talks on this issue have been held between the EU and the Malaysian authorities in Kuala Lumpur. In this matter, the EU refers to the sanitary and phytosanitary agreement of the World Trade Organization (WTO), stipulating the rules that WTO members are obliged to follow when governing food safety as well as animal/plant health. Thus, Malaysian halal understanding and practice are also dependent on international law that tries to standardize divergent halal classifications. Moreover, in these processes Islamic technoscience overlaps with food science and regulation.

As we have seen, a general trend following rising halal requirements in Malaysia is to separate halal and non-halal production, and most companies, the advisor tells me, have realized that it is easier not to mix the two in the same production plant. At the same time, halal in Malaysia is, to a large extent, about hygiene, so companies must bear in mind that they should not think of halal as an isolated Islamic food taboo. Another issue is how companies handle problematic ingredients such as alcohol and animal gelatin. Generally, issues are smoothly resolved between JAKIM and companies, and the embassy can play a constructive role in these processes. The embassy can also assist companies by "paving the way" for taking the issues of Danish companies to "a higher level of Malaysian authority," that is, bringing particular cases to the attention of contacts within the bureaucracy in Malaysia and arguing how the individual case actually follows official guidelines. These examples show that Islamic technoscience as material technology and specialized social expertise help standardize halal in the interfaces between food safety and religion.

The media in Malaysia often bring stories about companies that come into focus for allegedly violating halal requirements. Media exposure, such as that in the aftermath of the Ajinomoto scandal in Indonesia, for example, is of great concern to local Malaysian as well as multinational companies. Consequently, the Malaysian cake chain Bengawan Solo had to place an advertisement in several major Malaysian newspapers to assure its Muslim customers that its products did not contain pork or lard.[2] Another case was police investigations of emails that cast doubts on certain products. The company, Gardenia Bakeries (M) Sdn Bhd, for instance, had to call a press conference to refute e-mail allegations that its products were not halal. The most recent case involved e-mails targeting the Coffee Bean outlets, alleging that non-halal products were being used to make its specialty coffees.[3] In the Malaysian media, such rumors are at times said to have started in Singapore and elsewhere. Concerned over rumors and lies being circulated in cyberspace, the Malaysian government wanted to "police e-mails." According to rumors, the cappuccino served in Coffee Bean had pork gelatin in it, and the Chinese papers in Singapore have reported that Gardenia bread is made with non-halal substances.[4]

Before moving to the company ethnography, I discuss relevant points made in *Halal Food Production* (2004) that many companies use as a handbook for halal production. Enzymes (together with gelatin) are used in a multitude of food and nonfood processes, for example, in dairy and starch industries. Traditionally, the majority of enzymes used in the food industry were from animal sources, but now there are microbial alternatives. Enzymes from microbial sources or halal-slaughtered animals, it is argued, are halal, whereas an enzyme from a porcine source is haram (Riaz and Chaudry 2004, 21). Alcohol is ubiquitous and naturally present in all biological systems, and arguably it does not nullify the halal status of food products. What is more, alcohol in pure form is the best solvent and chemical available for extracting, dissolving, and precipitating functions in the food industry. Thus, religious scholars have realized its importance for use in the industry and ingredients made with alcohol or extracted by using alcohol have become acceptable as long as alcohol is evaporated from the final ingredient (Riaz and Chaudry 2004, 24).

Biotechnology and genetically modified organisms (GMO), in particular, are contested fields with regard to modern halal. Of course, there is no specific mentioning of (genetically) modified ingredients in the Koran because these scientific discoveries are recent (Riaz and Chaudry 2004, 137). Both Jewish[5] and Islamic scholars currently accept products made from simple genetic engineering. However, production conditions in fermenters must still be kosher/halal, and so must the ingredients as well as the processing. The Muslim community is still considering the issue of products with a porcine gene and a final ruling has not been established. The "leaning" seems to be toward rejecting such materials. Religious leaders of both communities have not yet determined the status of more complex genetic manipulations (Riaz and Chaudry 2004, 162). Enzymes that derive from microbial or biotech sources are acceptable as kosher, halal, and vegetarian. Enzymes extracted from kosher-killed animals are accepted as kosher, and enzymes extracted form halal-killed animals accepted as halal (Riaz and Chaudry 2004, 164–165). These points are all relevant to the two companies I now discuss. They are both located in industrial estates in Malaysian states that promote themselves as halal hubs, targeting investors and manufacturers.

HALAL BIOTECH: FOOD INGREDIENTS, ENZYMES, AND BIO-BASED SOLUTIONS

I am in an industrial estate to visit a European multinational company that produces food ingredients, enzymes, and bio-based solutions. The company has specialized in offering manufacturers new opportunities to meet growing consumer demand for halal-labeled products and halal certification plays a key role in this. All the company's raw materials comply with halal requirements, and thus the certification process was relatively uncomplicated. This is an example of a company in which the application of Islamic technoscience is essential; that is, material technology and specialized social expertise shape the way in which this company as a social organization understand and practice halal.

I am discussing halal in the work of the company with two representatives from the Halal Committee that is mandatory for halal-approved companies to set up. The first representative is a man who has been working for the company for 19 years. He is a chemistry graduate who was initially involved in production and then shifted to work on implementing system requirements on safety and health and ISO standards on environmental management. The company chose to focus on the good manufacturing practices and food safety, which is internationally recognized instead of the local Malaysian standard for halal MS 1500 (production, preparation, handling, and storage of halal food). The Halal Committee member is responsible for managing halal compliance and certification including application for and renewal of certificates with JAKIM. Encouraged by JAKIM he also participated in trainings to enhance knowledge of halal technology and management. In his own words, he is the plant's "halal manager." His colleague is a woman who has worked for the company for 13 years. For example, she handles JAKIM halal online registration and certification, as well as quality control, product services, product specification, and customers' requirements.

The company is also kosher certified by the largest global kosher certifier, Orthodox Union (OU). Therefore, the company frequently has visits from both JAKIM and OU inspectors. Inspections often target the introduction of new raw materials and their religious status. For both types of inspections, the tendency is that they have changed from being announced to unannounced, and my ethnography shows that companies use many resources on constantly being prepared for many types of inspections and audits. Thus, unannounced inspections that in most cases take about a couple of hours almost exclusively occur when halal certificates are about to expire and renewal is due. A standard inspection or audit is not very detailed but is far stricter if a new raw material or ingredient is animal based. Hygiene and containing risk of cross contamination are other aspects looked into during inspections. Before or during inspections the company provides JAKIM with documentation in the form of production flowcharts and lists of ingredients used and combined. Flowcharts, a type of diagram that represents a process indicating the steps as boxes of various kinds and their order by connecting these with arrows, play an important role in giving inspectors a quick overview. They are important technologies for communicating about halal processes in different stages of production.

When we discuss the company's Halal Committee, I learn that it includes five Malays, who are "appointed from executive level." JAKIM informs the company about training seminars, and Halal Committee staff members have attended a few, but mostly they do not. The focus in most of these seminars is the process of application for halal certification, and the company has more than 18 years of experience with this. The cost of certification has been stable over the years. One of the major challenges for a company such as this one is that it takes "too long" for JAKIM to process an application, approximately four to six months. When a new product is introduced, the company has to wait another four to six months to obtain the halal certificate for that new product, the Halal Committee members explain. Another crucial aspect is to control the halalness of raw materials from a wide range of suppliers. Using the same supplier for longer periods simplifies this process. The company is faced with two groups of officers from JAKIM: first, a group specializing in technical knowledge with particular reference to food. Second, another group with an Islamic background is more focused on religious aspects such as the halal–haram binary. In connection with inspections or more informal visits, these two groups accompany each other and divide tasks between them. One of the halal committee members is occasionally invited by JAKIM to discuss about technical developments with regard to flavors and emulsifiers, for example. In this way JAKIM tries to keep up with industry innovation, and companies can discuss potential innovations with JAKIM before these are finally implemented in production. An important aspect is that company representatives and JAKIM officers not only exchange knowledge but also develop rapport that helps smooth cooperation.

JAKIM's halal logo can be found on boxes and bags with raw materials around the plant. Because of requirements from MUI and other halal certification bodies it is compulsory to put the halal logo on product labels. To sum up, a company such as this one, on one hand, is subjected to increasingly strict halal requirements by JAKIM, but, on the other hand, it also develops more refined processes to comply with such requirements. Even if the underlying principle behind halal remains a system of religious precepts and beliefs, Islamic technoscience is a privileged domain that highlights the interplay and compatibility of standardized forms of halal compliance, for example, with regard to training, establishing the Halal Committee, and raw-materials traceability.

HALAL IN A FOOD MANUFACTURING COMPANY

I also did fieldwork in a food manufacturing company. The general manager and the head of the company's Halal Committee explain that in 1995 the company first applied for JAKIM halal certification. At the time, there were no actual halal "standards," merely localized halal classifications—JAKIM representatives simply inspected the premises to ensure that it was free of alcohol, that raw materials were halal, and that hygiene in the form of toilets and washing facilities were in order. JAKIM inspectors wanted to know if the company was using any non-halal products such as brushes made out of pigs' hair or alcohol. Moreover, inspectors wanted to know if any "harmful" chemicals were part of production. All that has changed, and today halal is far more regulated and linked to the Malaysian MS 1500 standard and a whole range of management practices. These changes parallel those in the consumer behavior among the Malays, and the general manager and the head of the Halal Committee tell me that this fastidiousness has made it impossible to sell any food product to Muslims in Malaysia that is not fully halal certified. Even for non-Muslims in Malaysia halal has come to represent a form of wholesome, clean, and state regulated consumption.

The company's products started carrying the JAKIM logo in 1998, and over the years the logo has changed a number of times. We look at different generations of designs of the company's label on its products and how the

JAKIM halal logo has also been redesigned. Today, even the logo also has to be halal in itself, the company representatives explain to me, in that products can only be halal if no haram glue is used for labels or packaging altogether. The head of the Halal Committee learns about these requirements and many other types of new standards when he attends JAKIM training. The latest of these changes is JAKIM's focus on halal logistics and transport. The company is ISO 9002 (Quality Management) certified, and it is also complying with food safety regulations by the Malaysian Ministry of Health. When a company has this kind of certification, JAKIM inspectors tend to be more "confident" in issuing halal certificates. If not, inspectors will ask for much more information, the representatives explain. Thus, certification standardized individualized halal understandings or classification.

The company has formed the mandatory Halal Committee including at least two Muslim staff involved in the production process—previously it was any Muslim member of staff, but now JAKIM insists that it has to be Muslim staff directly involved in the production process. Establishing the Halal Committee was not very resource demanding because about half the company's staff are Muslims. Regarding the cost of certification, JAKIM charges the company when renewing certificates. Previously, JAKIM wanted to charge companies for each product, but protests from this and other companies changed this procedure. Now the certification process has been streamlined. Similarly, the general manager and the head of the Halal Committee recall that previously when imported raw materials were not formally halal certified and the mother company in Europe was not halal certified either, this was a major challenge because of problems with customs clearance in Malaysia. The mother company in Europe is now certified by IFANCA, which does inspections at the plant in Europe and is on JAKIM's list of recognized certifying bodies.

A particular case caught my attention during fieldwork with this company when we discussed ingredients that may or may not be recognized by JAKIM. The company decided to remove a coloring agent from one of its products. While IFANCA recognizes this coloring agent, JAKIM was unclear about this point. There are always ongoing debates in Malaysia over issues such as this one and clearly the company was uninterested in becoming subject of debate in the media or elsewhere so they removed the coloring agent from the product, which is problematic, because this cannot be replaced with a coloring agent that adds a comparable color. The company has had other similar debates with JAKIM, for example, over coloring agents in other products that resulted in the replacement of various ingredients, but this was not possible in the case of this particular coloring agent. However, after some negotiation JAKIM issued a *fatwa* stating that it agreed to the use of the coloring agent as long as the content did not exceed a certain quantity. Hence, halal certification can be a process of personalized and routinized negotiation that hinges on the social relations between the certifier and the certified.

Once JAKIM approves ingredients, normally the decision is not changed and this is extremely important for companies. Today such procedures are more formalized, and the company representatives feel that JAKIM is also interested in setting standards for decisions such as the one on the coloring agent. While the company took out the coloring agent to avoid it becoming an "issue" they now are assured that its acceptance in certain quantities is a new form of standard with which they comply. One thing that puzzles the general manager, however, is that there does not seem to be a shared "standard" on an issue such as this one among various certifiers: IFANCA accepted the coloring agent all along while JAKIM was much harder to convince. This is an example of regional and theological differences, or classifications, as it were, among certifiers and the *ulamas* they often consult in cases such as this in and across global halal zones.

An issue such as the preceding one can also be discussed when the head of the Halal Committee attends halal training arranged by JAKIM and HDC. In the last seminar he attended, representatives from Standards and Industrial Research Institute of Malaysia were also present, and a woman asked about JAKIM's stand on coloring. The head of the Halal Committee then explained about JAKIM's *fatwa* and about how the company now complied with that particular "standard." During my stay with this company we looked at JAKIM's written regulations on halal. It is mentioned that *najis* (filth), alcohol, and a whole range of haram ingredients cannot be part halal production, but other issues that are important for this company's production are not listed, and this testifies to the fact even if halal has become standardized there are still areas that are open to divergent types of classifications and, thus, negotiation.

Once a year an unannounced JAKIM inspection takes place in the company. This inspection is carried out by a *ulama* or *ustaz* (religious teacher) together with a food technologist coming from Kuala Lumpur. The local state Islamic authorities also visit the factory, but these visits are separate. Different people carry out inspections so the company does not have the opportunity to establish a personal relationship with these inspectors. The inspection normally takes about an hour, and inspectors are especially "confident" about the production process when they see the company's food safety certificate. When the company applied for halal certification and was JAKIM approved, JAKIM inspectors first came to the factory after the office was closed, and staff responsible for halal had to rush to the factory to participate in the inspection. Since then, inspections have become "standardized," and there are no real surprises, even if inspections are unannounced.

The company representatives recall how shifting agencies have been involved in regulating halal over the years. For example, in 1998 the government privatized halal certification and inspections and outsourced responsibilities to a company called Ilham Daya, which was criticized for excessive fees (discussed in Chapter 1). Ilham Daya's involvement in halal was also felt in the company; that is, there were excessive fees for individual products and unclear rules more generally. Hence, the state looked into the level of fees companies had to pay, and eventually JAKIM took over all these responsibilities.

The placement of the JAKIM logo begins with JAKIM sending the logo electronically to the company together with a certificate. JAKIM is not very specific about the color and size of the logo. Thereafter, the company places this logo in the final design at labels and in advertisements. The general manager stresses that “the halal logo has become very important to customers, without it we can’t sell our products.” In most factories, halal logos are not ubiquitous: they are mostly found on certificates and in some instances on raw materials such as sugar. However, in this company the JAKIM logo could be seen on the large number of packaged products on the conveyor belts around the factory. I could observe this when I was shown the parts of production that halal inspectors often want to see. However, there is no fixed route during inspections, and while some inspectors are focused on particular production processes, others are more interested in the equipment used.

This factory is a good example of a food manufacturing company that has adapted to rising halal requirements by applying and adapting to localized forms of Islamic technoscience and regulation. The case with the coloring agent shows how a company such as this one can negotiate sensitive issues with religious authorities. This discussion also shows how the standardization of halal products, production processes, people, and the setting up the Halal Committee, for example, has taken place. From being a religious injunction left to individualized interpretation or classification among Islamic bureaucrats and inspectors, halal is now centrally regulated and more simple to comply with.

THE WORLD LEADER IN HALAL

Nestlé Malaysia exports its products to more than 50 countries worldwide with export sales of over RM 1 billion in 2011, and the company was the first multinational to “voluntarily request” halal certification of all its food products in 1994. Certification of Nestlé Malaysia products provides assurance that these are manufactured, imported, and distributed under the strictest hygienic and sanitary conditions in accordance with the Islamic faith. Moreover, products and premises for manufacturing have been inspected and have earned halal certification by recognized Islamic bodies. The halal logo on packaging testifies to the fact that products are prepared according to “stringent Islamic requirements” (http://www.nestle.com.my/AboutUs/Nestle_in_Malaysia/Pages/halal_policy.aspx). What is more, advertisements for Nestlé halal products are ubiquitous not only in Malaysia but also globally. For example, a Nestlé advertisement in *The Halal Journal* (Nestlé 2010) shows a Muslim woman wearing a *tudung* (long headscarf) eating a KitKat chocolate bar in front of a computer in her office with London's Big Ben and Parliament in the background. The heading reads "Bringing Peace of Mind around the World." The text states that halal "benefits everyone" and that since the 1980s Nestlé Malaysia has been manufacturing products according to guidelines on halal. This has earned Néstle Malaysia the recognition as the halal center of excellence for the Nestlé Group worldwide. Following the text is a clear image of JAKIM's halal logo. An important insight from Nestlé's engagement with halal is that with regard to food, global capitalism has made peace with cultural diversity (Wilk 2006, 197).

Nestlé's unique position and history in the global market for halal make the company's presence at halal network events such as the one held by HFCE in Brussels evident. In his Brussels speech, the committee chairman of Nestlé Halal Committee Regulatory Affairs explains that the company has come a long way having taken halal to its global position today. He joined the company in 1988 and has worked there since. He is educated in food technology from Universiti Putra Malaysia (which today runs a Halal Products Research Institute as we saw in Chapter 4). He started in the production of noodles and moved on to research and development at the company's headquarters in Switzerland to learn about pasta.

Néstle established its halal policy in 1992 in close cooperation with the Malaysian state represented by JAKIM. Prior to state institutionalization of halal in Malaysia a plethora of Islamic revivalist groups produced halal products without a proper certification process, the committee chairman argued. Islamic revivalism and Malay ethnicity in Malaysia since the 1970s have been major factors behind pushing halal to become a global market force, which Nestlé has a deep knowledge of and expertise in marketing. The committee chairman recalled that he visited Pusat Islam or the Islamic Center in Kuala Lumpur (set up primarily to reduce vice and upgrade Muslim morality instead of regulating halal in a systematic manner) to ask for halal certification.

As a "human company" with "social responsibility" Nestlé started producing halal seriously on a global scale. In 1997 the company implemented a plan that would give customers "global access" to halal. Nestlé has 86 halal-certified factories globally, the committee chairman showed on his slides, and several standards are in place and are to be implemented to increase halal reliability. The company also set up its Halal Committee composed of senior Muslim executives from various disciplines to be responsible for all matters pertaining to halal certification and training workers on complying with halal standards and auditing Nestlé factories worldwide. What is more, more than 1,200 small and medium-sized companies have enrolled in a Nestlé Corporate Social Responsibility mentoring program that aims to build halal knowledge and skills of productivity, marketing, quality assurance, and efficiency measurement. The company's production is certified by JAKIM in Malaysia while other credible halal-certification bodies certify products manufactured outside Malaysia.

The committee chairman explained that "knowledge" is key in Nestlé's handling of halal and that the following aspects are essential: cooperation with JAKIM, learning from global experience in settings such as the UK; commitment and sincerity, knowledge of raw materials and ingredients, utensils, sanitation/hygiene, food safety, cross contamination, critical Muslim consumers and consumer groups in Malaysia that claim their rights, as well as training of non-Muslims involved in halal. The committee chairman ended by stating that third-party assurance or certification is essential concerning all the points he raised. As a Muslim he always checks labels for halal logos, and if no proper logo is to be found on products in stores, especially outside Malaysia, he looks for "sensitive" ingredients on the labels. All this testifies to how Néstle, as a multinational company, has helped shape halal as a global assemblage. Simultaneously, it is also clear how Néstle as an organization adapted to rising halal requirements historically, that is, the story of standardization in this particular company.

After the committee chairman's presentation, a company representative in the audience wanted to know if it is advisable to have logos printed on raw materials. The committee chairman answered that it is often a good idea in order to avoid contamination, especially in connection with the certification of batch production. He passed this question on to the JAKIM representative in the audience, because he would perhaps be better qualified to answer this question. Halal logos are the visual manifestation of the company's history of certification and standardization. Another company representative asked, "Why is there no global harmonization of halal standards?" The representative suggested that a harmonization of standards would make it easier for his company to comply with often conflicting or overlapping understandings of halal. The committee chairman answered that future harmonization could become a key element, but that it is not yet possible because of the multiple approaches to halal understanding and practice. A last question concerned the accepted level of alcohol in industrial processes. The committee chairman replied that alcoholic beverages are not allowed at all, and if a company needs to use ethanol only as a processing aid (e.g., to extract flavor), it must not come from alcoholic beverages. Based on scientific evidence and techniques from labs in Malaysia, the residual limit must not exceed 0.5 percent, and as a "best practice" Nestlé Malaysia does not use alcohol in its products.

During my fieldwork in Malaysia I visited Nestlé's headquarters, which is located in a suburban setting about 15 kilometers west of Kuala Lumpur. The headquarters are not far from the suburb where I did my doctoral research on Islam, consumer culture, and halal among Malay Muslim middle-class families and the headquarters of the HDC. I discussed Nestlé's involvement in halal with the committee chairman and a staff member who works in halal production. He is educated in food science in Malaysia and joined the company in 2000. Since his appointment he has been sitting on the Halal Committee, and he is currently involved in developing new halal chocolate products. One of the topics we discuss is the Halal Committee. It is a requirement for halal products manufacturers to set up the committee, and it includes 16 Muslim staff representing various departments in the company, including the factories and supply chains. Besides the fact that now this committee has become a legal requirement, it predominantly acts as a focus for sharing halal knowledge and commitment enhancing halal practices within the manufacturing sites. The two representatives explain that the company set up the Halal Committee on its own initiative long before it became mandatory. Similarly, Nestlé also developed its halal policy before other companies, which gave the company a global advantage.

Nestlé is pleased with the Halal Act. The representatives argue that in the global market for halal the old Trade Description Act of 1975 is far from effective in protecting halal integrity and that is it unsatisfactory that "anyone" can declare that their products are halal without serious legal regulation and enforcement. Because Nestlé has such a long history of halal policy and compliance, the company also possesses in-depth knowledge about how the state and JAKIM, in particular, have understood halal over the years, that is, how the leadership has stressed the importance and possibilities in promoting Malaysia as a "halal hub" on a global scale. Former prime minister Tun Abdullah Haji Ahmad Badawi, for example, was the driving force behind setting up the HDC and promoting Malaysian halal more generally.

In collaboration with stakeholders, Nestlé's status as a leader in halal globally has made the company more resilient, and thus, the company did not really experience major difficulties during the shifting of authority from HDC back to JAKIM. The present prime minister, Datuk Seri Najib Tun Razak, has taken halal to greater heights with the establishment of halal parks creating initiatives for industries and especially small and medium-sized enterprises to grow. Around the world, consumers can find Nestlé products with halal logos on them, and the company's design department has great influence on how the JAKIM logo fits in with the design of packaging of products. JAKIM is very flexible about the placement of the logo and its color, as long as this is put in a "proper place," that is, where consumers can notice the logo that should live up to a "minimum size" and not be placed in any "obscene" contexts. Over the years, there have been many versions of the JAKIM logo, and this has followed more general trends in the design of wrappings for the vast number of Nestlé products. Nestlé's design department also considers how the JAKIM logo fits together with other types of logos on individual wrappings.

Nestlé is experienced when it comes to handling inspections by JAKIM. These inspections, in line with tightened regulation of halal in Malaysia, take place "very frequently" at the company's factories and their duration is about a day or less. Inspectors and JAKIM have the "power to do what they find necessary during inspections"; that is, there is not really a standard route inspectors might take. "We are open and have nothing to hide," the committee chairman says. Normally there is rotation of new inspectors who visit Nestlé so there is no "personal relationship" between the company and inspectors. Nestlé maintains a good collaboration and ongoing work with JAKIM directly or via the Federation of Malaysian Manufacturers and other Malaysian government agencies to further improve the certification process.

What is more, for each application for having a new product certified there would be an inspection. While inspections normally were unannounced they are now "moving to announced." However, what the chairman calls unannounced "enforcement audits" occasionally take place. The Nestlé representatives approve of this form of audit culture, and they explain that it exists because of a general lack of halal understanding among companies and specific instances in which companies purposely or accidentally have failed to comply with halal regulation. This, in turn, has created a form of "surveillance audit" culture that should be in place, the representatives agree, for companies that have limited knowledge of halal. Conversely, Nestlé as a "respected" and "trusted" company that has "internal halal assurance, logistics management, and a Halal Committee" has "disciplined" the company to be "outstanding" in "instilling" halal "discipline" within the company.

Nestlé is a good example of a global company that has adapted to increasing halal requirements in Malaysia and then taken these experiences to a global level. Néstle's history of standards and certification is also the history of the emergence and consolidation of halal as a global assemblage across a multitude of zones. So since 1992 Néstle has not only standardized halal production through JAKIM certification, the company has also itself been rationalized, systematized, and differentiated to adapt to modern halal production and regulation. In Malaysia, the state certifies Nestlé's production. Imported products produced by Nestlé are certified by IFANCA. These certifying bodies are competitors in the global market for halal certification, and a company such as Nestlé is meticulous about selecting certification that is acceptable in particular regional, national, and local markets. I now discuss halal understanding and practice of companies based in Europe that are certified by JAKIM-recognized bodies. These discussions are of specific relevance to the way in which the halal network actively shapes halal as a global assemblage in and across zones. JAKIM cannot possibly certify companies around the world, so it "outsources" regulation to smaller certifiers such as IFANCA or HFCE. In effect, these smaller bodies are themselves regulated by JAKIM, and as we shall see this form of "indirect" certification poses challenges to companies.

NOVOZYMES

Novozymes is the leading enzyme manufacturer globally. The company's history starts with Nordisk founded in 1923 and Novo in 1925. These were merged into Novo Nordisk in 1989, and Novozymes was founded by demerger in 2000. The company has enzyme plants in six countries, three in Denmark, two in the US, two in China, two in India, one in Brazil, and one in Canada. Novozymes has more than 6,000 employees, and in 2013 annual revenues were about US$2 billion. The company makes about 900 enzyme products purchased by many different industries manufacturing detergents, foods, beverages, textiles, biofuel, and animal feed among other things. Novozymes started undergoing auditing for Jewish dietary law (*kashrut*) compliance in the late 1980s. In 2000 the position of global kosher and halal coordinator was created. He has been with Novozymes for many years and has been involved in quality assurance and several other areas of enzyme production. Novozymes is a good example of a company that takes global kosher and halal challenges seriously, and this has had an impact on certification, staff policies, and innovation in the company. Practically, all the company's food-grade enzymes are kosher and halal certified. Comparatively, more enzymes are kosher certified because some of these are for the production of alcoholic beverages only; that is, halal certification is irrelevant.

Novozymes's relationship with Malaysia and Singapore is as follows: the company has offices in Malaysia, but it does not produce enzymes in these two countries. I visited Novozymes's office in an industrial estate ("Technology Park") outside Kuala Lumpur in 2006. The Novozymes representatives stressed that even if Novozymes does not have production facilities in Malaysia and thus is not certified by JAKIM, halal has "immense importance" for the company because "Malaysia is Malaysia" and halal is inseparable from JAKIM authority and law. The representatives also emphasized that kosher in countries such as Thailand and Indonesia is vital for Novozymes's activities. To have only one company standard for kosher and halal certification, the representatives explained that this is "centralized" so that the kosher and halal coordinator in Denmark is in charge of everything to avoid having "different versions of certifications." The chairman of the HFCE, which inspects Novozymes's production, is also vice president of the influential halal-certification body IFANCA, based in Chicago. He was born in Malaysia, where he worked with JAKIM, and has been involved in setting up Malaysia's state regulated form of halal certification since the early 1980s. This chairman of the HFCE is also the inspector who carries out inspections in Novozymes Denmark, as we shall see.

A particular issue is of importance in the relationship between JAKIM and Novozymes: Novozymes is not halal certified by JAKIM or the MUIS, but it is essential to the company that its current halal certification by other certifiers is recognized by JAKIM. This aspect is also important for Novozymes's customers in Malaysia. The coordinator's job involves clarifying questions such as these, that is, what certification bodies currently recognize which types of certification in particular countries or zones as it were. More specifically, the coordinator contacted JAKIM with several inquiries. The first inquiry was about products from Novozymes's plants in China certified by IFANCA and MUI. The coordinator asked if these products would need a third certification by one of the JAKIM recognized Chinese certifiers if they were to be sold in Malaysia. An assistant director from JAKIM's Halal Hub in Cyberjaya outside Kuala Lumpur answered that if Novozymes's products were manufactured in China, as was the case, and were to be exported to Malaysia as halal products these products must be certified by Chinese certification bodies. A similar inquiry and answer concerned India. Another enquiry was about products from Novozymes's plants in Denmark certified by HFCE and about whether this certification was sufficient for exporting and selling in Malaysia. The assistant director answered that according to JAKIM circular "exemption" is given to the countries in the EU in which halal certificates issued by the Recognised Foreign Halal Certification Bodies originate; that is, certifiers within the EU are recognized. In the eyes of JAKIM, China and India, like all other countries, compose individual halal zones in which local and recognized halal bodies must certify local production by multinational companies. EU member states, however, are exempted from this requirement according to the answers given in this case and are seen to compose one zone.

The coordinator gave a specific example of the way in which the company complies with both kosher and halal requirements: these necessitated change to ingredients and production processes in connection with replacing porcine gelatin with fish gelatin to produce an immobilized lipase for eatable oils. Although Novozymes has complied with steadily growing kosher requirements since the 1980s, the coordinator explains to me that inquiries about halal certification from Southeast Asia, especially Malaysia, Singapore, and Indonesia, finally culminated in new practices in 2001 following the food scandal in Indonesia discussed above. Thus, in Novozymes the histories of religious regulation, standardization, and technoscience are of special importance.

However, before this food scandal, there was already increasing interest in halal and Novozymes, and the coordinator started learning about halal and its similarities to and differences from kosher—also in terms of locating and ultimately choosing certifiers. In the eyes of the coordinator, there is not too much difference in handling kosher and halal, respectively: pork avoidance is similar in both systems, but most important, there are similarities with respect to the understanding and practices surrounding the approval of raw materials, product certification, and audits/inspections. Alcohol is allowed in kosher, and more generally, kosher is more complex in terms of avoiding cross-contamination. Consequently, kosher inspections are often more detailed.

To comply with divergent halal requirements set by Islamic organizations globally the company's products are certified by five different certifiers, among which is the HFCE. The reason for needing several certifiers is that these, in many cases, do not (continually) recognize one another. Hence, to ensure global coverage in and across different halal zones regulated by divergent halal certification bodies more than one certifier is needed. The researcher learned from certifiers and companies that typical forms of tensions between certifiers include unwillingness to share information, misrecognizing each other's certification, a lack of cooperation, competition, neglecting to invite other certifiers to conferences such as the one in Brussels, and disregard of standards and the attempts to set them up, as well as theological and scientific disputes—for example, regarding allowed levels of alcohol in halal production as discussed in connection with Néstle.

The move from animal to plant, fish and synthetic ingredients was not only resource demanding and costly it also generated forms of innovation that benefit the company today, that is, in many ways non-animal ingredients are more unproblematic in the globalized market in an era of food scares such as Bovine Spongiform Encephalopathy (BSE) and rising religious requirements. Novozymes complies with a number of International Organization for Standardization (ISO) standards and certifications—for example, quality, environmental, and food safety systems. The company is inspected and audited not only by several parties in connection with these types of standards and certifications but also by local authorities and customers in countries where production takes place. When we discussed standards and standardization the coordinator contended that halal standards similar to those of ISO would be desirable. It is confusing that different halal certifiers compete and have different halal understandings and practices, resulting in tensions and a constant uncertainty about recognition and misrecognition between certifiers. However, despite calls for such standards by certifiers and companies, there is no sign that actual halal standardization is being institutionalized on a global scale. Such standards could ideally also include inspections, and this would perhaps soothe different certifiers' skepticism about the inspection qualifications, competences, and capabilities of other certifiers that can lead to a certifier being misrecognized.

Novozymes trains all staff involved in kosher and halal production, that is, basic rules/regulations, approved ingredients/raw materials and their handling, and certification procedures. The coordinator is responsible for such training, and he participates in training arranged by the MUI, for example. Novozymes's training of staff takes place at different levels at the company's sites around the world. The coordinator functions as the company's overall authority on kosher and halal globally, but at each of Novozymes's sites one member of staff is appointed local coordinator responsible for kosher and halal expertise. Worldwide, the company has about seven local coordinators, one per site. Consequently, training takes place centrally in Denmark and at local sites of production in each country. Moreover, training also addresses communicative aspects such as how to cooperate with halal certifiers and especially their specific requirements when getting products and production processes through the certification process. An important question in this respect is how these recognized certifiers understand and practice MUI requirements.

At the 4th International Halal Food Conference in Brussels, discussed earlier, the global halal coordinator ends his talk by presenting a wish list aimed at the company's certifiers: quick and clear responses, precise and realistic requirements, realistic time frame for new requirements, specification of requirements—*not* how to comply with them, and common standards, as well as mutual full recognition between different certification bodies. In many ways handling halal is more "straightforward" in Novozymes's production compared to kosher, but often halal certifiers' theological, bureaucratic, and scientific interpretation is unclear, varies over time, or varies from product to product. The aspect of the halalness of products and raw materials from suppliers is another challenging area where more consistency would be desirable. As in the case of many other companies, Novozymes does not critique rising religious requirements, per se, but, rather, that at times these are unclear, diverging, and not "standardized."

In the eyes of the coordinator these network events are especially important because during the breaks issues such as certification and recognition can be discussed and potentially negotiated. Companies such as Novozymes participate in quite a number of these network events, and here they learn about other companies' experiences with halal challenges. Novozymes together with other multinationals in biotech, dairy, and food ingredient production, for example, have formed a network that at regular meetings and electronically share experiences with both kosher and halal. This network started as a kosher experience network, but now also includes halal. These companies have appointed kosher and halal coordinators to comply with rising requirements and this network gives them an opportunity to meet and exchange experiences with religious requirements in their particular types of companies. These "alliance structures" or intercorporate alliances are forms of institutionalized relationships among firms based on localized networks of stable frameworks for exchange, and collective action (Gerlach 1992, 3).

In 2009 MUI announced that with effect from October 1, the organization would only recognize halal certificates and logos from a very limited number of certifiers. To the surprise of the coordinator, a couple of the company's certifiers were not on the list of recognized certification bodies. This list, however, was apparently not conclusive, and the whole situation was "confusing," to say the least. To deal with this issue the coordinator worked hard to establish certification by another and recognized certification body. A move like this by MUI in Indonesia means that extra resources must be put into securing alternative forms of certification in companies around the world, as we shall see in the case of more companies below.

In 2010 MUI's Assessment Institute for Foods, Drugs, and Cosmetics held the Indonesia International Halal Business & Food Expo in Jakarta—a combined halal network event and training. This included training on MUI's Halal Assurance System and harmonization of international halal standards. The coordinator explained to me that MUI halal requirements are "very strict" and that its Halal Assurance System complements the ISO quality management systems. The coordinator participated in this training in Indonesia, and as we have seen, this training is a disciplining of both companies and recognized certifiers, but these sessions also give companies and certifiers an opportunity for more informal and personalized interaction and exchange of ideas that can help smoothen cooperation and tensions. One of the main challenges for a company such as Novozymes is that MUI and its recognized certifiers insist that the products and raw materials suppliers sell to halal-certified companies are also halal. Comparing MUI to its recognized halal certification bodies, MUI tends to be stricter about documentation of the halal status of products and raw materials. Consequently, recognized certifiers must examine the halalness of certified companies' suppliers. This poses a challenge, a "turbulent situation," as the coordinator explains, as many of these suppliers do not have proper halal certification.

Novozymes's contracts with certifiers have been through Novozymes's legal department. It is not extremely detailed because both company and certifier are mutually interested in a constructive relationship. The cost involved in certification is important to a company such as Novozymes. The amount paid for kosher and halal certification is fixed, and it includes one yearly inspection. Additional inspections are covered by certifiers. In the case of MUI inspections, these take place every two years. In the eyes of MUI its Halal Assurance System ensures the halalness of production and products in the period between. Certifying bodies pay for expenses in connection with additional inspections.

In Novozymes the researcher found halal logos from various certifiers on certificates for raw materials. Certificates state that the products are properly certified and it contains all necessarily product information. Logos on products themselves are not very common because it is not a formal requirement to put logos on packaging or boxes. When logos can actually be found on product boxes or packaging this is mostly because the company wishes to display the logo and thus make it a part of the company's branding (Fischer 2012). In general, Novozymes's customers are not too interested in pursuing the option of having logos on products themselves—the certificate that accompanies products is the central form of documentation.

I was given the opportunity to carry out participant observation at a halal inspection in Novozymes. The halal inspector is the chairman of the HFCE, the organization that arranged the Brussels conference. He is also vice president of the influential halal certification body IFANCA, based in Chicago. HFCE can be seen as a kind of subsidiary organization of IFANCA in Europe. The inspector was born in Malaysia, where he worked with JAKIM, and has been involved in setting up Malaysia's state regulated form of halal certification since the early 1980s. The mission and objectives of HFCE are to promote the concept of halal globally in the interfaces between Islamic organizations and scholars, Muslim consumers and companies, research, and training.

When a company requests halal certification an audit/inspection of the production facility is done to review the production processes, ingredients, and sanitation aspects of the facility, and this was also the case in Novozymes. Companies must provide necessary documentation and information pertaining to specification sheets, labels, flow charts, cleaning/sanitation procedures, and other production details. A contract is signed between HFCE and the company on the agreement by both parties. HFCE is recognized by JAKIM, MUIS, and MUI. It is essential to Novozymes being certified by a body that enjoys the most widely recognized type of certification. Even if HFCE and IFANCA closely cooperate, they carry out independent inspections at Novozymes. For example, Novozymes's factory at its headquarters in Denmark only has inspections from HFCE whereas the company's factory in China is the only one inspected by both MUI and IFANCA. The HFCE inspector explains that kosher is a term similar to halal, but there are many differences; while Islam prohibits all intoxicants, Judaism regards alcohol, among other things, as kosher. He is fully aware that Novozymes has been fully kosher certified since the 1990s.

The regular inspections of Novozymes by HFCE take one to two days, during which the HFCE inspector explores the production process. The inspector does not concentrate on the biotechnological details as much as on hygiene in the production process to ensure that no cross-contamination with haram substances occurs. Similar to kosher, these inspections are resource demanding for Novozymes. However, they allow the company to develop and refine their production methods to comply with increasing religious requirements. For example, Novozymes does not introduce new ingredients or production processes without consulting its halal certifiers. Consequently, these organizations influence the innovation process within the biotechnology industry. Unannounced inspections are allowed, but unsurprisingly Novozymes and other companies prefer announced inspections that they can prepare for and schedule. The HFCE inspector is more focused on visual aspects of the production processes as well as scrutinizing logos, certificates, and accompanying documents. The HFCE inspector is well aware that Novozymes has been fully kosher certified for many years and that this limits his main concern to alcohol and that Novozymes has very few ingredients and production processes that can be considered problematic.

Similar to what we saw in the case of Nestlé, Novozymes is a global and leading company in its field that has chosen to fully comply with both kosher and halal. However, the company has not developed its halal policies and practices in close cooperation with JAKIM in the context of ethnic politics and Islamic revivalism in Malaysia, and this is a main difference between these two multinationals. Kosher certification has helped Novozymes comply with rising halal requirements, and the company's coordinator equally divides his time between halal and kosher. The coordinator puts a lot of effort into ensuring that the rising requirements of not only Southeast Asian halal certifiers such as MUI and JAKIM, but also their recognized halal certification bodies are met. As a global company, Novozymes must generate in-depth knowledge about halal in and across many halal zones, that is, how a large number of regulatory bodies work and interact in divergent settings. This point is different from kosher and certification by OU in that a company such as Novozymes works directly with this organization and not with any recognized kosher bodies. Certification, standards, staff policies, training, networking, and many of the other issues discussed in this book meet in this company. Obviously, religion and regulation with a particular emphasis on technoscience is central to the company's history of halal standardization.

HALAL BIOTECH: FOOD, HEALTH, AND ANIMAL FEED

At the conference in Brussels I met a senior chemist who was also halal and kosher coordinator of a company that is a global supplier of bioscience-based ingredients to food, health, and animal feed industries. More specifically, the company produces cultures and dairy enzymes, probiotics, and natural colors. The company is certified by several kosher bodies and halal certified by HFCE, IFANCA, and Halal Feed and Food Inspection Authority (HFFIA) based in the Netherlands. The company has offices around the world including Malaysia and Singapore. Halal certification is essential for this company due to demands from customers. The coordinator explained to me that MUI had "uplifted" itself to become a form of global authority on halal, in fierce competition with JAKIM and MUIS. More specifically, this means that if the halal certifying bodies that certify the company's production are not on MUI's or JAKIM's lists of recognized bodies, the company will have problems in Asian markets in particular. On a number of occasions, MUI has temporarily taken European certification bodies off its list of recognized bodies and this led to a "tsunami" of concerned requests to the company from customers in Asia. JAKIM is also essential for the company's sales, but mainly in Malaysia, where JAKIM has uncontested authority. Comparatively, MUI's authority is more widespread in Asia, and this is why MUI, most of all, is important to the company.

During my fieldwork at the company's factory, the coordinator and a colleague of his who is also involved in halal and kosher explain that the work with halal started a few years back. When requirements from customers "escalated" the company discussed two possible halal strategies or approaches: first, an ad hoc or "take it as it comes" approach that included a relaxed attitude toward halal requirements, that is, having individual products certified and not the whole production process. Second, a "once and for all" approach that was ultimately chosen and included having all possible products and production processes halal certified similar to the way in which the company did with kosher. This transition was not overly resource demanding as only a few raw materials and ingredients were haram and had to be replaced. Being kosher certified also smoothened this process, as alcohol was the only real concern.

The company has been halal certified by HFCE, IFANCA, HFFIA, and MUI for some years, but Halal Control, a German halal-certifying body, was also considered for a shorter period. This happened when MUI stopped recognizing HFCE when the organization faced internal problems. The company then needed an alternative plan for certification and chose Halal Control as a viable option. When HFCE yet again appeared on MUI's list, the company reverted to HFCE certification for production in Europe and IFANCA certification for US production. What is more, the company is also certified by HFFIA based in the Netherlands for some enzyme products, because some local customers require this. These customers argue that MUI recognizes this certifier, the coordinator explained. However, at one point HFFIA was also misrecognized by MUI but then again recognized at a later stage. The coordinator thought this is strange because HFCE is also on MUI's list of recognized bodies and speculates that this is a question of "market shares and authority" in the global market for halal.

When the workload involved in halal became heavier, more staff became involved in this area. A colleague in the company assists the coordinator, and she explains to me that she cooperates with the coordinator and specifically looks into documentation in connection with the large amount of products that need certification. What is more, she tries to "streamline" and "optimize" procedures surrounding halal application processes—for example, retrieving product certificates from certifiers and a lot of other "practical" issues. More generally, staff policies in the company changed when the focus on halal intensified within the last decade or so. The company management, and the marketing manager, in particular, needed to make strategic decisions about the cost of transforming production and hiring and training staff to meet halal requirements. It took much more work than they ever dreamed of, and this is still the case. As we saw earlier, the company decided on a wholehearted approach having as many products and production processes halal certified; that is, all that could possibly be halal was certified as such. This also meant that locating and choosing certifiers, organizing inspections, and ordering appropriate documentation were needed. The company also made sure that halal fits into the overall production processes.

Working with halal certification is similar across different types of products and to maintain efficiency it is important that the same approach and procedures can be used in different applications such as dairy production and cultures for salamis, which are in big demand among Muslim consumers in Germany, for example. "Doing everything in the same way," the halal coordinator explained, is not only easier it also makes it possible to avoid doing ritual cleansing that takes up valuable production time when halal and non-halal production meet. What is more, complying with halal in a concerted way standardizes halal production procedures, and this is a general trend in highly specialized production processes in which halal is only one question among many others, such as avoiding allergens. This is an important point because it shows that when companies such as this one go wholeheartedly into halal, they actually set halal standards that are not based on requirements from consumers or certifiers.

The coordinator and his assistant made it explicit to the various halal certifiers that requirements about Muslims being involved in the production processes would not necessarily be met. Instead, the company argued that ISO standards and quality assurance ensured that production meets halal requirements. In response, the company was offered a one-day training course by Halal Control in Frankfurt, Germany, on how to handle halal as a non-Muslim company. The company accepted the offer and participated in the training that proved to be educational for both certifier and company. From companies and certifiers I learned that there is now a common understanding that outside Southeast Asia, certifiers are well aware that requirements about employing Muslims are sensitive and even illegal. This is an example of the way in which certifiers and companies negotiate important issues in the globalized market for halal—and that training can play an important role in this.

When the company was first halal certified and awaited its first halal audit/inspection the inspector asked if the company was kosher certified and when the coordinator confirmed that this was the case the inspector was pleased because as he explained there are so many similarities between halal and kosher. Actually, halal certifiers often see the Jewish system of kosher certification as a model for the institutionalization, standardization, and certification of halal. In the eyes of the coordinator and his assistant, there is a major difference between working with kosher and halal certifiers. Kosher certification and regulation is "extremely efficient" and "modern." The company chose to be kosher certified by OU and OK Kosher (Circle K), another leading kosher certifier, because these were seen to be the most reliable choices recognized by other major certifiers. For certification of individual kosher products around the world, the company is also certified by Star K, yet another leading kosher certifier. More specifically, these certifiers recognize each other's certificates, and this is a big advantage both for companies and for kosher organizations and their inspectors. Hence, when inspectors do inspections they can easily spot and approve raw materials, ingredients, and products that are certified by these organizations.

Efficiency for the company, for example, means that Circle K's kosher communication is digitalized so that on Circle K's website, the company can list the product that contains this or that raw material. Then Circle K sends the certificate electronically the next day. This makes this process unproblematic as Circle K knows about all the company's raw materials. What is more, Circle K also updates certificates once a year and contacts the company's suppliers so that all raw material lists are fully updated. Conversely, halal certification is less efficient. Several certifiers the company has worked with are slow to respond to important inquiries about acceptance of new raw materials, for instance, and there are often errors in their processing. Other companies face similar problems, the coordinator put in plain words. He knew this from discussions with other companies in the kosher/halal network that gives them an opportunity to meet and exchange experiences with religious requirements in their particular types of production. Anecdotal evidence suggests that companies rank Southeast Asian certifiers in the following way starting with the smoothest certifier to work with: MUIS, JAKIM, and MUI.

For both halal and kosher certification, the cost is outlined in a contract that was written up when an agreement on certification came into effect. The company pays an annual fee that includes annual routine inspections, and there are extra costs in connection with additional inspections. Altogether the company receives about four or five types of auditors/inspectors from ISO, customers, as well as local and foreign authorities. Hence, halal and kosher inspections/audits are only one category among a whole range of others and not really considered to be that different. The main thing for companies is that requirements and regulations are clear so that they can comply with these to obtain certificates they can show to their customers.

When the HFCE inspector inspects the company he is most of all interested in any changes in production that may involve non-halal products or ingredients. There is a big difference between halal inspectors and the way in which they inspect—some are thorough and systematic while others seem unqualified and focused on issues that do not have anything to do with halal. The general tendency is that when inspectors are not educated in food technology or biotechnology they tend to focus on "standard" issues instead of the particular production process. Kosher inspectors from the major certifiers are for the most part properly educated to do inspections. Normally, a halal inspection takes about half a day and it is always announced, but in principle it could be unannounced. This means that the company is highly prepared for these announced inspections and during my stay at the company's factory I was given the tour that inspectors normally take. During inspections ingredients list covering acceptable ingredients are also discussed. These lists are normally valid for one to two years.

Until MUI started regulating halal, requirements were "fluffy," to say the least. Before the company was halal certified and could get a standardized certificate from a certifying body it would send out a simple questionnaire for suppliers to fill in: Is there any ethanol or gelatin in this or that raw material? At the time, the answers given by suppliers were sufficient, but this is far from the case with halal requirements and "standardization" coming from MUI, in particular. Now MUI "outsources" the regulation of these standards to its recognized halal bodies in Europe. In this company most kosher and halal logos are to be found on accompanying documents and certificates and not so much on products themselves. Comparatively, more kosher logos than halal logos are found in this company.

Some kosher and halal requirements can be "negotiated." For example, kosher rules stipulate that if you have produced non-kosher and will produce kosher afterwards you have to do a kosherization cleansing of equipment and leave this inactive for 24 hours before a final scald of equipment. Unsurprisingly, a multinational company such as this one is uninterested in leaving equipment inactive for 24 hours because this is inefficient and expensive. Hence, the company negotiated alternatives with the rabbinic supervisor from the kosher certification body in question, and an alternative and more "suitable" solution was found. This type of negotiation is often premised on the degree to which the kosher/halal inspector, on one hand, and the company and its coordinator, on the other, have a personal relationship. If it is the first time a new inspector comes to the company, the coordinator explained to me, one does not know whether one can negotiate or not. However, in most cases a suitable compromise is found "because inspectors are also businessmen."

An example of such as compromise was when the German certification body Halal Control visited the company and discussed ritual cleansing after the manufacturing of a haram product. The halal inspector suggested that "clay detergent" was applied to perform the "*najis* cleansing" of the production equipment. The company's engineer protested and argued that clay would definitely damage the equipment. Hence, a compromise had to be worked out: the company now applies its standard cleaning of the equipment.

The material from this company shows how religion, science, and technology are fully compatible in the market for biotech products. This point is quite similar to what we saw in Chapter 4 on halal science and research in Malaysia. The difference, however, is that while halal is being promoted by the state in Malaysia, a European company such as this one must set up its own forms of self-control to live up to halal requirements that originate in Southeast Asia. These requirements are then outsourced to European halal certification bodies to enforce in connection with production in Europe, and this complicates processes of certification and standardization. The ethnography from this company shows that not only is kosher important for halal understanding and practice, kosher is also seen as a model or ideal in terms of efficiency that some halal certifiers could benefit from being inspired by.

HALAL DAIRY

During my fieldwork in Malaysia I visited a multinational food company that supplies products such as dairy, seafood, meat, and vegetables to wholesale, food service, and industrial customers worldwide. The company does not manufacture its products in Malaysia, but it imports many food products into Malaysia. Hence, the company is not directly certified by JAKIM, but it is heavily reliant on JAKIM's list of recognized Islamic certification bodies worldwide. The company's foodservice manager explains to me that this list is the company's "guideline" that is always consulted for specific recognized certification bodies. The foodservice manager, like the company's other staff I did fieldwork with, is educated in food technology and trade, and he has working experience from other Muslim countries. If for some reason there is doubt about the halal recognition status of these bodies, which is not uncommon, the foodservice manager calls or e-mails a contact in JAKIM, which will verify if the certification body in question is recognized or not. The company cannot in any way influence JAKIM's decision; that is, the company does not have any right to appeal this decision. "This matter," the foodservice manager states, "is strictly between JAKIM and the halal certifying body in the country in question."

The recognition of JAKIM by MUI in Indonesia is also an important issue. During my fieldwork in 2010, a staff explained that because JAKIM is not recognized by MUI, a JAKIM logo cannot "get products into Indonesia because this is not recognized by MUI." It was not until July 2012 before the Indonesian government for the first time recognized JAKIM's logo permitting Malaysia to trade its halal products also in Indonesia (Fischer 2012). In 2010 MUI made new rules that limited the number of recognized certifiers in Europe to only one, namely, HFCE. At the same time, MUI required that all products must have a valid halal logo. However, as one of the company's staff argued this was merely a "rule to be bent." The problem with MUI, the foodservice manager argues, is that it continuously changes its halal regulation and policies. Previously, MUI was more "relaxed," but this is certainly not the case after the major food scandal in 2001 and fierce competition with MUIS and JAKIM, in particular, about enforcing halal in the "strictest possible way," leading to a steady increase in halal requirements. The heavy promotion of halal network events in Malaysia and making the country a halal hub add to this, the staff member contends. In the eyes of the foodservice manager, JAKIM is more stringent and efficient in its halal regulation compared to MUI.

Staff agree that in Malaysia, where the company is most active, halal has taken on special meaning within the last 25 years, but within the last decade it has accelerated and with the last four to five years it has "culminated." Now, "everything," including raw materials, must carry or be accompanied by a recognized halal logo: if products are manufactured in Malaysia, it is the JAKIM logo, and if imported, a logo issued by a recognized certifier such as IFANCA and HFCE is needed. All this is a challenge for a company such as this one that imports products into Malaysia.

If the company's products were simply produced and consumed in Malaysia it would only have to deal with JAKIM and not so much shifting recognition of certifiers around the world. Hence, developments over the last decade or so has caused considerable confusion among many companies now that there is far more "control" in the market, as one staff member put it, and the latest development in 2010 was that JAKIM would also look into packaging, that is, if glue for labels as well as edible printing and dyes used directly on food contained prohibited ingredients.

All these developments have spread to the company's headquarters in Europe that now receive halal inspectors from European halal bodies recognized by JAKIM. What is more, the company has to accept that certification is expensive and allocate finances to this part of production. At the time of the fieldwork, the company has not yet hired staff that are responsible for halal, in particular, but the foodservice manager explains that it can soon be the case as more and more questions about halal is asked at the company's headquarters in Europe—in many cases, headquarters redirects questions to the foodservice manager in Malaysia, and this is a resource-demanding and not always efficient way of dealing with enquiries from around the world. Often headquarters do not understand what Southeast Asian halal requirements are about and why they are so difficult to comply with. The quality assurance department at headquarters often complains about logo and certificate requirements in particular. Hence, hiring a global coordinator may be a more efficient way to centralize halal knowledge and responsibilities. Because the company does not produce in Malaysia, it is not mandatory to set up a Halal Committee. What is more, the company has Muslims employed at many of its factories around the world, so this has not posed a problem.

A particular case in the company concerns rennet (a complex of enzymes), which is an essential part of cheese production. Traditionally, rennet was produced in calf stomachs, but today this can be produced artificially using microbial technology in laboratories. The production of rennet is not only easier to control in laboratories—halal certifiers are not concerned that modern rennet could be from a calf that was not ritually slaughtered, so this development is both scientifically as well as religiously an advantage for companies. What is more, in the opinion of many Islamic scholars intestines cannot be halal. This example shows that technoscience in many cases can provide solutions to the challenges faced by companies.

An advertisement for one of the company's products states that it is an Italian original hard cheese produced in Eastern Europe. It is fully certified by HFCE and comes with a proper certificate. The Italian recipe for this cheese stresses that it must be traditionally produced using calf rennet. Hence, the cheese cannot be halal except if production is moved to a country where it can be manufactured using modern and artificial rennet produced in a laboratory, and this is what the company did when it moved production of this particular cheese to Eastern Europe. In this way the company can produce halal hard cheese accepted by certifiers the world over.

The certification process of specific products normally follows a general procedure: headquarters in Europe receives notice and instructions about products that warrant certification and then looks into the "halal status" of the factory in question. Factories must guarantee that they do not produce anything non-halal, the foodservice manager explains. On the halal certificate that should accompany products it must be specified which products the certification covers. The certification process normally takes about two and three months, depending on whether it is a new product that is being certified or it is a renewal of an existing certification. A staff at the company's office in Kuala Lumpur involved in this process stresses that within the last four or five years "certificates have become more important than the price"; that is, proper halal certification has become a value added in itself. Moreover, ingredient lists are a constant source of concern to a company such as this one. In dairy production, alcohol (except for cognac cheese) and pork are not major issues, but MUI is not consistent, staff told me, about complete ingredient lists that are valid for a specified time.

As the company does not manufacture its products in Malaysia the aspect of halal inspections is not really important. However, inspections by JAKIM-recognized bodies at the company's factories around the world are extremely important. During one of my visits to this company it was the first time I saw a copy of JAKIM's list of recognized halal bodies. Products manufactured outside Malaysia and certified by JAKIM-recognized organizations must be accompanied by a certificate whereas logos on wrappings are optional.

Printing logos on products is more resource demanding for companies in terms of designing the packaging so that the logo fits in naturally. JAKIM only requires an accompanying logo so this is the option many companies prefer. During my fieldwork in supermarkets, as we shall see in detail in the subsequent chapter, it was apparent that most food products, but not all, carry halal logos, and the question is what effect this has on consumer choices. When I discussed this point with the company representatives they were somewhat ambivalent about this point: on one hand, Malay consumers tend to look for logos, and on the other hand, putting logos on products is resource demanding. As long as a certificate is available, it is basically JAKIM's responsibility together with the supermarket to attest that the product is halal.

Because the company specializes in dairy production that is relatively uncomplicated in terms of halal, JAKIM seems to be very focused on hygiene and the risk of cross-contamination when dealing with the way in which its recognized certification bodies enforce halal at the company's factories outside Malaysia. As in many other companies, in this one, rumors about mandatory ritual cleansing demanded by JAKIM to obtain certification are ever present. One staff member told me about a friend of his working in a similar company that had to perform ritual cleansing using "sand from Mecca." In general, staff are concerned that the fierce competition is driving up halal requirements and that no global halal standard is in sight. However, there is one advantage to all this: when a company such as this one fully complies with strict Southeast Asian halal requirements and build in-depth knowledge of this it "helps keep other companies out of the market," as the foodservice manager jokingly explains.

This company is an example of the way in which halal compliance can take place in modern dairy production. The company has not hired a global halal coordinator as of the time of this fieldwork, but much effort goes into ensuring that the company's JAKIM-recognized certifiers in Europe remains on JAKIM's list of approved halal bodies.

HALAL UNCERTIFIED

A multinational company based in Europe contacted me in connection with a new and promising product that was ready to be put on the market. The company was stunned to say the least when it learned that the product had to be halal certified to enter Asian markets and Southeast Asian ones, in particular. The company asked my advice regarding how to comply with halal in the context of its particular product and regarding what certifier to choose. At a meeting at the company's headquarters the group of employees at the company responsible for ensuring halal certification told me that they could not believe it when they learned that the company's product had to be halal certified. As far as they knew, halal was something that had to do with "meat and Islam only." I asked staff whether the company was already kosher certified, and it was not. Halal certifiers often see existing kosher certification as helpful during the halal certification process. A central question we discussed was which certifiers would be ideal, and ultimately the company chose to contact JAKIM to move the certification process forward.

Soon after, JAKIM visited the company's headquarters to negotiate a potential certification of the product in question. Before the meeting with the JAKIM delegation, I discussed the company's strategy for receiving the JAKIM delegation with staff. The visit caused some concern among the company's staff responsible for negotiating certification: What kind of institution was JAKIM in the first place? What was the company to expect from the delegation coming from Malaysia? What costs would be involved in the visit and certification? What should they serve the JAKIM delegation; that is, what did halal mean in terms of proper food and drinks for the delegation during the visit? Staff also wanted to know how much JAKIM was expected to learn about the company's production process and how it should document this: Was documentation enough, or would JAKIM want a detailed tour of the relevant factories during the visit?

The whole certification process and JAKIM's visit could also be "turned around"; I suggested that JAKIM would definitely be interested in certifying this well-respected multinational and that this would stress the authority and reliability of JAKIM in competition with other certifiers. After the meeting with JAKIM at the company's headquarters, staff thought that it was constructive and held in a good atmosphere. The JAKIM delegation explained about halal requirements in this type of production and was shown around the production site. JAKIM had also made it clear that to get the product certified the halal status of all raw materials, that is, valid halal certificates, had to be in place for all critical raw materials. In spite of all this, the company was not halal certified by JAKIM or any other certifier at the time. Unsurprisingly, these are sensitive issues for a company such as this one, and it is hard to tell precisely what happened in the process. The other companies discussed in this and the next chapter develop and market products according to halal requirements. However, in the case of this particular company, these requirements came as a surprise once the product in question was already developed. This point was reinforced by the fact that the company was not kosher certified in the first place.

In this chapter I have explored how companies that rely on JAKIM certification, in particular, in one way or the other try to live up to rising halal requirements. Within the last decade or so JAKIM has "disciplined" companies, as one company representative explained, and all these companies are confronted with this fact. In other words, in the halal zone of Malaysia, regulatory institutions are disciplining companies with regard to halal understanding and practice, but companies have also become more skilled in negotiating standardized halal requirements. A central aspect of audit culture is the pushing of control and self-control further into companies to satisfy the need to connect internal organizational arrangements to public ideals. Many companies argue that even if requirements and control have intensified, halal is more professionally regulated and standardized today compared to the unclear and confusing requirements of the past. Simultaneously, these companies have developed and refined (Islamic) technoscientific solutions to comply with halal requirements. It is clear from the above that a multitude of divergent halal classifications are now being overshadowed by processes of standardization and that companies themselves are rationalized to deal with these challenges. The case of the coloring agent in the food-producing company highlights several of the points raised in this chapter. The company decided to remove the coloring agent because of JAKIM requirements, and then after some negotiation JAKIM issued a *fatwa* stating that it agreed to the use of the coloring agent as long as the content did not exceed a specified amount. This case shows that halal understanding and practice are open to negotiation between state and market. It is clear that halal as an Islamic injunction influences the social organization of business, that is, how companies understand and practice halal requirements as social organizations. However, both religious authorities and companies that increasingly are relying on science and scientific evidence in the regulation of halal give evidence that halal training is important for them. I have explored halal in the histories and cultures of companies and the webs of interpersonal networks linking different people in different constellations for different intents and purposes. Interestingly, several of these companies were kosher certified and this emphasizes that halal as a global assemblage is only one religious market among others.

Many of the conclusions drawn from comparable companies certified by JAKIM are also valid for these companies certified by recognized halal-certification bodies. However, a particular area of tension is the significance of JAKIM's and MUI's recognition or misrecognition of other certifiers. Novozymes and other companies have "standardized" the design and qualities of products, as well as the proper conduct with regard to the production, preparation, handling, and storage of halal. Halal requirements formulated in the Southeast Asian zone characterized by strong regulatory institutions with legal backing are outsourced to recognized certification bodies in other zones in which halal regulatory institutions do not really exist. In effect, complying with halal in and across divergent zones presents companies with multiplicity and ambiguity—especially in the context of ever-shifting recognition/misrecognition. Even if the underlying principle behind halal remains a system of religious precepts and beliefs, technoscience is a privileged domain that highlights the interplay and compatibility between regulation and audit culture. The more halal proliferates as a globalized religious market, the more technoscientific modes and methods of production and traceability become important for producers, traders, and certifiers. The increased focus on such methods to verify commodities as halal based on technoscience constantly expands the requirements to cover new types of commodities and practices. Both religious authorities and companies are increasingly relying on technoscientific evidence in the regulation, innovation, and proliferation of halal.

NOTES

1. Parts of this chapter are republished with kind permission from Springer Science+Business Media from *Contemporary Islam*, "Manufacturing Halal in Malaysia," 2015, Johan Fischer. DOI: 10.1007/s11562–015–0323–5
2. *New Straits Times* September 10, 1998: No pork, lard used, says cake chain.
3. *New Straits Times* September 15, 2004: Mimos to police e-mails.
4. *New Straits Times* September 17, 2004: Uphill task to police e-mails.
5. The Hebrew term *kosher* means "fit" or "proper," and it signifies foods that conform to Jewish dietary law (*kashrut*) dating back 2,000 years. Halal parallels the Jewish kosher, which includes a number of additional prohibitions, for example, a number of marine species. Contrary to halal, kosher requirements have a longer history of systematic institutionalization, certification, and standardization. Most companies explored in this chapter are also kosher certified and a more detailed discussion of kosher can be found in my article "Keeping Enzymes Kosher: Sacred and Secular Biotech Production" (2015).

BIBLIOGRAPHY

Fischer, Johan. 2011. *The Halal Frontier: Muslim Consumers in a Globalized Market*. New York: Palgrave Macmillan.

Fischer, Johan. 2012. "Branding Halal: A Photographic Essay on Global Muslim Markets." *Anthropology Today* 28(4): 18–21.

Fischer, Johan. 2015. "Keeping Enzymes Kosher: Sacred and Secular Biotech Production." *E M B O Reports*. DOI: 10.15252/embr.201540529.

Gellner, David N. and Hirsch, Eric. 2001. "Introduction: Ethnography of Organizations and Organizations of Ethnography." In *Inside Organizations: Anthropologists at Work*, edited by David N. Gellner and Eric Hirsch, 1–18. Oxford and New York: Berg Publishers.

Gerlach, Michael. 1992. *Alliance Capitalism: The Social Organization of Japanese Business*. Berkeley: University of California Press.

Kipnis, Andrew B. 2008. "Audit Cultures: Neoliberal Governmentality, Socialist Legacy or Technologies of Governing." *American Ethnologist* 35(2): 275–289.

Mazzarella, William. 2003. *Shoveling Smoke: Advertising and Globalization in Contemporary India*. Durham and London: Duke University Press.

Mitchell, Marilyn. 1998. *Employing Qualitative Methods in the Private Sector*. Qualitative Research Methods Series 42. Newbury Park: Sage.

Miyazaki, Hirokazu. 2013. *Arbitraging Japan: Dreams of Capitalism at the End of Finance*. Berkeley: University of California Press.

Nestlé. 2010. Bringing Peace of Mind around the World. *Halal Journal* 35 July/August: 10.

Riaz, Mian N. and Chaudry, Muhammad M. 2004. *Halal Food Production*. Boca Raton: CRC Press.

Urciuoli, Bonnie. 2008. "Skills and Selves in the New Workplace." *American Ethnologist* 35(21): 211–228.

Wilk, Richard. 2006. *Home Cooking in the Global Village. Caribbean Food from Buccaneers to Ecotourists*. Oxford and New York: Berg.

7 Shops and Restaurants

In this chapter I first discuss how shops—super-/hypermarkets, in particular—live up to increasing halal requirements with special emphasis on Singapore, not only in terms of keeping halal/haram products separate but also the way in which more and more super-/hypermarkets are designed according to halal requirements. Second, I explore halal in smaller and larger local restaurants as well as global chains such as McDonald's in the two countries. Moreover, many local Chinese restaurants are being halal certified because they want to attract Muslim customers, and I examine the transition from serving pork and alcohol to halal status. An important issue that runs through these discussions is the display of halal logos in shops and restaurants as a technology or technique that marks properties or products as being properly certified.

My previous research showed that the majority of middle-class consumers in Kuala Lumpur shop for everyday groceries and food in super-/hypermarkets (Fischer 2008), and this is the case in Singapore. As halal proliferated in the 1980s in urban Malaysia and Singapore, it contributed to new forms of space making lifting halal out of its base in halal butcher shops and wet markets into standardized space such as super-/hypermarkets. Economic growth, the emergence of large middle-class groups, and globalization of the food market have pluralized shopping choices; that is, in urban Malaysian and Singaporean shops and restaurants, there is availability of a very wide range of local and imported foods.

Before super-/hypermarkets became dominant, halal was mainly about trusting the authority of the local halal butcher shop, older Malay middle-class informants in Malaysia told me. Conversely, contemporary halal consumption among my informants suggested a religious and ethnic identity that, to a large extent, is impersonal and technological in nature, because halal has been lifted out of not only local halal butcher shops but also the domain of traditional religious authority. Hence, from trusting the authority of the local halal butcher consumers now rely on the authority involved in proper Islamic branding through marking commodities with logos or accompanying certificates. These transitions can be conceptualized as a move from a "bazaar economy" to a "standardized" economy

(Fanselow 1990) characterized by standardized and substitutable commodities in terms of quality/quantity. The buyer can collect information about highly standardized and economically substitutable halal commodities prior to purchase through direct comparison, precedent, or consultation with other buyers (Fanselow 1990, 252). Hence, in the standardized commodity market, brand names and trademarks work as classificatory devices by which the provenance of goods becomes identifiable and therefore their quality more predictable (Fanselow 1990, 253). With the declining importance of personal loyalty (e.g., in halal butcher shops and wet markets) in the labor market, the importance of previous experience, training, skill, and formal qualifications among staff increases (Fanselow 1990, 258) as we have seen it throughout this book. In standardized shopping spaces such as super-/hypermarkets, a vast amount of information on product logos and labels is transmitted. Hence, this form of standardized and impersonal shopping warrants detailed information on labels and in the form of logos signifying certification by a recognizable certifier. What is more, super-/hypermarkets are themselves standardized spaces in terms of design that allows for the proper handling of halal on the one hand and readiness for audits/inspections on the other.

At the 4th International Halal Food Conference in Brussels a Malaysian woman in the Q&A session wants to know why and how it could happen that "halal pork" turned up in the Supermarket NTUC FairPrice Co-operative in Singapore when everybody knows that pork cannot possibly be halal. The MUIS representative agrees that pork can never be halal and that it would compromise Syariah if it were labeled as such. She explains that the incident referred to arose because of a rumor in an email that halal pork was on sale in Singapore. The MUIS inspectors did not find any halal pork when investigating, and the MUIS representative calls this a "sabotage" incident. The subsequent police investigation could not place responsibility. This incident was big in the media, and the picture of "halal pork" was widely displayed. A FairPrice spokesman said the organization regarded the case as a deliberate and willful act of mischief and would take necessary steps to ensure that such an act is "halted immediately with no repetition thereafter." The MUIS carried out its own checks at eight FairPrice outlets and found that none of the specified items bore the MUIS logo. An MUIS spokesman said, "We treat the case of the MUIS halal certification mark on the packaging containing pork very seriously as the halal mark has been abused." He added that under AMLA, an abuser of the MUIS halal certification mark is liable to a fine not exceeding $10,000 or to a jail term not exceeding 12 months, or both. This means the perpetrator is culpable even if the mark is a sticker, is a fake, or was digitally added.[1]

I now discuss another case that attracted attention in the Singaporean media during my fieldwork in 2009. In a news release (NTUC FairPrice 2009) FairPrice launched Singapore's first supermarket audited by a local halal consultancy organization at Joo Chiat Complex in Eastern Singapore. This supermarket addressed the needs of Muslim customers by introducing a wider range of halal-certified "offerings" within its store catering for the "significant" Muslim population residing in the vicinity of this new store. FairPrice at Joo Chiat Complex was the first supermarket to appoint a local halal consultancy organization, the Chairman of NTUC FairPrice announced. Moreover, FairPrice had plans to extend this to other bigger stores. To attain the audit approval by the halal consultancy organization, FairPrice stores undergoing the Audit Program set up by this consultant had to complete a series of at least four stringent audits. The program covers the processes of handling halal products, training of key staff on halal requirements, and recommendations on areas for improvement (NTUC FairPrice 2009). This Audit Program, the chairman stressed, supplemented ongoing efforts to build a closer relationship with the Muslim community. In addition to the variety of products offered at other FairPrice stores, in the newly launched outlet at Joo Chiat Complex, a third of its in-store products were halal certified. Of these, about 400 are new halal products, including a wide range of baking needs, spices, meat products, and toiletries (NTUC FairPrice 2009).

The halal consultancy's objective was to ensure that all facilities, practices, and processes in FairPrice outlets comply with requirements recommended by MUIS. This work was done through a series of steps by the halal consultant that include spending a month minimum with the outlet to develop halal process flows and food handling procedures to ensure compliance with MUIS requirements; training of key staff to understand more about halal and the processes that will ensure halal status of products; auditing the branches (minimum four times) that have been trained, reporting, and recommendations to FairPrice; and regular meetings with FairPrice for exchange of ideas (NTUC FairPrice 2009). In the media[2] this move was described as FairPrice "stepping up its standards in the stocking of halal foodstuffs" in its new store in Joo Chiat Complex that was audited by the halal consultant meeting "strict requirements" as recommended by MUIS. However, that same day another article heading read "Only MUIS can certify."[3] It was stated that MUIS had "taken issue" with FairPrice's new halal auditing program. In the article, MUIS's president stressed that the council is the sole authority that can certify establishments and products as halal. FairPrice had helped its Muslim customers with a halal auditing program of another Muslim body. MUIS emphasized that it had not yet certified the Joo Chiat outlet. The day after this point was repeated in the article with the heading: "MUIS sole authority on halal certification."[4] In the article, FairPrice's managing director explained that the halal consultant's audit would give Muslim customers a greater level of assurance, but MUIS "threw a question mark over the claim," stating that it had not yet certified the Joo Chiat outlet and that FairPrice had merely approached the council for advice on choosing a consultant. In response to this request MUIS had earlier referred FairPrice to the halal consultant. A spokesman for the halal consultant confirmed this and argued that MUIS should speak to both the consultant and FairPrice about the issue so that people would know what MUIS's "jurisdiction" and "scope" were.

It was established that the consultant's role was only to consult and audit and not to provide any form of certification for halal. The main outcome of this case was that it was firmly established that MUIS is the sole authority on halal certification in Singapore. FairPrice stated that it fully recognized this authority. All this should be seen in relation to some wider transformations outlined in the same article: halal certification in Singapore and overseas had boomed and as the Singapore "halal mark" had become a recognized one, the number of certified establishments has nearly quintupled from 500 to 2,300. On August 23 it seemed to be "business as usual" when the FairPrice supermarket in Joo Chiat Complex offered "new halal products for keen cooks."[5]

At MUIS's halal training discussed earlier, I met a FairPrice director of food safety and quality. FairPrice received its first International Organization for Standardization (ISO) certificate in 1993 and food safety certification around the same time, and these types of certification work as "platforms and procedures for standardization and standardized practices in all FairPrice outlets," she explained. Around 2006 FairPrice started to receive more and more requests about halal from Muslim customers and as a cooperative it was necessary to address all needs from organic to halal, but the question was how to do it. "A specific halal counter is not enough. There has to be a mindset in terms of a system," the director reasoned. Halal has become increasingly important for FairPrice and the organization has tried to focus on "mass requirements" and "streamline basic platforms" to address issues such as standard operating procedures for doing things. However, during my fieldwork in 2009, halal was mainly to do with counters in individual outlets and this posed challenges to a company such as FairPrice. Thus, as an organization FairPrice moved from more localized classifications of halal understanding and practice towards standardization and certification.

This was the case in the FairPrice outlet in Joo Chiat Complex discussed earlier that I frequently visited during fieldwork. The director shared that it was challenging to comply with the individual store approach when MUIS had introduced the Halal Quality Management System, or HalMQ, in 2008—a new certification scheme that was to ensure new levels of halal standardization in Singapore. FairPrice suggested that HalMQ had to be a "quality system" similar to ISO, which was "companywide and not store specific." However, after discussions between FairPrice and the MUIS, implementing halal became more standardized, establishing the Halal Corner or "partition," that is, a designated halal-certified service corner. This is different from Malaysia (as we shall see later) where local and multinational super-/hypermarkets keep non-halal products in a separate room because strict Muslims would not accept a partition only, the director tells me. Previously, halal was more of an ad hoc question or classification—"where to put the freezer" in this or that outlet—but now procedures have been standardized and centralized in the Halal Team including representatives from various departments of FairPrice from corporate communication to purchasing administration. The director explains that the Halal Team is a constructive forum for discussing and standardizing halal.

When we discuss the advantages and disadvantages of halal becoming big business not only in Singapore but also globally, she comments that it is important for Singapore to take part in this market as the country is strategically located between Malaysia and Indonesia that are major halal markets. Even if the number of Muslims is limited in Singapore, shops must cater for all "races," and the Chinese do not mind the proliferation of halal as long as this does not replace products such as pork. This shows that even though the local market for halal products is limited in Singapore the awareness of halal as a lucrative and ever-expanding global market and Singapore's rightful role in this market is a powerful idea. For instance, the FairPrice Joo Chiat Complex is located in an area with many Malays, and naturally this outlet must "adapt to the surrounding community. We're a cooperative doing what's best for the community," the director stresses. Thus, this supermarket like many other super-/hypermarkets around the world adapts to the specific requirements of local consumers, and this is why there was special attention to halal in the Joo Chiat Complex outlet that caters to the Malay community. In this outlet some customers ask for Muslim staff that can advise them on halal. In general, halal and non-halal products are both available in FairPrice outlets and other supermarkets in Singapore except for the Halal Corners in which only halal products can be found.

FairPrice designs all packaging for their own brands, and they take into account how the MUIS halal logo fits in with the general design of their house brand products. The director explains that packaging is designed so that it is "suitable" for all Singaporeans. Many products carry the nutritional information under the Food Act on top. Below that is the Healthier Choice Symbol issued by the Health Promotion Board under the Singaporean Government. Under this logo is the MUIS halal logo. The FairPrice design department is, to a large extent, responsible for these designs, and MUIS and other parties are flexible about this. However, MUIS does not accept red logos, for instance, and prefers green or black ones. With respect to the process behind the halal logo on specific packaging this is as follows: the supplier applies for the halal certificate, and normally it takes between 9 and 12 months for the final approval to go through. When the supplier receives the logo from MUIS this is sent to FairPrice, which fits it into the overall design of the packaging. Having the MUIS halal logo on products helps FairPrice when consumers enquire about the halal status of products. At the same time, industry players in Singapore and MUIS are aware of the growing demand for halal-certified products together with increased competition from Malaysia and elsewhere. FairPrice finds itself in the zone between the industry, consumers, and MUIS, and this is the reason it takes halal so seriously. Hence, marking or tagging products with halal logos has become essential technologies or techniques for halal standardization in super/hypermarkets.

During my fieldwork in Singapore I found a wealth of different halal logos in FairPrice outlets: MUIS/JAKIM logos on a bag of honey almonds (Figure 7.1) together with a number of additional logos; an MUIS logo on coffee (Figure 7.2), a Halal Authority Australia logo on muesli bars (this product was also kosher certified and labeled as *pareve* (foodstuff made without milk, meat, or their derivatives; Figure 7.3), and IFANCA logos among many other halal logos.

A particular case concerns the separation of frogs' legs and crabs in one of FairPrice's hypermarkets. Muslim customers were concerned about frogs' legs, which are considered a delicacy among some Chinese, in particular, being stored next to crabs that are halal, and consequently these two products were separated (Figure 7.4). In FairPrice, as in other super-/hypermarkets in Malaysia and Singapore, by far, the most (food) products are halal certified; that is, it is by no means only halal meat and other products in the designated Halal Corner that are halal certified (Figure 7.5).

Halal inspections are important for FairPrice. As more and more outlets were halal certified in Singapore, MUIS subcontracted inspection duties to Warees Halal Division, a subsidiary of MUIS, which helps firms attain

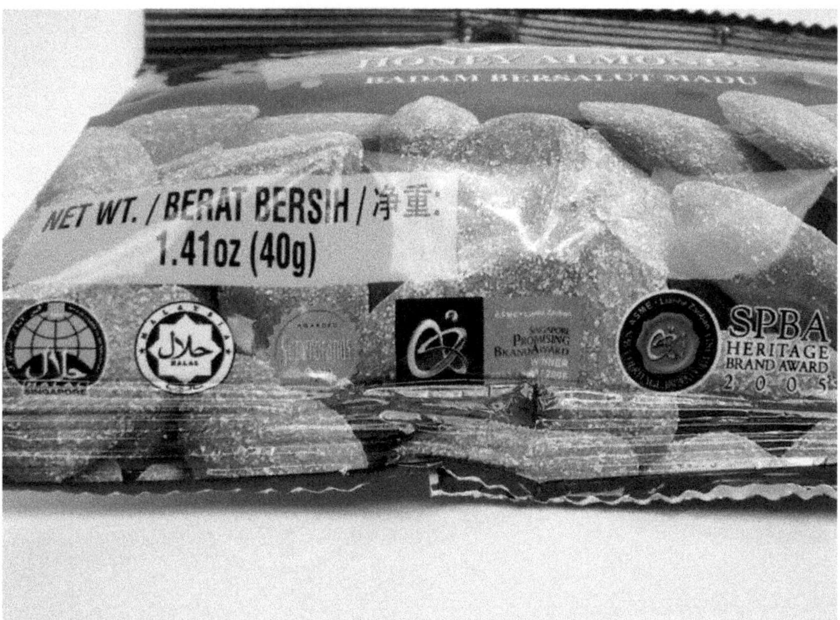

Figure 7.1 MUIS/JAKIM logos on a bag of honey almonds

Figure 7.2 An MUI logo on coffee

Figure 7.3 A Halal Authority Australia logo on muesli bars

Figure 7.4 Crabs and frogs' legs in FairPrice before they were separated

Figure 7.5 Amocan canned chicken in FairPrice

MUIS halal certification through the process of consultation and the organization is also responsible for halal training, as we have seen. Once companies are certified, Warees Halal undertakes the task of ensuring that firms comply with requirements of the halal certification, that is, conducting site audits, engaging local Muslim organizations abroad to conduct regular periodic audits, and sending halal-certified products for laboratory tests. Typically, inspections take place in the wake of "customer feedback"; that is, customers inform MUIS about issues they would like to have checked, and the MUIS then contacts Warees Halal, which performs an inspection. When its certification expires, FairPrice contacts MUIS, and inspections take place as part of the process of renewing certification. Last, because of HalMQ, more inspections take place. Inspections are both announced and unannounced, and the director does not feel that there is any real difference between the two. After an inspection in a FairPrice outlet, this outlet then e-mails a report back to headquarters. Halal consultants carry out halal "integrity audits" so that certified stores follow halal standards at all times.

After the FairPrice Halal Quality Management system was established in 2010 the organization fully complied with MUIS's halal standard requirements. The management system of the Food Safety and Quality Department in FairPrice also involves audits at suppliers and food safety partners all along the supply chain. The Operational Halal Integrity Program FairPrice set up ensures that the halal control points are properly monitored at the stores with three key focuses: each store is designed to properly review the store layout to ensure minimal cross-contamination, product control, and facility/equipment control.

FairPrice set up the mandatory Halal Team that attends halal training. Before this became a mandatory requirement it was just a "working team," in the words of the director. Every FairPrice outlet with a halal certificate must send one staff for training. This training was constructive for FairPrice in that it laid out the basic MUIS "halal principles, standards," the director explains to me. "If we know that these are the mandatory standards then it's easier to talk to the officers and inspectors and to form our own system," she argues. In addition to the preceding, employees at FairPrice must participate in an on-the-job-training program to ensure that staff are aware of receiving, handling, and displaying halal certified products. Finally, the organization has a communication program including various platforms with suppliers, staff, and customers to ensure all parties are aware of the proper handling of halal-certified products.

In conclusion, the FairPrice case shows how an organization can comply with rising halal requirements. This process can be challenging at times, but by now this whole process has been "standardized," meaning that in super-/hypermarkets, as particular "zones," the roles of and relationship between MUIS as a regulatory institution and FairPrice have been settled. FairPrice's transition from localized halal classifications to halal standardization has taken place through certification technologies and techniques: training of staff, close cooperation with MUIS, and marking products and space with halal logos.

HALAL SHOPPING ZONES

Earlier, the director of FairPrice explained that establishing the Halal Corner or "partition" was very different from Muslim countries such as Malaysia, where super-/hypermarkets keep non-halal products in a separate room because strict Muslims would not accept a partition only. Shops and super-/hypermarkets in Malaysia live up to the increasingly tight halal requirements, not only in terms of keeping halal and non-halal products separate but also in the way in which more and more super-/hypermarkets are designed according to halal requirements. Since I started doing research in Malaysian shops in the mid-1990s this tendency has become much more clear. *Tidak halal* (non-halal) products, such as pork, are, for the most part, stored in a small, secluded room away from the main shopping area in both super-/hypermarkets. Wine and other alcoholic drinks are often stored in another room in hypermarkets and supermarkets (Figure 7.6).

Figure 7.6 Non-halal products in a separate room in a supermarket outside Kuala Lumpur

Non-halal products can also be located in a specific counter (Figure 7.7). In contemporary Malaysian convenience stores this trend is also noticeable (Figure 7.8).

Store managers in these shops told me that "normally" JAKIM does unannounced inspections twice a year. A store manager in a supermarket in central Kuala Lumpur explained, "We have to make sure that the standard of handling the halal counter meets requirements and City Hall will do the same"; that is, city hall will check on the freshness, expiration, or damaged products, as well as the halal certificate. Hence, halal is inseparable from wider concerns about cleanness and proper handling of products in super-/ hypermarkets. In all these stores it is essential that management have a valid halal certificate to show customers.

In the Malaysian state of Kelantan, which is often considered the Malay Muslim heartland, I could not find any non-halal products such as alcohol or pork anywhere in the huge Tesco hypermarket. At the same time, lines for customers are separated so that women who shop alone have a particular line while other lines are designated for families. In all these shops in Malaysia and Singapore, halal logos are ubiquitous, and they signify a transition toward impersonal, regulated, and standardized ways of shopping in the relationship between seller, certifier, and buyer.

Figure 7.7 The non-halal counter in a Malaysian supermarket

Figure 7.8 Non-halal products in a convenience store in central Kuala Lumpur

RESTAURANTS

Many of the trends we saw earlier are visible in restaurants in Malaysia and Singapore. Actually, the transformation of shops and restaurants can be discussed as McDonaldization, that is, processes by which the principles of the fast-food restaurant are coming to dominate more and more sectors of the world and how this affects education, work, politics, religion, and many other aspects of society (Ritzer 2006, 5). Arguably, McDonald's has succeeded because it offers consumers, workers, and managers efficiency, calculability, predictability, and control (Ritzer 2006, 14). In Malaysia and Singapore McDonald's underwent rigorous inspections by Muslim clerics to ensure ritual cleanliness and these restaurants are fully halal certified (Watson 2006, 295), and in Indonesia, restaurants are owned by Muslims to avoid criticism of Americanization (Watson 2006, 304–305). I return to the case of McDonald's later.

Restaurant owners, including those of McDonald's franchises, mainly become certified to expand their customer base among the local Muslim population. In Singapore, a Chinese owner of a restaurant that specializes in Indonesian cuisine employs Muslim workers, and the menu does not contain pork. He explains that he has no choice but to become halal certified and putting up the halal sign (Zainal 2009, 30). Other restaurant owners likewise reveal that they attract more Muslim customers after being halal certified. Restaurants have to make the choice of finding a satisfactory way in connection with unlawful foods or eliminating it altogether. A manager of an eating establishment that specializes in international cuisine removed mustard containing alcohol (Zainal 2009, 49). For instance, this transition is more difficult in Japanese restaurants in which sake is an important cultural ingredient (Zainal 2009, 50). Most restaurant owners consider halal certification a necessary but complicated decision (Zainal 2009, 52).

Before entering into a discussion about halal in restaurants, I outline some more general points about food culture in Malaysia and Singapore. Chinese, Indian, Thai, Western, and many other influences have shaped the Malaysian and Singaporean national cuisines. *Rempah*, a spice paste, is central to many Malay dishes, and this is also the case with *belancan* (shrimp paste or sauce). As could be expected, rice plays an important role in the culinary traditions of Malays, Indians, and Chinese in Malaysia and Singapore. Festive occasions call for dishes such as *nasi himpit* (compressed rice cubes), *rendang daging* (rich coconut beef), and *sayur lodeh* (curried vegetable stew) among the Malays. Other popular dishes are *satay* (pieces of diced or sliced meat, fish, or tofu that are grilled and served with various spicy seasonings including peanut sauce), varieties of *nasi goreng* (fried rice), *mee goreng* (fried noodles), *ayam percik* (grilled chicken dipped in rich coconut gravy and spices), and *nasi lemak* (rice cooked in coconut milk served with a spicy pasta, boiled eggs, and anchovies).

Indian food includes banana leaf rice (white rice served on a banana leaf with an assortment of vegetables, curry meat or fish, and *papadum*, which is a crispy flatbread), *biryani* (a mixture of spices, basmati rice, meat/vegetables, and yogurt), curries, and *roti canai* (a thin bread that is fried and served with condiments). Indian Muslims, Mamak, developed a particular and popular cuisine in Malaysia that includes *nasi kandar* (rice served with other dishes of curry with chicken, fish, beef, or mutton and often together with vegetables) and *mee mamak* (fried eggs and noodles).

Basically, Chinese food is inspired by mainland Chinese cuisine, but it has been blended with local food cultures. Many Chinese dishes involve pork as a subingredient. Often these dishes are also available in versions with chicken to accommodate Muslim tastes. An example of a popular Chinese dish is *bak kut the* (pork ribs soup). Malays enjoy many other Chinese dishes such as *nasi ayam hailam* (chicken rice) as long as they are seen to be properly subjected to halal requirements.

Nyonya food, a mix of Chinese and Malay cuisines, is the food of the Peranakan people of Malaysia and Singapore, descendants of Chinese immigrants who, to a large extent, have adopted local Malay culture. Nyonya food is one aspect of the millennia-old and diverse interaction between East and Southeast Asia (Anderson 2007). Typical dishes are *asam laksa* (rice noodles served with fish, vegetables, and spices in a soup) and *laksa lemak* (laksa served in a rich coconut gravy). In sum, the Malaysian and Singaporean national cuisines are heavily influenced by the countries' multiethnic composition.

However, the proliferation of halal has reconfigured these culinary exchanges. This does not mean that Malays typically will only eat traditional Malay dishes, but that the dishes of the other are subjected to novel forms of halal requirements. On top of these types of ethnic or "national" foods, a wide range of mainly Western and Asian restaurants and fast-food outlets are prominent in urban Malaysia and Singapore. What is more, food is a primary marker of class in the interfaces between the state, marketplace, and revivalist Islam in modern Malaysia and Singapore.

In the popular media in Singapore restaurants and rising halal requirements and concerns started to surface in the early 1980s. These trends and discussions are comparable to what happened in Malaysia. MUIS clarified that Muslims are forbidden to eat meat at restaurants without halal certificates. At the same time, Kentucky Fried Chicken (KFC) was "looking into" setting up halal chicken branches in areas with many Malays. In 1981, KFC burgers were "pork-free," but the meat was not prepared the "Muslim way." Simultaneously, McDonald's considered getting beef prepared the "halal way" in Australia when the Malaysian McDonald's opened.[6] The move to halalize products by fast-food chains was not unproblematic. For example, two local fast-food restaurants were said to have "run afoul" of MUIS with the halal signs they put up. MUIS stated that the two restaurants did not have the necessary certificates to make the claim and the food sold was not halal unless it was cooked free of lard or pork. The cooking utensils also must not have been used to cook pork or lard.[7]

By 1990 only one fast-food outlet was MUIS halal certified: Arnold's Foods at City Plaza.[8] When I visited this restaurant in 2009 it was packed during lunchtime, and it was not possible to be seated. Later in 1990, however, several of the major fast-food chains such as Kentucky Fried Chicken, Texas Fried Chicken, and A&W applied for MUIS halal certificates to "boost sales" by capturing the Muslim market.[9] When the decision to go halal by fast-food giants such as McDonald's became public, letters to the editor in *Straits Times* expressed concern about this move. A reader wrote that he had reservations about McDonald's decision to go halal as the fast-food chain served pork sausage during breakfast.[10] In response, fast-food restaurants planning to go halal, McDonald's, A&W, Kentucky Fried Chicken, and Texas Fried Chicken assured that the food they served fully complied with Islamic regulations even if this meant removing pork or other non-halal ingredients. MUIS stressed that meat slaughtered according to Islamic specifications cannot be eaten by Muslims if during the preparation, processing, or storing it comes into contact with forbidden foods in Islam. However, halal meat mixed with non-halal food could still be consumed by Muslims after ritual cleansing. For outlets to be certified halal, "everything" from ingredients used to preparations and serving must conform to Islamic standards. To obtain halal status, MUIS also required restaurants to hire at least two Muslim staff at each outlet to ensure that regulations are complied with.[11] MacDonald's and corporations more generally take letters to the editor and similar inquiries extremely seriously. In response to the preceding letter, McDonald's issued a statement saying that the company worked closely with MUIS for halal certification and that all terms and conditions as stipulated by MUIS for halal certification would be "implemented and strictly conformed and adhered to."[12]

A&W was the first fast-food chain to be fully halal certified by MUIS and after an inspection of the applicant's premises all conditions and requirements had been met.[13] More restaurant chains were following A&W's move, especially when this company announced a 30 percent increase in sales since the chain went halal.[14] In 1992, McDonald's was fully halal certified by MUIS: the slaughtering of animals, preparation of food, cleaning of utensils all have to be done by Muslims, two Muslim employees were present to verify the halal status of the food at all times, and MUIS must be allowed to carry out spot-checks to ensure that standards are kept.[15]

A particular case concerns McDonald's. In 2010 the company removed pig characters from its latest toy promotions. The pig soft toy was expected to have been part of a 12-character Doraemon set depicting the animals of the Chinese zodiac calendar. Customers wanting the toy would have to pay S$2 on top of making a food purchase. However, McDonald's decided not to include the pig toy to avoid offending Muslim customers and had a Doraemon Cupid toy in its place instead. The move upset Chinese customers keen on collecting all 12 toys in the series and caused a public debate in Singapore about religious requirements in the public sphere.[16] This case shows how sensitive even multinationals are in a globalized world where bad news travels fast on the Internet, in particular.

It was not until 1995 McDonald's and many other fast-food giants were halal certified by JAKIM in Malaysia. In *New Straits Times* this move by McDonald's and other restaurants was discussed as necessary now that McDonald's was fully halal certified in Chinese majority Singapore. During my fieldwork I spent a lot of time in McDonald's restaurants in Malaysia and Singapore. McDonald's in Malaysia was so kind to give me permission to take pictures in these restaurants. I was particularly interested in the visual representation of halal logos on signs and in certificates. Even if halal in these Malaysian McDonald's outlets have been standardized or McDonaldized, as it were, there are differences. In Chinatown in Kuala Lumpur, for example, the outlet not only displays the JAKIM logo on the store front, inside, and on the visible halal certificate, it is also stated in Malay on a sign that the food is *ditanggun halal* ("guaranteed halal"; Figure 7.9). The

Figure 7.9 McDonald's in Chinatown, Kuala Lumpur

photo in Chapter 1 from Chinatown in Singapore is an example of the same trend—here the MUIS logo is clearly displaced on the restaurant's door. This was not the case in other McDonald's outlets I visited in Singapore. In McDonald's in the state of Kelantan, Malaysia, the word *McDonald's* is written in both Arabic and Roman characters (Figure 7.10).

KFC's 48 restaurants were MUIS certified in 1994, and KFC said that Muslim staff was "stationed" at every outlet to receive and keep records of halal food suppliers. Staff were not allowed to bring non-halal food or drink into the outlets.[17] When this major transition to halal certification and standards came about in the mid-1990s, MUIS published its conditions for halal certification: pork avoidance; ritually slaughtered meat; proper handling of crockery, utensils, stoves, chillers, and cold rooms that must be cleaned by a qualified Muslim if they have been used previously for preparing pork; and "authorized Muslim employees" present. These Muslims were responsible for receiving halal food or meat supplies, verifying that all food prepared met the manner prescribed by Islam, and verify/sign all records on orders, bills, invoices, and halal certificates.[18]

When Burger King was halal certified in 1996, not only was pork bacon replaced by turkey bacon; restaurant outlets also had to undergo ritual cleansing.[19] However, using halal turkey ham and bacon was confusing to some Muslim consumers, who contacted MUIS.[20] The following years more

Figure 7.10 McDonald's in the Malaysian state of Kelantan

and more restaurants such as Pizza Hut were halal certified and many had to undergo ritual cleansing. A restaurant owner explained that it was a tedious ritual, but it had to be done. Reportedly, Pizza Hut's sales went up by almost 50 percent after it went halal.[21]However, complaints about food courts were also being heard. The complaints were usually about food stalls, which claim to serve halal food but cannot produce a halal certificate issued by MUIS. In 1998, MUIS received 20 complaints involving six food courts. MUIS officers checked out the complaints, informed the environment ministry about operators claiming to serve halal food without proper certification, and advised them to apply for one. There were also cases of forged halal certificates. MUIS would report such cases to the police. MUIS also prepared a list of halal eateries and food stalls for the Muslim community to refer to[22] (Figure 7.11). However, most food stalls in urban Malaysia and Singapore are not halal certified. Instead, these stalls, which, for the most part, are run by Muslims, display different types of Islamic paraphernalia such as plaques with Islamic calligraphy, and/or they write halal in Arabic/Roman characters.

Local entrepreneurs in Singapore also set up hawker centers selling halal food to compete with Starbucks that is fully halal certified in both Malaysia and Singapore (Figure 7.12) and Coffee Bean.[23] This was also the case in large food courts in malls,[24] hotels,[25] and "exotic cuisines," such as that of a new and expensive French restaurant.[26] In 2003 the Zipangu Japanese

Figure 7.11 An MUIS-certified food stall in Singapore

Figure 7.12 A halal-certified Starbucks in central Kuala Lumpur

Restaurant of Shangri-La Hotel Kuala Lumpur introduced halal Kobe beef, beef from cattle reared with a special diet.[27] Many Chinese restaurants were also halal certified (Figure 7.13), but others are not (Figure 7.14).[28]

In this chapter I have tracked the way in which shops and restaurants have been halal standardized in Malaysia and Singapore. Halal logos and certificates play major roles in standardized shops and restaurants selling standardized halal products. Standardization makes halal impersonal, and in turn, this stresses the need for third-party visual assurance that also has legal implications. These points also stress the fact that as these halal spaces or landscapes are halalized they are subjected to new forms of halal audit culture. What is more, the FairPrice case shows that in Singapore, halal certification is fully centralized in MUIS. As we saw in the case of both FairPrice and McDonald's, companies are extremely sensitive to consumer criticism. Standardization of halal in shops and restaurants smoothen compliance for companies, but ironically, compliance is also driving up halal requirements to cover more and more products and processes, that is, audit culture pushes control and self-control further into shops and restaurants. This exploration situates modern and global halal technologies and techniques in a framework of new governing practices. With regard to staff policies, training, innovation, and certification, shops and restaurants work hard to comply with halal. Another important issue was halal inspections in super-/hypermarkets that can be said to be a new form of religious audit culture.

Figure 7.13 A Chinese MUIS-certified restaurant in Singapore

Figure 7.14 A Chinese non-halal restaurant in Malaysia

NOTES

1. *Straits Times* November 25, 2007: FairPrice alerts police to halal pork photo on Net.
2. *Straits Times* August 21, 2009: Halal audits for FairPrice outlets.
3. *Straits Times* August 21, 2009: Only MUIS can certify.
4. *Straits Times* August 22, 2009: MUIS sole authority on halal certification.
5. *Straits Times* August 23, 2009: Halal food at supermart.
6. *Straits Times* June 16, 1981: Three fast food centres to make their meat "halal" for Muslims.
7. *Straits Times* May 6, 1984: Fast food chains run foul of MUIS.
8. *Straits Times* June 4, 1990: Only one fast-food joint certified halal.
9. *Straits Times* November 29, 1990: Fast-food bid to go halal.
10. *Straits Times* December 12, 1990: Reservations about McDonald's halal move.
11. *Straits Times* December 14, 1990: Fast-food outlets give assurance on halal switch.
12. *Straits Times* December 20, 1990: McDonald's working with MUIS on halal food move.
13. *Straits Times* March 23, 1992: A&W the first fast-food chain to get halal cert.
14. *Straits Times* June 18, 1992: Fast-food chains looking into going halal.
15. *Straits Times* August 27, 1992: McDonald's food and drinks now halal.
16. *Straits Times* January 9, 2010: McDonald's pulls pig toy.
17. *Straits Times* January 26, 1994: Kentucky Fried Chicken outlets go halal; February 1, 1994: KFC hopes to earn up to 5% more by going halal.
18. *Straits Times* February 1, 1994: MUIS conditions for a halal restaurant.
19. *Straits Times* June 25, 1996: Going turkey with the bacon.
20. *Straits Times* April 23, 1997: Burger King menu confuses Muslims.
21. *Straits Times* May 11, 1998: Pizza chain aims to go halal.
22. *Straits Times* November 19, 1998: More firms taking the halal path.
23. *Straits Times* February 20, 1999: Kopi kulture—Coffee, tea and halal food too.
24. *Straits Times* October 13, 2006: Satisfy your appetite this weekend.
25. *Straits Times* November 7, 2010: More hotels go halal.
26. *Straits Times* October 23, 2011: Ooh-la-la halal.
27. *New Straits Times* June 21, 2003: "Halal" Kobe beef delights at Zipangu.
28. *Straits Times* November 25, 2005: $7m plan to improve restaurants' standards.

BIBLIOGRAPHY

Anderson, Eugene N. 2007. "Malaysian Foodways: Confluence and Separation." *Ecology of Food and Nutrition* 46: 205–219.

Fanselow, Frank S. 1990. "The Bazaar Economy or How Bizarre is the Bazaar Really?" *MAN New Series* 25(2): 250–265.

Fischer, Johan. 2008. *Proper Islamic Consumption: Shopping among the Malays in Modern Malaysia*. Copenhagen: NIAS Press.

NTUC FairPrice. 2009. *News Release*. Singapore: FairPrice.

Ritzer, George. 2006. "An Introduction to McDonaldization." In *Mcdonaldization: The Reader*, edited by George Ritzer, 4–24. Thousand Oaks: Pine Forge Press.

Watson, James L. 2006. "Transnationalism, Localization, and Fast Foods in East Asia." In *Mcdonaldization: The Reader*, edited by George Ritzer, 292–305. Thousand Oaks: Pine Forge Press.

Zainal, Muhammad Firduas bin. 2009. *MUIS Halal Certification: Local Causes, Global Impacts?* BA Thesis Dept. of Geography. Singapore: National University of Singapore.

Conclusion

In this book I explored global halal production and trade among Islam, standards, and technoscience. From the late 1990s onward, the market for halal has become fully globalized; that is, from around that time halal emerged as a global assemblage in and across diverse zones. In 2000, a seminal article discussed capitalism at the new millennium calling it "millennial capitalism" that is capitalism in its messianic, salvific, and magical manifestations (Comaroff and Comaroff 2000, 293). In many ways my ethnography fits well with central points discussed in that article. The religious aspects of millennial capitalism are central. Occult economies are economies with a material aspect based on the effort to conjure wealth or to account for its accumulation by appealing to techniques that defy practical reason and ethical aspects transmitted in moral discourses generated by production of value through magical means (Comaroff and Comaroff 2000, 310). I think halal as a global assemblage conditions and is conditioned by occult economies. This is also the case concerning the way in which such economies have become a major focus of popular attention with respect to the place of the arcane in the everyday production of value (Comaroff and Comaroff 2000, 310).

This point was clear when reading newspapers in which halal was described as an ever-expanding global market that Malaysia and Singapore must "tap" with the help of their unique forms of state certification. Simultaneously, the states in Malaysia and Singapore promote halal as a neutral, self-evident, and lucrative business. The age of millennial capitalism has complex and controversial effects on the state. For example, there is a tendency for states to appeal to new or intensified magicalities, rituals, and fetishes (Comaroff and Comaroff 2000, 327), not unlike what we have seen in the case of halal. All this comes together in millennial capitalism and markets. Thus, millennial capitalism both feeds into and is fed by new Islamic ideas and state power. The proliferation and standardization of the kosher market is another example of these trends. Malaysia and Singapore are examples of the emergence of such a complex, and often highly ambiguous, millennial capitalism. In these two countries, capitalism is more than ever before inseparable from and subjected to elaborate religious ethics and standards. Simultaneously, the religious market transcends international boundaries and expands within a framework of advertisement and accessibility to the public. In other words, millennial capitalism in Malaysia and Singapore is infused with much more than Westernized market rationality, and as we have seen, companies around the world must relate to this form of millennial capitalism or occult economy as it were.

In the new millennium, 9/11, taking place only a few months after the food scandal in Indonesia, can be said to have transformed Islam into both an agent and a product of globalization. Moreover, my ethnography took place in the current climate of the global economic crisis that seemed to reinforce halal as a global assemblage: on one hand, halal, including Islamic finance, can be contextualized as a moral remedy against the immoral ways of the West that had generated the current economic crisis and, on the other, as a global lucrative market that expands even in times of crisis.

In January 2013 McDonald's and one of its franchise owners agreed to pay US$700,000 to members of the Muslim community in Detroit to settle allegations about a restaurant that falsely advertised its food as being prepared according to Islamic dietary law. In the settlement notice, the management said it had a carefully designed system for preparing and serving halal so that halal chicken products are labeled, stored, refrigerated, and cooked in halal-only areas. The company added that it trains its employees in preparing halal food and requires strict adherence to this process (http://www.usatoday.com/story/money/business/2013/01/21/mcdonalds-islamic-diet-lawsuit/1852147/). I think this recent example shows how halal has been lifted out of its Southeast Asian zones, where the Ajinomoto and Cadbury incidents took place, to be fully globalized. In other words, the particular relationship between regulatory institutions and markets in countries such as Malaysia, Singapore, and Indonesia is now reconfiguring other zones across the globe as we saw in the case of European companies.

Four overarching themes have permeated discussions throughout this book: economics in relation to Islam and Malaysia and Singapore's role in the global market for religious/ethnic commodities; technoscience as a privileged domain highlighting the role of Islam in divergent halal zones; authority linked to the power involved in halal standardization and legislation embedded in contemporary Malaysian, Singaporean, and Islamic institutional discourses and practices; and the multiplicity, ambiguity, and strategizing that arise among organizations from the earlier mentioned transformations.

The first theme taken up in this book is economics in relation to Islam and Malaysia's and Singapore's roles in the global market for religious/ethnic commodities. Halal production, trade, consumption, and standardization as forms of economic life or activities are evident in Malaysia and Singapore and globally. In powerful discourses, halal legitimizes the existence of ethnicized markets in contexts where ethnicity and religion are often sensitive issues. This point was clear in the media in Malaysia and Singapore where halal visions and strategies are ubiquitous. The halal network is fueled by the revival and expansion of ancient Islamic trade networks. Now Malaysia and Singapore try to export this indigenous halal model to other zones around the globe. Sovereign rule in Malaysia and Singapore creates new economic possibilities, spaces, and technologies/techniques for regulating, standardizing, and marketing halal such as an increased legal focus on halal and zoning technologies. Technoscience, standards, economy, and government all converge in such zones. Audit culture is, to a large extent, about cultural and economic authority granted to auditors; that is, the halal economy is not only about a lucrative global market. Certification is also a service that companies must pay for, and because the production, trade, and regulation of halal took off and was standardized, a particular certification economy emerged. Third-party certification is essential to companies and these have allocated resources to not only pay for certification, per se, but also to establish new positions such as the global halal coordinator as seen in the case of several companies. Increasingly companies allocate resources to monitor halal compliance, also in technoscientific terms, and to this point I now turn.

The second theme is how technoscience as a privileged domain highlights the role of Islam in divergent halal zones. The more halal proliferates as a global assemblage, the more technoscientific modes and methods of production and traceability become important for producers, traders, certifiers, and consumers. The increased focus on such methods to verify commodities as halal based on Islamized knowledge and technoscience constantly expands the requirements to cover new types of commodities and practices. At the same time, the fusion of religion and technoscience is inseparable from state/political support and funding. Both religious authorities and companies are increasingly relying on technoscience and scientific evidence in the standardization, innovation, and proliferation of halal.

During my work with scientists in Muslim universities, Islamic organizations, certifiers, and companies I learned that religion and technoscience are fully compatible in the market for a wide range of halal products and services. My ethnography from the Islamic Science University of Malaysia demonstrates how science and research, also in terms of allocating research funding, is a major focus area for the state while halal science institutions cooperate with companies in terms of product development, innovation, and testing. In laboratories in Malaysia and elsewhere, scientists make use of haram-detection technology and techniques not only to locate alcohol and pork but also to focus on broader issues of health and hygiene, contaminants, heavy metals, cholesterol, and edible products. This point shows that modern halal as an assemblage is also about hygiene, wholesomeness, and health. More and more types of technologies and tests can verify, and thus move beyond, the symbolic approach to determining, whether a substance is "religious" or not, as we saw in the case of kosher.

The third theme relates to authority, particularly linked to the power involved in halal standardization and legislation embedded in contemporary

Malaysian, Singaporean, and Islamic institutional discourses and practices. In both Malaysia and Singapore halal is inseparable from the way in which Islam and religion more generally are regulated by the state. In Malaysia, the state nationalized Islam and halal, fearing the implications of the reflowering of Islam. Thus, state institutions gradually developed the vision of becoming the world leader in halal production, trade, and regulation. In Singapore, halal evolved from being a sensitive Malay minority question to becoming a major national focus of both state and market. Singapore's "double minority" setting is a driving force in the promotion of halal in that Malay Muslims are simultaneously seen as a "problem" as well as instrumental to the production, promotion, regulation, and consumption of halal in the region and vis-à-vis Malaysia, in particular. The stress on Chinese ethnicity, ethics, and values also embodied a powerful narrative about the hard-working and economically successful Chinese that must "tap" the global and expanding market for halal helped by "instrumental Malays."

In both countries halal is entangled in complex webs of political, ethnic, and national significance, and at the same time, it is promoted as an example of the compatibility of the ethnicized state, modern Islam, business, and proper Islamic consumption. To my mind, the main tension involved in modern halal in Singapore and Malaysia is the way in which the state through forms of economic nationalism, support, and legislation promotes and regulates halal as a national and neutral business disregarding the major societal transformations it brings about. This point is inseparable from new forms of audit culture and audits/inspections in manufacturers, shops, and restaurants seem to take on a life of its own.

My empirical material shows that even if the underlying principle behind halal (and kosher) remains "divine order," technoscience, and audit culture are increasingly evoked as authoritative fields of knowledge in the way in which halal is understood, practiced, regulated, and standardized. The Malay entrepreneur Altaf, discussed earlier, argued that halal has become a career for paid employees rather than a calling. The point here is that bureaucratization and rationalization can be seen to empty halal of its religious or spiritual contents, which are linked to personalized religiosity and transactions between seller and buyer. This transformation prompts the major focus on a wide range of standards—for example, that Muslims with certain qualifications, knowledge, or skills must be involved in halal.

The fourth theme deals with the multiplicity, ambiguity, and strategizing that arises among companies (manufacturers/shops/restaurants) from the preceding transformations. A very visible transformation in companies is the proliferation of halal logos on products, facades, advertisements, and certificates. These logos testify to the fact that a recognizable body certifies products and production processes among producers, sellers, buyers, and certifiers. State regulation, economy, technoscience, audit culture, training, and Muslim consumer activism are all aspects of modern halal as a global assemblage that is essential to the everyday work of and in companies in

Southeast Asia and globally. It is in companies that halal standards and audit culture are quite specifically translated into practices such as complying with quality assurance and a host of other standards discussed in this book. Changing landscapes of halal legality and regulation are also of major concern to companies. I explored how companies that rely on JAKIM certification in one way or the other try to live up to rising halal requirements. Within the last decade or so, JAKIM and MUIS has "stepped up" its control of companies as one company representative explained and all these companies are confronted with this fact. Many companies argue that even if requirements and control have been "stepped up," halal is more professionally regulated today compared to the unclear and confusing requirements of the past.

It is clear that halal as an Islamic injunction influences the social organization of business, that is, how companies understand and practice halal requirements as social organizations. At the same time, both religious authorities and companies are increasingly relying on science and scientific evidence in the regulation of halal. Several companies also give evidence that halal training is important for them when they try to comply with halal. I have explored halal in the histories and cultures of companies and webs of interpersonal networks linking different people in different constellations for different intents and purposes.

There is quite a difference between being halal certified directly by JAKIM or MUIS, on one hand, or by one or more "recognized certifiers," on the other. My ethnography shows that recognition or misrecognition of other certifiers is a critical point for companies and that this creates multiplicity and ambiguity. In other words, when halal requirements formulated in the Southeast Asian zone characterized by strong regulatory institutions with legal backing are outsourced to recognized certification bodies in divergent halal zones, halal production and regulation become more complex. Two examples of how companies can negotiate or tackle halal requirements stand out. The case of the coloring agent in the food-producing company in Malaysia highlights this point. The company decided to remove the coloring agent because of JAKIM requirements, and then after some negotiation JAKIM issued a *fatwa* stating that it agreed to the use of the coloring agent as long as the content did not exceed a specified amount. In effect, this is also an example of how a new standard comes into being. One particular case concerned rennet in a dairy manufacturer that was certified by a JAKIM-recognized body. Traditionally, rennet was produced in calf stomachs, but today this can be produced artificially using microbial technology in laboratories. The Italian recipe for this particular cheese stresses that it must be traditionally produced using calf rennet, and the company decided to move its production to a country where the cheese can be manufactured using artificial rennet. In this way the company can produce halal cheese that can be exported to Malaysia.

Not only is kosher important for halal understanding and practice among companies and halal bodies; kosher is also often seen as a model or ideal in terms of efficiency that some halal certifiers could benefit from being inspired by. What is more, kosher is in many ways comparable to the way in which halal as a global assemblage proliferates in and across global zones. Thus, kosher testifies to the fact that halal is only one type of global religious market in millennial capitalism (Lever and Fischer 2016).

BIBLIOGRAPHY

Comaroff, Jean and Comaroff, John. 2000. "Millennial Capitalism and the Culture of Neoliberalism." *Public Culture* 12(2): 291–343.

Lever, John and Fischer, Johan. 2016. *Between Religion, Regulation, and Consumption: Globalising Kosher and Halal*. Manchester: Manchester University Press.

Index

For Product Safety Concerns and Information please contact our EU
representative GPSR@taylorandfrancis.com
Taylor & Francis Verlag GmbH, Kaufingerstraße 24, 80331 München, Germany

www.ingramcontent.com/pod-product-compliance
Ingram Content Group UK Ltd.
Pitfield, Milton Keynes, MK11 3LW, UK
UKHW022118190926
475702UK00013B/1523

9781138060272